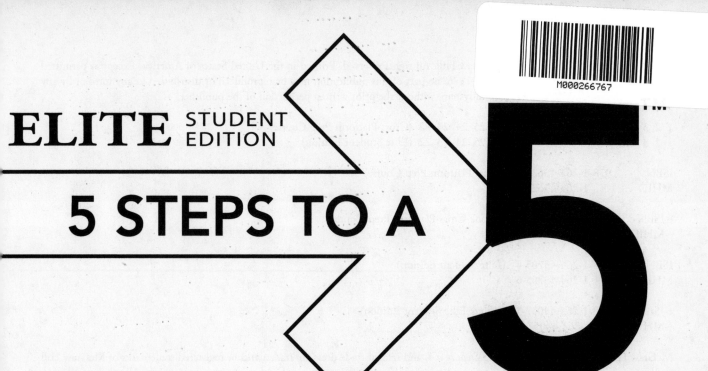

ELITE STUDENT EDITION

5 STEPS TO A 5

AP Computer Science Principles

2023

Julie Schacht Sway

Mc
Graw
Hill

New York   Chicago   San Francisco   Athens   London   Madrid
Mexico City   Milan   New Delhi   Singapore   Sydney   Toronto

1 2 3 4 5 6 7 8 9   LHS   27 26 25 24 23 22 (Cross-Platform Prep Course)
1 2 3 4 5 6 7 8 9   LHS   27 26 25 24 23 22 (Elite Student Edition)

ISBN   978-1-264-43629-3   (Cross-Platform Prep Course)
MHID   1-264-43629-7

e-ISBN   978-1-264-43661-3   (e-book Cross-Platform Prep Course)
e-MHID   1-264-43661-0

ISBN   978-1-264-43705-4   (Elite Student Edition)
MHID   1-264-43705-6

e-ISBN   978-1-264-44057-3   (e-book Elite Student Edition)
e-MHID   1-264-44057-X

McGraw Hill products are available at special quantity discounts to use as premiums and sales or for use in corporate training programs. To contact a representative, please visit the Contact Us pages at www.mhprofessional.com.

McGraw Hill is committed to making our products accessible to all learners. To learn more about the available support and accommodations we offer, please contact us at accessibility@mheducation.com. We also participate in the Access Text Network (www.accesstext.org), and ATN members may submit requests through ATN.

CONTENTS

STEP 5

Build Your Test-Taking Confidence

ELITE
STUDENT
EDITION

5 Minutes to a 5

Appendix

PREFACE

Welcome to the future! Your future, that is. It will be filled with technology because technology is well integrated into many aspects of our lives. The good news is that computer science is not that hard! You've just had little, if any, experience with it and this course exposes you to several key aspects in the field. Even if you do not become a programmer, data analyst, or network engineer, the more you understand about how these skills work, the more valuable you will be to a future employer or the more prepared you will be as a future business owner.

This review book is designed to help you prepare for the AP Computer Science Principles exam and performance task. Reviewing the concepts helps you confirm those you are confident about and identifies those you need to better understand before the exam. This book also guides you through preparing your project and written response for the performance task to earn as many points as possible. Let's get started!

ABOUT THE AUTHOR

Julie Sway serves as the technology department chair and education technology and innovation director at Brookstone School, a 3K–12 independent school, and serves as an AP reader for Computer Science Principles. During her career, she has worked for Coca-Cola USA, Coca-Cola Enterprises, Coca-Cola GesmbH in Vienna, Austria, and Southwest Airlines as a software developer, project manager, auditor, and software quality assurance manager. While her experience in the business world provides insight into the skills and knowledge needed by introductory programmers, she is thankful she discovered the joy of teaching computer science to students and helping teachers integrate technology. She has previously worked as an instructional technologist, technology director, and classroom teacher. She is the founder of EdCamp Columbus, GA, and the Chattahoochee Valley Regional Technology Competition. She has presented at GISA and GaETC conferences on a variety of topics and helps evaluate applications for the Innovation grants awarded by GaETC. Julie earned her BS in Computer Science from UNC Chapel Hill and an MBA from Georgia State University. She has completed coursework toward a master's degree in Instructional Technology from St. Joseph's University.

Julie wants to thank her three children, Michael, Kathleen, and Elyse, for always providing inspiration and her husband, Richard, for his support.

INTRODUCTION: THE FIVE-STEP PREPARATION PROGRAM

This book is organized as a five-step program to prepare you for success on the AP Computer Science Principles exam. These steps are designed to provide you with the skills and strategies vital to the exam and the practice that can lead you to that perfect 5. Here are the five steps.

Step 1: Set Up Your Study Program

In this step you'll get an overview of the AP Computer Science Principles exam and gain an understanding of the format of the exam, the topics covered, and the approximate percentage of the exam that will test knowledge of each topic. You will also find advice to help you set up your test-preparation program. Three specific options are discussed:

- Full school year: September through May
- One semester: January through May
- Six weeks: Basic training for the exam

Step 2: Determine Your Test Readiness

In this step you'll take a diagnostic exam. This test should give you an idea of how well prepared you are to take the real exam. It will also identify the content and skills you most need to review and practice. The multiple-choice questions on the diagnostic test are similar to those on the real AP Computer Science Principles exam, so time yourself and discover what taking the test will be like.

Step 3: Develop Strategies for Success

In this step you will learn strategies that will help you do your best on both the multiple-choice exam and the performance task. Learn how to attack the multiple-choice test and the Create performance task in the most effective and efficient way possible. Some of these tips are based upon an understanding of how the questions are designed, others have been gleaned through experience helping students prepare for the exam, and still others are based on experience grading the performance task.

Step 4: Review the Knowledge You Need to Score High

In this step you will review the material you need to know for the test. The chapters are organized around the "big ideas" that form the backbone of the AP Computer Science Principles course and exam. Here you'll find:

- A comprehensive review of the concepts you'll need to know for the AP Computer Science Principles exam

- Key terms, listed at the beginning of each chapter, that you need to understand and be able to use

- Practice multiple-choice questions for each of the concepts tested on the exam

Step 5: Build Your Test-Taking Confidence

In this final step you will complete your preparation by testing yourself on practice exams. This book provides you with two complete exams, answers, and explanations. Be aware that these practice exams are *not* reproduced questions from an actual AP Computer Science Principles exam, but they mirror both the material tested by AP and the way in which it is tested. Use the exams to practice pacing yourself and build your confidence. You're now ready for the test!

Introduction to the Graphics Used in This Book

To emphasize particular skills and strategies, we use several icons throughout this book. An icon in the margin will alert you that you should pay particular attention to the accompanying text. We use three icons:

This icon points out a very important concept that you should not pass over.

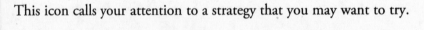

This icon calls your attention to a strategy that you may want to try.

This icon indicates a useful tip.

Set Up Your Study Program

CHAPTER 1

What You Need to Know About the AP Computer Science Principles Assessment

IN THIS CHAPTER

Summary: This chapter provides basic information on the AP Computer Science Principles assessment. You will learn about the exam, the topics covered, and the types of questions asked. You will also learn about the in-class performance task (30% of your final AP score), which must be completed and submitted to the College Board by the 2023 published deadline by 11:59 p.m. Eastern time before you take the exam later in May.

Key Ideas

✪ The multiple-choice exam, administered Monday, May 9, 2022 at noon, contains 70 questions and is two hours long without a break.

✪ In addition to the multiple-choice exam, you must submit a Create performance task by the deadline specified by the College Board.

✪ Your total score (on a scale of 1–5) is determined by your scores on the component parts:

 ✪ 70% of your total score is based on the multiple-choice exam

 ✪ 30% of your total score is based on the Create performance task

✪ Most colleges and universities award credit for earning a score of 4 or 5. Some award credit for a score of 3. A list of individual college policies can be found on the College Board site, and you should always check with the colleges and universities you are applying to for their current AP policy.

The Basics

The AP Computer Science Principles exam was first offered in spring 2017. More than 45,000 students took the first multiple-choice exam and submitted their performance task projects. The following year, enrollment grew to 76,000—a 55% increase! In 2018–2019, over 100,000 students took the exam. In 2019–2020, 150,000 students were registered and 110,000 submitted their performance tasks, even with the pandemic! One key goal of this course, according to the College Board, is to make computer science more inclusive and accessible to all students. This course is an introductory course, equivalent to a one-semester course in college. No prior computer science coursework or knowledge is required to take it. Students should have successfully completed high school algebra prior to taking the course. It's the *computer science for noncomputer science majors* course. For computer science majors, it may fulfill another requirement, such as an ethics in computer science requirement.

The Format

The AP Computer Science Principles assessment consists of a multiple-choice exam (70% of your score) and a Create performance task (30% of your score). You'll want to focus more time preparing for the exam since it counts more. However, you cannot ignore or do minimal effort on the Create performance task and still expect to earn a good score.

The Multiple-Choice Exam

There are 70 questions on the multiple-choice exam; you'll have two hours without a break to complete them. Since there are 70 questions and the exam counts for 70%, each question counts for 1% of your final score. For the first 62 questions, select only the best answer. For the remaining eight questions, you must select two answers. This is clearly noted in each of the last eight questions. Starting this year, there will also be a set of stimulus-response questions included in the 70 questions. Students will review a provided computing innovation and respond to five multiple-choice questions about it. This is in place of the former "Explore performance task" required in prior years. Unlike other AP exams, there are no free-response questions.

There is no penalty for wrong answers, so do NOT leave any questions blank. As with any multiple-choice question, if you are not sure, try to eliminate one or more of the answers. Then either go ahead and mark your best guess (recommended) or skip a line on the answer sheet. You can mark questions in your test booklet that you want to come back to. Later questions may help trigger your memory to determine the correct response for a question you were not sure about.

The Performance Task

The AP in-class performance task assesses skills that cannot be measured in the multiple-choice exam. Prior to the exam, you must submit a Create performance task project to the College Board using the digital portfolio site. This project accounts for 30% of your overall AP score.

The Create performance task requires you to develop a computer program, submit a video of the program running, and answer free-response questions about the program you created. You will have at least 12 hours of in-class time to work on this project.

Your AP teacher will give you a handout that contains instructions for the project. The handout is also available on the College Board's website in a PDF publication called the *AP Computer Science Principles Student Handouts*. You can find this publication at https://apcentral.collegeboard.org/pdf/ap-csp-student-task-directions.pdf.

Download and print out this document for future reference. You will need to refer to it often when working on the performance task. It also contains a copy of the exam reference sheet that you'll be provided when you take the multiple-choice exam.

Your AP Score

The multiple-choice exam is graded automatically by a computer. The Create performance task is graded by college professors and high school AP teachers who are teaching the course. They are trained and each project is evaluated and reviewed to ensure projects are graded consistently and fairly.

In the end you will be given a score that ranges from 1–5. The following table shows the meanings of the scores:

AP Score	Recommendation
5	Extremely well qualified
4	Well qualified
3	Qualified
2	Possibly qualified
1	No recommendation

Most colleges and universities award one-semester course credit if you earn a score of 4 or 5. Some colleges award credit for a score of 3. You should check with the colleges and universities you are applying to for their current policy regarding this AP exam. The College Board website has a list of the AP policies of individual colleges and universities, but to be sure, check directly with the school.

Being awarded college credit while you are still in high school has its advantages. You may be able to skip an introductory course and jump right into the elective courses you want to take in college. If you earn enough AP credits, you may be able to graduate early. Even if you don't want to graduate early, earning AP credit will give you more flexibility, making it easier to obtain a double major or to study abroad. Another benefit is that you'll probably save money by not having to pay college tuition for course credits you've earned in high school. Perhaps most important, doing well on AP exams will help you stand out in the college admissions process, showing colleges that you're serious about studying and that you're able to handle college-level courses.

What's on the Exam?

The AP Computer Science Principles Exam and performance task are designed to test your proficiency with six computational thinking practices and the five "big ideas" covered in the course content. In this AP course, you'll not only learn about technology but also about how it affects our lives.

The "Big Ideas"

Taking this course introduces you to a broad survey of technology-related topics. These include the five "big ideas" the course covers:

1. Creative Development
2. Data
3. Algorithms and Programming
4. Computing Systems and Networks
5. Impact of Computing

Step 4 in this book, where you'll review the content you need to know, is organized around these "big ideas."

The following table shows the percentage of multiple-choice questions you can expect from each of the Big Ideas in the AP exam:

Big Idea 1: Creative Development	10–13%
Big Idea 2: Data	17–22%
Big Idea 3: Algorithms and Programming	30–35%
Big Idea 4: Computer Systems and Networks	11–15%
Big Idea 5: Impact of Computing	21–26%

Computational Thinking Practices

Computational thinking is a driving concept in this course. There are six computational thinking practices the course references. They are:

- Computational Solution Design
- Algorithms and Program Development
- Abstraction in Program Development
- Code Analysis
- Computing Innovations
- Responsible Computing

These practices are interwoven throughout the course. All but the last one are evaluated through questions on the multiple-choice exam. More detailed information on what's covered in the AP course and exam is available on the College Board's website in the PDF publication *Computer Science Principles Course and Exam Description*. You can find it by searching by the title or you can go to https://apcentral.collegeboard.org/pdf/ap-computer-science-principles-course-and-exam-description.pdf.

Who Writes the Questions?

AP exam questions are designed and tested by a committee of college professors and high school AP teachers. The process of introducing a new course takes years, and once available, the questions continue to be evaluated. This committee is also responsible for determining the criteria and rubric for the Create performance task.

The AP Computer Science A Course—How Is It Different?
The AP Computer Science A exam teaches programming concepts using the JAVA programming language. It focuses more on developing solid programming and problem-solving skills. Taking one course does not preclude taking the other. They can even be taken at the same time. See the College Board site for more information about the AP Computer Science A course and exam.

Taking the AP Exam

How to Register

If you are taking AP Computer Science Principles at school, the school's AP coordinator will contact you and help you sign up. If you are not taking the class, you should contact the AP coordinator at your school or school district for assistance in registering. Home-schooled students should either contact the AP coordinator for their school district or their assigned school to register. Beginning with the 2019–2020 school year, students had to register for the AP exam by November 15. Students in classes that only meet second semester had to register by March 15. Do not miss this registration date or you will be charged a $40 late fee.

The fee to take an AP exam in 2022 was $96 in the United States and $126 if taken outside of the United States. Check the College Board website for the most up-to-date information on fees. You can get a refund of most of your fee if you end up not submitting your performance task and not taking the exam. You may be entitled to a reduced fee if you have significant financial need; check with the AP coordinator at your school for more information about eligibility for fee reductions.

The Dates

You should plan to complete the AP Computer Science Principles performance task by mid-April. The project for the performance task must be submitted via an online submission process by May 1st, 2023, at 11:59 p.m. Eastern time. Check with your AP teacher or the College Board website for the instructions for submitting your project.

The AP Computer Science Principles multiple-choice exam will be administered on Monday May 8, 2023, at noon. The actual date varies each year. You may also view this information at the College Board's website: https://apcentral.collegeboard.org/exam-administration-ordering-scores/exam-dates.

Test-Day Policies

On test day, you need to bring the following items:

- Several pencils and an eraser that doesn't leave smudges
- A school-issued or government-issued photo identification
- A standard non-internet connected watch so you can easily keep track of test time in case there is no clock in the testing room

Items you are NOT to bring into the test room include:

- Any electronic device that can access the Internet or be used to communicate with others
- Any food or drink, including bottled water
- A smartwatch or any watch that beeps or has an alarm
- Cameras or photographic equipment
- Any music device, including ear buds

CHAPTER 2

Planning Your Time

IN THIS CHAPTER

Summary: Preparing for the exam is important. The right preparation plan for you depends on your study habits, your own strengths and weaknesses, and the amount of time you have to prepare for the test. This chapter will help you get off to a good start by developing a personalized plan to prepare for the multiple-choice exam and the performance task of the AP Computer Science Principles assessment.

Key Ideas

✪ Do not wait until the last minute to begin preparing. Develop a study plan and stick with it.

✪ Your study plan should be tailored to your needs, your study habits, and the amount of time you have available.

✪ Prioritize your review based on your strengths and weaknesses. Take the diagnostic exam in the next chapter to identify the areas you most need to review and practice.

Three Approaches to Preparing for the AP Computer Science Principles Assessment

It's up to you to decide how you want to use this book to study for the multiple-choice exam and prepare for the performance task. This book is designed for flexibility; you can work through it in order or skip around however you want. In fact, no two students who purchase this book will probably use it in exactly the same way.

The first step in developing your plan is to take the diagnostic test in the next chapter. This is a practice exam that closely mirrors the actual multiple-choice exam. By taking the diagnostic test, you'll find out exactly what the exam is like as well as what you are reasonably good at and what things you need to review. Identify your weaknesses and focus on these first.

The School-Year Plan

If you are taking the AP Computer Science Principles course as a one-year class, and if you find the course difficult, a full school-year test preparation plan may be right for you. Following this plan will allow you to practice your skills and develop your confidence gradually. You can use the chapters in this book for extra practice and another explanation of the concepts as you cover the same material in your class. Starting your study plan for the exam at the beginning of the school year will allow you to get to all the practice exercises in the book and maximize your preparation for the exam.

If you choose the option of beginning early, you can still start by taking the diagnostic exam in the next chapter. This will show you exactly what the multiple-choice exam is like so you know what you are up against. You can also find out what you already know. For this plan (and for the semester review plan), you have time to take the diagnostic exam at the beginning and again later in the year to check your progress and understanding.

The One-Semester Plan

Starting in the middle of the school year will give you plenty of time to review and prepare for the test. This is a good option if you have only limited time on a daily basis to devote to test preparation either because you need to prepare for other AP exams as well, or you're super busy with extracurricular activities.

With the one-semester plan, you should start by taking the diagnostic test in the next chapter. This will give you an accurate idea of what the multiple-choice test is like. You'll get a sense of how hard the test will be for you, how much time you need to devote to practice, and which types of questions or tasks you most need to work on. You can skip around in this book, focusing on the chapters that deal with the things you most need to work on. Be sure to find time to take both practice exams at the end of this book. Take the final practice test a few days before you take the actual test.

The Six-Week Plan

OK, maybe you procrastinated a bit too long. But if you're doing well in your AP Computer Science Principles class, you don't need to worry too much. And whether you're doing well or not, you still have time to improve your score by reviewing weak areas and practicing taking the test.

Start by taking the diagnostic test in the next chapter to find out what the actual multiple-choice test will be like and to identify the content areas you most need to review. You don't have time to do everything in this book, so prioritize based on your weaknesses. If you find the diagnostic test difficult, try to devote as much time as possible to the review chapters. Save time to take at least one practice test and preferably take both of them. Even if you do really well on the diagnostic test and don't need further content review, you should take the practice exams at the back of this book to practice pacing yourself within the time limits of the exam.

The Practice Exams Are Your Friends

The practice tests are probably the most important part of this book. Taking them will help you do all of the following:

- Practice with the types of questions on the AP Computer Science Principles multiple-choice exam.
- Measure progress and identify areas you need to focus on in your test preparation.
- Practice pacing yourself within the time limits imposed by the test.

Save the last practice test for a final check at the end of April or beginning of May. But don't wait until the night before the test to take the practice tests. Staying up and trying to do some last-minute cramming may be counterproductive.

Planning for the Performance Task

If you are in a traditional classroom setting, your teacher will determine when you begin to work on the Create performance task and time will be provided in class. The Create performance task requires 12 hours of class time be provided. You may work more than the 12 hours of class time allocated on your own. But don't get bogged down and spend too much time on it; stay cognizant of the preparation time you will need for the multiple-choice section and other AP exams you have. Remember, the multiple-choice exam counts for 70% of your total score. While you cannot do poorly on the Create performance task and still get a high score, you do need to do well on the multiple-choice questions to achieve a 4 or 5.

If your class is a yearlong class, your teacher may do a full or partial practice Create project first. This will help you better learn how to prepare the written response, video, and program code. If you are taking this course as a semester-long course, your teacher may opt for a practice performance task on a smaller scale or one performed in groups.

If you are working in an independent study environment or home-school setting, you should not begin the Create performance task until you have a good understanding of data abstraction and procedural abstraction, algorithms, and programming selection and iterative statements, along with lists and procedures. All of these need to be incorporated into your program and the written response. These are covered in Big Ideas 1 and 3. If you are working on your own, begin the Create performance task in mid-March at the latest. If you are new to programming, you may need the additional time to learn programming fundamentals, and it may take longer to implement the concepts into your code.

Remember that once you begin the actual Create performance task, you cannot get help on the content of your project. Your teacher, or anyone else, is only allowed to answer questions related to the project task, timeline, components, and scoring in general and not about your specific project.

Once this is finished and submitted to the College Board, 30% of your AP score is set. You then only need to spend time preparing for the multiple-choice section on exam day.

Calendar: The Three Plans Compared

Month	School-Year Plan	Semester Plan	Six-Week Plan
September	Diagnostic Exam		
October	Big Idea 1		
November	Big Idea 3		
December	Big Idea 2		
January	Big Idea 4	Diagnostic Exam Big Ideas 1 and 3	
February	Big Idea 5	Big Ideas 2 and 4	
March	Review as needed Practice Exam 1	Big Idea 5 Practice Exam 1	Diagnostic Exam Review weak areas
April	Review concepts as needed Submit Create performance task Practice Exam 2	Review concepts as needed Submit Create performance task Practice Exam 2	Practice Exam 1 Review concepts as needed Submit Create performance task Practice Exam 2

STEP 2

Determine Your Test Readiness

CHAPTER 3   Take a Diagnostic Exam

CHAPTER 3

Take a Diagnostic Exam

IN THIS CHAPTER

Summary: Taking the diagnostic exam will help you identify the areas that you need to review as well as give you an idea of what the questions on the actual multiple-choice exam will be like. After you've completed the test, use the evaluation tool at the end of this chapter to identify specifically what chapters you most need to review and adjust your study plan accordingly. This diagnostic exam includes questions from all of the "big ideas" covered in the AP Computer Science Principles course.

Key Ideas

KEY IDEA

✪ Taking the Diagnostic Exam will allow you to familiarize yourself with the AP Computer Science Principles exam.

✪ Evaluate your performance on this test to identify your own strengths and weaknesses and then modify your study plan to prioritize the types of skills or areas of content you most need to work on.

How to Take the Diagnostic Test

Take this diagnostic exam when you begin to review for the exam. It will help you determine what you already know and what you need to spend time reviewing. It will also give you an idea of the format of questions on the AP exam.

Take the diagnostic exam in a simulated testing environment. Be in a quiet location where you will not be disturbed. Use the answer sheet in this manual and a pencil to answer the multiple-choice questions. The AP Computer Science Principles exam is still a pencil-and-paper exam! However, in 2021, the exam was also given in a digital format. Schools were able to select either digital or paper formats. One drawback of the digital format is that you cannot go back to review or change your answer for prior questions. The make-up exam dates only used the digital option.

Set a timer for two hours and try to pace yourself so you finish the exam. If you are not finished when the time is up, note how far you got, and then complete the rest of the exam. Answering all the questions will provide a better evaluation of what areas you need to review.

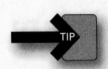

As you take the test, mark all the questions you were not sure about so you check the answer explanations for them as well as those you miss. But do not check an answer until you have finished all the questions after the two-hour testing period.

Test yourself in an exam-like setting. Take this diagnostic test and the practice exams at the end of this book in a place where you won't be interrupted for two hours. Time yourself. If you use your cell phone to time yourself, make sure it's completely silenced in airplane mode so you won't be interrupted.

In the next section of this book, you'll find helpful strategies for attacking both the multiple-choice exam and the Create performance task. The strategies were developed to help you prepare in the most effective and efficient way. Then in Step 4, you'll begin the review of the concepts and skills tested. After taking this diagnostic exam, you will know which of these chapters you need to review the most.

AP Computer Science Principles
Diagnostic Test

Multiple-Choice Questions
ANSWER SHEET

1 (A) (B) (C) (D)	26 (A) (B) (C) (D)	51 (A) (B) (C) (D)
2 (A) (B) (C) (D)	27 (A) (B) (C) (D)	52 (A) (B) (C) (D)
3 (A) (B) (C) (D)	28 (A) (B) (C) (D)	53 (A) (B) (C) (D)
4 (A) (B) (C) (D)	29 (A) (B) (C) (D)	54 (A) (B) (C) (D)
5 (A) (B) (C) (D)	30 (A) (B) (C) (D)	55 (A) (B) (C) (D)
6 (A) (B) (C) (D)	31 (A) (B) (C) (D)	56 (A) (B) (C) (D)
7 (A) (B) (C) (D)	32 (A) (B) (C) (D)	57 (A) (B) (C) (D)
8 (A) (B) (C) (D)	33 (A) (B) (C) (D)	58 (A) (B) (C) (D)
9 (A) (B) (C) (D)	34 (A) (B) (C) (D)	59 (A) (B) (C) (D)
10 (A) (B) (C) (D)	35 (A) (B) (C) (D)	60 (A) (B) (C) (D)
11 (A) (B) (C) (D)	36 (A) (B) (C) (D)	61 (A) (B) (C) (D)
12 (A) (B) (C) (D)	37 (A) (B) (C) (D)	62 (A) (B) (C) (D)
13 (A) (B) (C) (D)	38 (A) (B) (C) (D)	63 (A) (B) (C) (D)
14 (A) (B) (C) (D)	39 (A) (B) (C) (D)	64 (A) (B) (C) (D)
15 (A) (B) (C) (D)	40 (A) (B) (C) (D)	65 (A) (B) (C) (D)
16 (A) (B) (C) (D)	41 (A) (B) (C) (D)	66 (A) (B) (C) (D)
17 (A) (B) (C) (D)	42 (A) (B) (C) (D)	67 (A) (B) (C) (D)
18 (A) (B) (C) (D)	43 (A) (B) (C) (D)	68 (A) (B) (C) (D)
19 (A) (B) (C) (D)	44 (A) (B) (C) (D)	69 (A) (B) (C) (D)
20 (A) (B) (C) (D)	45 (A) (B) (C) (D)	70 (A) (B) (C) (D)
21 (A) (B) (C) (D)	46 (A) (B) (C) (D)	
22 (A) (B) (C) (D)	47 (A) (B) (C) (D)	
23 (A) (B) (C) (D)	48 (A) (B) (C) (D)	
24 (A) (B) (C) (D)	49 (A) (B) (C) (D)	
25 (A) (B) (C) (D)	50 (A) (B) (C) (D)	

AP Computer Science Principles
Diagnostic Test

Multiple-Choice Questions

Time: 2 hours
Number of questions: 70
The multiple-choice questions represent 70% of your total score.

Directions: Choose the one best answer for each question. The last eight questions have two correct answers; for these, you will be instructed to choose two answer choices.

Tear out the answer sheet on the previous page and grid in your answers using a pencil.

AP Computer Science Principles Exam Reference Sheet

On the AP Computer Science Principles exam, you will be given a reference sheet to use while you're taking the multiple-choice test. A copy of this six-page reference sheet is included in the appendix of this book (reprinted by permission from the College Board).

To make taking this practice test like taking the actual exam, tear out the reference sheet so you can easily refer to it while taking the test. Save these reference pages since you'll need to use them when you take AP Computer Science Principles Practice Exams 1 and 2 at the end of this book. If you misplace the Exam Reference Sheet, you can print another copy located at the end of the Student Handouts document: https://apcentral.collegeboard.org/pdf/ap-csp-student-task-directions.pdf?course=ap-computer-science-principles.

GO ON TO THE NEXT PAGE

1. How are procedures abstract in computer science?
   (A) They are blocks of code that do something specific.
   (B) They represent the lowest level of code for the computer to run.
   (C) They use actual values to represent concepts.
   (D) They can be used without understanding or seeing the code used.

2. What do parameters used in a procedure provide?
   (A) They allow software reuse for different values.
   (B) They return calculated values from the procedure to the calling program.
   (C) They provide a way to call a procedure from within another procedure.
   (D) They provide the connection of an API to the procedure.

3. What happens when you "clean data"?
   (A) Corrupt data records are corrected or removed.
   (B) Incomplete data records are completed or removed.
   (C) Duplicate records are removed.
   (D) All of the above.

4. What causes an algorithm to be considered one that runs in an unreasonable amount of time?
   (A) The solution is too inefficient for large datasets.
   (B) There is not an algorithm that can solve it.
   (C) It is solved most efficiently with large datasets.
   (D) Multiple algorithms exist with different levels of efficiency.

5. What are statements, procedures, and libraries examples of?
   (A) Low-level machine code that the computer uses to run the code
   (B) Abstractions used in writing software because they can be used without knowing the details of how they work
   (C) Algorithms that provide suggestions on how to approach writing the code to solve a problem
   (D) Pseudocode that helps design a solution for coding challenges

6. What is an issue that organizations must handle when dealing with datasets?
   (A) Ensuring that enough staff are on hand to process the data
   (B) Ensuring that the bandwidth can handle the processing of the data
   (C) Ensuring that people's private data is not exposed
   (D) Ensuring that the system can scale down after the data are sent to the cloud

7. How does the Internet work with the different equipment in use?
   (A) The routers adjust for the different equipment manufacturers by sending data on the same equipment brands.
   (B) Specific companies are approved to make equipment for the Internet.
   (C) Vendors follow the protocols established to enable data to be sent and received across any equipment.
   (D) The server farms handle the data once the data reach the Regional ISP (Internet Service Provider).

8. What is the binary equivalent of the decimal number 158?
   (A) 10011111
   (B) 10011110
   (C) 10011101
   (D) 10011000

9. How do selection statements determine which section of code to execute?
   (A) Through the use of the Turing algorithm for analysis
   (B) Through random number generators
   (C) Through conditions that evaluate to true or false
   (D) Through variables initialized to execute these statements

GO ON TO THE NEXT PAGE

10. You are writing a program to help the school assign lockers each year. You have a list of student names and a separate list of locker numbers. The locker numbers match the index position for the list. Assume the lists are correctly initialized. What can replace <missing code> to assign the student to the next available locker?

```
students←[list of student names]
lockerNum←[list of locker numbers]
index ←1
FOR EACH name in students
{

        <missing code>
        index ← index + 1

}
```

(A) lockerNum ← name
(B) lockerNum[index] ← name
(C) students ← lockerNum
(D) students[index] ← lockerNum

11. What do logical conditions always evaluate to?
(A) A Boolean value
(B) A value stored in a constant
(C) A "string" text field
(D) A real number

12. What is the process where algorithms are used with historical data to attempt to predict human needs or requests for information?
(A) Data excavation
(B) Trend prediction
(C) Social analysis
(D) Machine learning

13. What would be the starting and ending index positions for the substring function to extract everything up to but not including the "@" if you are given the following string: person@apcsp.org?
(A) 0, 5
(B) 0, 6
(C) 1, 6
(D) 1, 7

14. How is analog data converted to digital data?
(A) The analog curve is extrapolated and converted into x, y coordinate values.
(B) The analog data values are converted precisely to digital data.
(C) Samples of the analog data are taken and converted to bits.
(D) Samples of the analog data are approximated to mimic the smooth curve.

15. How do APIs simplify writing programs?
(A) By providing step-by-step instructions on how to use the programming language
(B) By importing the newly written software to the API for others to use
(C) By providing documentation on how to code the needed functionality
(D) By connecting prewritten and tested software to a new program

16. While algorithms can be analyzed mathematically, what information does the testing process provide?
(A) How often program statements execute
(B) The maximum size dataset the algorithm can handle
(C) The validity of the algorithm
(D) The clarity of the algorithm

17. Why is there a need to find different algorithms for problems that already have a solution?
(A) Different algorithms could use heuristics rather than precise values.
(B) Different algorithms could be more efficient.
(C) Different algorithms could use frequency analysis.
(D) Different algorithms could provide intractability.

18. Algorithms can be written with a combination of what three statements?
(A) Sequence / Selection / Iteration
(B) Series / Procedural / Functional
(C) Connection / Collection / Recursive
(D) Selection / Sorting / Searching

19. What is the most common way computer viruses are spread?
(A) By people clicking on an infected file
(B) From phishing attacks
(C) Through a rogue access point
(D) From random botnet attacks

GO ON TO THE NEXT PAGE

20. Different levels of access to technological devices and the Internet due to economic or geographic reasons is referred to as:
    (A) Binary split
    (B) Demographic division
    (C) Digital divide
    (D) Technology rift

21. How does creating program components help with program development?
    (A) Individual components can be added without additional testing.
    (B) Adding tested components incrementally to working code helps create program functionality that is correct.
    (C) Multiple people can write the components and still ensure compatibility.
    (D) The components can be combined all at once to create the needed program functionality.

22. What is the name of the search method that provides *higher* or *lower* feedback with each iteration of the search?
    (A) Bucket search
    (B) Merge search
    (C) Linear search
    (D) Binary search

23. How does documentation help with maintaining programs?
    (A) It journals the history of program changes, showing how the program first worked before changes.
    (B) If code is modified, the documentation can guide the programmer in testing to ensure the functionality is still correct.
    (C) It documents how to run the program in multiple languages for a global audience.
    (D) It is useful for training new employees on how to learn the programming language.

24. Parallel computing consists of what two parts?
    (A) A sequential section and a parallel section
    (B) A parallel section and a distributed section
    (C) A sequential section and a distributed section
    (D) A sequential section and an iterative section

25. What could a binary number represent?
    (A) A number in decimal
    (B) A color
    (C) Text
    (D) All of the above

26. How can programmers avoid duplicating code?
    (A) Through the use of selection statements
    (B) Through the use of iteration
    (C) Through sequential statements to process all data once
    (D) Through the use of efficient algorithms

27. What is a problem that no algorithm exists to solve all instances called?
    (A) Indeterminable problem
    (B) Undecidable problem
    (C) Infinite problem
    (D) Exponential problem

28. Why should procedures be used?
    (A) They ease the workload on the processors.
    (B) They facilitate the storage of data.
    (C) They make writing and maintaining programs easier through reuse of code.
    (D) They control the flow of input and output data.

29. What can help with identifying and correcting program errors?
    (A) Revisiting requirements
    (B) Collaboration among team members
    (C) Clustering requirements and tests
    (D) Consolidating testing

30. How can financial transactions safely occur on the Internet?
    (A) Through the use of symmetric keys
    (B) Through certificates issued by Certificate Authorities (CAs) that validate the keys used
    (C) Through the use of double authentication methods
    (D) Through the use of frequency analysis

31. What is the definition of bandwidth?
    (A) The frequency at which data can be transmitted across the Internet
    (B) The speed at which data can be sent through the Internet
    (C) The amount of data that can be transmitted in a fixed amount of time
    (D) The delay between the request and the receipt of information on the Internet

GO ON TO THE NEXT PAGE

32. Which type of loop is most effective to iterate over a list?
    (A) Traversal loop
    (B) REPEAT UNTIL
    (C) FOR EACH
    (D) REPEAT n TIMES

33. What is one way to help ensure the correctness of algorithms?
    (A) By testing with small sets of expected data
    (B) Through reuse of existing correct algorithms to build new algorithms
    (C) Through documenting the functionality of the algorithm
    (D) Through the use of heuristic algorithms

34. You are helping write the code to register students for classes. What can replace <missing code> to make the program work? Assume all variables are initialized correctly.

```
desks ← 25
studentID ← " "
classRoster ← []
REPEAT UNTIL (<missing code>)
{
    studentID ← INPUT()
    IF (studentID ≠ "done")
    {
        APPEND(classRoster, studentID)
        desks ← desks - 1
    }
    ELSE
    {
        desks ← 0
    }
}
```

    (A) desks = 25
    (B) desks < 0
    (C) desks = 0
    (D) LENGTH(classRoster) = 0

35. An error that produces incorrect results is what type of error?
    (A) Syntax error
    (B) Runtime error
    (C) Overflow error
    (D) Logic error

36. Why is it important to write programs that are readable?
    (A) They are easier to modify and debug.
    (B) They run more efficiently.
    (C) They effectively process all cases of input.
    (D) They produce accurate results.

37. How is collaboration useful in defining requirements?
    (A) The multiple viewpoints can provide several outcomes for the program.
    (B) Applying differing experiences and skills provides better identification, analysis, and program development to meet requirements.
    (C) The analysis can be divided among several people, speeding up the development process.
    (D) Having multiple perspectives helps the group form alliances among the team members.

38. When would lossless data compression be preferred over a lossy one?
    (A) When you need to restore the original file
    (B) When the level of compression is more important than restoring to the original file
    (C) When you need to display the file on mobile devices and websites
    (D) When you have limited space available on your computer

39. How does the Internet process transactions securely?
    (A) The public key encryption model is easy to use to encrypt data but intractable for decrypting.
    (B) Frequency analysis is used to disguise the use of common letters in encrypted messages, which keeps passwords secure.
    (C) Symmetric keys are used to encrypt and decrypt messages for speed in processing to avoid interception.
    (D) Multiple alphabets are used to encrypt and decrypt messages to allow for use with different languages.

GO ON TO THE NEXT PAGE

40. When does an overflow error occur?
(A) When a program exceeds the limit of lines of code for a programming language
(B) When the lines of output exceed the programming language limit
(C) When a "divide by zero" condition occurs
(D) When an integer needs more bits than are available to represent it

41. Why are simulations useful abstractions?
(A) They can test hypotheses without real-world constraints.
(B) They can change multiple options at the same time, leading to new insights.
(C) They can precisely test real-world events to identify the ultimate outcome.
(D) They can confirm the cause of events.

42. What is one way that data can be intercepted over a public network?
(A) A router
(B) A successful phishing attempt
(C) Keylogging software
(D) A rogue access point

43. What is an example of lower-level abstractions combining to make higher-level abstractions?
(A) Dividing functionality into separate modules that are all part of one program
(B) Writing pseudocode to identify what the program needs to do
(C) Creating help documentation so the user will know how to use the program
(D) Using a flowchart to identify program decisions

44. How is the Internet scalable?
(A) Through the ability for additional networks and routers to be added without impacting service
(B) Through the ability to add longer public keys to keep data secure
(C) Through the ability to add additional authentication for users
(D) Through the ability to add additional bandwidth to requests

45. Having your personally identifiable information (PII) stored online enhances your online experience with making online purchases, filling out forms, and other uses. A risk is that your PII data could be vulnerable to exposure through hacking or accidental disclosure. Which piece of information is classified as PII?
(A) Zip code
(B) Internet search history
(C) Language preference
(D) Time zone

GO ON TO THE NEXT PAGE

Questions 46–50.

A GPS company is developing a new software app called "Find my car!" to work with self-driving vehicles. If you cannot remember where you parked your vehicle, or it's raining when you are leaving a location, you can press a button on an app to summon your vehicle. The self-driving car will exit its parking spot and drive to your GPS location for you to enter the vehicle.

Here is a flowchart of the process.

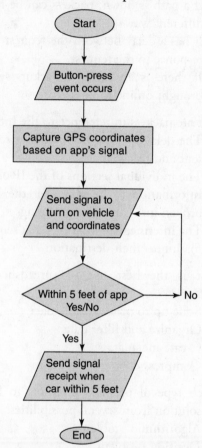

46. Is this a computing innovation? Why or why not?
- (A) A computer program is not needed, so the app is not a computing innovation.
- (B) The programming is completed by the GPS satellite, not this innovation, so the app is not a computing innovation.
- (C) The programming is controlled by the self-driving car's manufacturer, so the app is not a computing innovation.
- (D) The app sends GPS coordinates to the vehicle, along with the signal to drive to the location, so the app is a computing innovation.

47. What output does the app produce?
- (A) Instructions to start the vehicle and drive to the coordinates provided
- (B) The button event to be pressed
- (C) A signal to the GPS satellites to send current location coordinates
- (D) Directions to get from the parking spot to the current location

48. What is the most likely privacy concern of the app?
- (A) Two people using the app at the same location could cause the signal to be sent and recognized by both vehicles.
- (B) Location data would be available and potentially used by the company to identify future needed updates to the app.
- (C) Unauthorized individuals could use the app to summon someone else's vehicle.
- (D) People could enter the waiting vehicle before the driver gets to it.

49. Which of the following is the most likely potential harm of the app?
- (A) Traffic congestion for drivers and pedestrians at restaurant and shopping entrances that were not designed for multiple waiting vehicles
- (B) Increased air pollution if people leave their self-driving cars idling until they get to the vehicle
- (C) Car accidents when people driving vehicles are maneuvering around the self-driving waiting vehicles
- (D) Illegal parking as people leave their cars running to run into a store for a "quick" errand

50. What data is most likely to be needed for the app to work?
- (A) Fingerprint reader for valid entry to the vehicle
- (B) Accurate longitude and latitude coordinates
- (C) Cameras for the vehicle to safely navigate to the signaled location
- (D) Sensor to recognize the signal summoning the vehicle

GO ON TO THE NEXT PAGE

51. Tracing what your code is doing is an example of which of the following terms?
    (A) Discovery
    (B) Debugging
    (C) Traversing
    (D) Scaffolding

52. What is an example of "metadata"?
    (A) A line of code
    (B) A header in a document
    (C) Author of the document
    (D) Test data

53. Why should we use an iterative development approach?
    (A) Because each iteration improves or adds code to build a successful program
    (B) To meet the legal requirements for code to handle sensitive data
    (C) To be able to begin coding while remaining requirements are being defined
    (D) To minimize the amount of time needed for testing

54. You need to write a program named *calculate* to compute the average temperatures for an area. What would be the best variable name for this and why?
    (A) t—Variable names should be short so there is less opportunity for a typo.
    (B) avgTemperature—Variable names should be descriptive to help others understand their purpose.
    (C) calculateAvgTemp—Variable names should start with program name and then the variable name for ease of tracking.
    (D) 1Temp—Variable names should begin with a number starting with 1, followed by 2, and so on to know how many there are.

55. How can you defend a phishing attack?
    (A) Block incoming web traffic until the attack is over.
    (B) Open the website in question directly rather than clicking on the link provided.
    (C) Install antivirus software and keep it updated.
    (D) Never open unexpected e-mail attachments.

56. On the AP exam, compound expressions can be created using which of the following operators?
    (A) IS / IS NOT
    (B) NOT / NOR
    (C) IF / ONLY IF
    (D) AND / OR

57. What does it mean when we say the Internet is redundant?
    (A) Parts of it are unnecessary.
    (B) If a path is down, packets can be routed a different way.
    (C) It has a delay between the request and the response to the request.
    (D) If there is an error, a backup system is brought online to be used.

58. What are packets in reference to the Internet?
    (A) The delay in time from when a request is sent and received
    (B) The individual sections of the IP address
    (C) Information to be sent over the Internet broken into same-size groupings
    (D) The intermediate locations that send information to their destination

59. What is the best use of spreadsheets and databases?
    (A) Scale up to process more data
    (B) Organize and filter data
    (C) Create metadata
    (D) Compress data

60. Which type of problem attempts to find the best solution from several possibilities?
    (A) Algorithmic problem
    (B) Decision problem
    (C) Efficiency problem
    (D) Optimization problem

61. What describes the process of keeping common or similar features and functionality while removing details that are different?
    (A) Algorithm
    (B) Decomposition
    (C) Simulation
    (D) Abstraction

GO ON TO THE NEXT PAGE

62. A half-time program wants to randomly select a seat number for an attendee to come shoot baskets for the chance to win prize money. What code could randomly select a number from a list of seats checked in? Assume all variables are initialized correctly.

(A) `selected ← (RANDOM(start, stop))`

(B) `IF    (RANDOM(start,   stop)   =   LENGTH(availNums))`

(C) `REPEAT UNTIL (RANDOM(start, stop) = 0)`

(D) `FOR EACH num in availNums`

```
{
    IF (num = RANDOM(start, stop))
    <rest of code>
}
```

63. What is a method to confirm a person's credentials before providing access? Select two answers.

(A) Biometric identification

(B) Public key encryption

(C) A symmetric password

(D) A security token sent to a device such as a cell phone

64. Which of the following selection statements correctly tests if a number is less than 914? Select two answers.

```
Selection 1:    IF (number < 914)
Selection 2:    IF (NOT (number ≥ 914))
```

(A) Selection 1 is correct.

(B) Selection 2 is correct.

(C) Selection 1 is incorrect.

(D) Selection 2 is incorrect.

65. How can you legally use an image on your website that you found on the Internet? Select two answers.

(A) You can use it copyright-free from the Internet.

(B) You can use it after paying a fee for use or obtaining written permission from the owner.

(C) You can use it if you provide attribution to the owner.

(D) You can use it if the author provided a Creative Commons license allowing such use.

66. What are key steps of any development process to ensure user requirements are met? Select two answers.

(A) Planning

(B) Feedback

(C) Creating

(D) Reflection

67. Which of the following are events that could trigger event-driven programming? Select two answers.

(A) Using a remote control for your TV

(B) A sensor sending data to a robot

(C) A program to calculate paycheck amounts

(D) A voice command

GO ON TO THE NEXT PAGE

68. You have two procedures to select from to continuously loop through a series of digital billboard ads. Will both procedures successfully work? Assume the list of advertisements is correctly initialized and the programs will be restarted each time the ads change, usually weekly. There are 604,800 seconds in a week. Select two answers.

Block 1
```
PROCEDURE displayAds(listAds)
{
    index ← 1
    REPEAT UNTIL (index ≥ LENGTH(listAds))
    {
        DISPLAY (listAds(index))
        < wait 10 seconds >
        index ← index + 1
        IF (index = LENGTH(listAds))
        {
            index = 1
        }
    }
}
```

Block 2
```
PROCEDURE adDIsplay(listAds)
{
    x ← 1000000
    REPEAT x TIMES
    {
        FOR EACH ad in listAds
        {
            DISPLAY (ad)
            < wait 10 seconds >
        }
    }
}
```

(A) Block 1 runs correctly.
(B) Block 1 does *not* run correctly.
(C) Block 2 runs correctly.
(D) Block 2 does *not* run correctly.

69. Your organization has determined that data used for assigning managers to high-volume sales stores is unintentionally biased. How can the bias in the data samples be corrected? Select two answers.

(A) Collect more data for a wider sample of data.
(B) Include a different type of data to add to the collection.
(C) Analyze the source of the data to identify existing bias to remove it.
(D) Review the attributes to include or ignore in your data collection and analysis.

70. You have the following procedure that is not working as expected to add numbers that are divisible by 2 or divisible by 3 to the end of a list. You collaborate with a classmate to help identify the problem. Assume the list of numbers passed as an argument holds valid numbers. What are the errors? Select two answers.

```
Line 1  PROCEDURE divisible (numList)
Line 2  {
Line 3      FOR EACH num in numList
Line 4      {
Line 5          IF (num MOD 2 = 0 OR num / 3 = 0)
Line 6          {
Line 7              INSERT (numList, num)
Line 8          }
Line 9      }
Line 10 }
```

(A) Line 5 should use MOD in both places.
(B) Line 5 should use division "/" in both places.
(C) Line 7 should use APPEND rather than INSERT.
(D) Line 10 has an extra closing brace.

STOP. End of Exam.

› Answers and Explanations

If further review is needed, the Big Idea where information can be found about the topic is included at the end of each question.

1. **D**—We do not need to know how a procedure works, only that it does. We need to know what input to provide and what output to expect. The details are hidden or abstracted away inside the procedure's code. Big Idea 3: Algorithms and Programming

2. **A**—Parameters allow a procedure to be more flexible by permitting different values from the program to be sent to the procedure. Code does not have to be duplicated each time it needs to be used in the program. Big Idea 3: Algorithms and Programming

3. **D**—Cleaning data refers to taking raw data and checking it for errors. These errors could be corrupt, incomplete, or duplicate data. Cleaning could include either correcting or removing the identified data, depending on the specifications for a particular dataset. Big Idea 2: Data

4. **A**—Unreasonable problems may have an algorithm that can work for a small number of values, but as the dataset grows large, the time or memory requirements to run it are beyond current capabilities. Big Idea 3: Algorithms and Programming

5. **B**—These are some of the abstractions that can be used in writing software. Both procedures and libraries provide algorithms that can be used without knowing the details of how they work—which is the definition of procedural abstraction in computer science. Big Idea 3: Algorithms and Programming

6. **C**—Organizations handling datasets must protect the data to ensure that people's private information is not accidentally revealed or able to be deduced or identified with basic data already publicly available. Big Idea 5: Impact of Computing

7. **C**—Protocols are a set of rules for a variety of services on the Internet. Data will move across any brand of equipment as long as the protocols are followed. Big Idea 4: Computing Systems and Networks

8. **B**—The decimal number converts to 10011110. Take the binary number and create a table of the powers of 2, starting with 2^0 in the rightmost position.

2^7	2^6	2^5	2^4	2^3	2^2	2^1	2^0
128	64	32	16	8	4	2	1
1	0	0	1	1	1	1	0

Subtract the largest value from the second row that is the same or less than the number, 158. In this case, subtract 158 – 128. Your remainder is 30. Place a 1 in the 128 column.

You can't subtract 64 or 32 from 30 without ending up with a negative number, so place 0 in those two columns.

You can subtract 16 from 30 and have a positive result. Therefore, subtract 30 – 16 = 14, and place a 1 in the 16s column.

You can subtract 8 from 14, so place a 1 in the 8s column and subtract 14 – 8 = 6.

You can subtract 4 from 6, so place a 1 in the 4s column and subtract 6 – 4 = 2.

Since 2 – 2 = 0, place a 1 in the 2s column and a 0 in 1s column.

Big Idea 2: Data

9. **C**—The code associated with the selection statement is executed when the Boolean condition evaluates to be true. Additional code can be executed if the condition is false using the ELSE statement. Big Idea 3: Algorithms and Programming

10. **B**—The FOR EACH loop traverses the list of student names. Therefore, we have to keep track of our position in the lockerNum list with the *index* variable. We need to set the lockerNum list to the assigned student name and the locker number is the index position. Remember that lists start at index 1 for these exam questions. Big Idea 3: Algorithms and Programming

11. **A**—Logical conditions are in a Boolean format, using relational operators such as >, <, =. This means that each condition will always evaluate to either true or false. Big Idea 3: Algorithms and Programming

12. **D**—Machine-learning algorithms learn from and make predictions based on data to improve the experience for those using it. One example is search algorithms. These often infer additional details of your search criteria, such as showing the Mustang car versus the mustang horse if your other search criteria include automobiles. Big Idea 2: Data

13. **C**—The index starts at the first position, 1, and includes the "n" in *person* at index position 6. Remember that the index position starts at 1 for this exam.

Character	p	e	r	s	o	n	@	a	p	c	s	p	.	o	r	g
Index	1	2	3	4	5	6	7	8	9	10	11	12	13	14	15	16

Big Idea 3: Algorithms and Programming

14. **C**—Analog data is converted to digital data by taking samples at regular intervals. These samples are converted to bits to represent the analog data in a digital format. Big Idea 2: Data

15. **D**—APIs provide prewritten, pretested program modules to be used by other programs, greatly simplifying the process of writing a new program. This helps speed up writing and testing the code as well. Big Idea 3: Algorithms and Programming

16. **A**—Testing involves implementing the algorithm through code and executing it to determine how often statements execute. These are used to informally determine the algorithm's efficiency. Big Idea 3: Algorithms and Programming

17. **B**—Different algorithms can be created to solve the same problem. These algorithms could provide new insights to the problem as well as be more efficient. Big Idea 3: Algorithms and Programming

18. **A**—All algorithms can be written with a combination of sequential, selection, and iterative statements.
    - Sequential statements run one after the other.
    - Selection statements are run only if the criteria are met.
    - Iterative statements repeat while the criteria are met.

Big Idea 3: Algorithms and Programming

19. **A**—Viruses must be spread via an infected file. These are transmitted in ways to get people to click on them, and e-mail attachments are the most common way. Big Idea 5: Impact of Computing

20. **C**—The digital divide is the term used to denote the different levels of access to the Internet and/or access to computing devices based on geographic, demographic, or socioeconomic attributes. Big Idea 5: Impact of Computing

21. **B**—Developing program components and testing them before combining them with other working, tested code helps create larger, correct programs. Big Idea 3: Algorithms and Programming

22. **D**—A binary search uses the "divide and conquer" method to halve (divide by 2) the size of the dataset, and continues to search the half of the dataset the number could still be in. The "higher" or "lower" feedback is required to determine which half of the dataset to keep. This search is very efficient, and the dataset must be sorted for it to work. Big Idea 3: Algorithms and Programming

23. **B**—By documenting what the program does, if code is changed, the programmer changing it can test to ensure that the program still works as intended. Big Idea 1: Creative Development

24. **A**—Parallel computing systems have a sequential part and a parallel part. The parallel part spreads out the processing among multiple devices to reduce the time needed. The sequential part combines the results from the parallel processing. Big Idea 4: Computing Systems and Networks

25. **D**—The same binary number could represent a number, color, or text field. The program using the binary number knows how to interpret its meaning. Big Idea 2: Data

26. **B**—Iteration sets up conditions where code can be repeated either a specified number of times or until a condition is no longer met. Big Idea 3: Algorithms and Programming

27. **B**—Undecidable problems do not have an algorithm that can solve all cases. Big Idea 3: Algorithms and Programming

28. **C**—Procedures are blocks of code that can be reused through calling them as many times as needed in a program, rather than duplicating code. This makes the program more readable and easier to maintain. Big Idea 3: Algorithms and Programming

29. **B**—Collaboration is the process of working with one or more individuals on an activity or task. It is an effective way to test and correct code. Team members can test each other's code and help each other correct any errors that are found. The collaborative efforts could occur in person or in a virtual format. Big Idea 1: Creative Development

30. **B**—Certificate Authorities (CAs) issue digital certificates that allow others using a site to confirm that the identity of that site is authentic. Big Idea 5: Impact of Computing

31. **C**—Bandwidth measures how much data can be transmitted from a location to another in a given amount of time. Big Idea 4: Computing Systems and Networks

32. **C**—A FOR EACH loop will check each element in a list from start to end without having to specify each one individually. Neither an "index out of bounds" error nor an infinite loop will occur. Big Idea 3: Algorithms and Programming

33. **B**—This is the concept behind libraries and APIs. Prewritten and tested algorithms and code can be used by other programs needing the same functionality in their program. It saves time as well as helps ensure that the new algorithms are correct. Big Idea 3: Algorithms and Programming

34. **C**—The classroom has 25 available desks, so the REPEAT UNTIL loop should continue until the number of available desks is 0. Big Idea 3: Algorithms and Programming

35. **D**—Logic errors occur when the program runs but there are unexpected results either in the steps the program executes or the output. An example would be using the wrong variable in a calculation that would give incorrect results. Big Idea 1: Creative Development

36. **A**—Readability makes code easier to understand and therefore easier to debug, maintain, and enhance. Big Idea 3: Algorithms and Programming

37. **B**—Having people with different perspectives and backgrounds helps identify new trends or ideas and potential solutions more easily than someone working alone or a in homogeneous group. Big Idea 1: Creative Development

38. **A**—Lossless data compression techniques enable the original, uncompressed file to be restored. Lossless techniques do not provide as much compression as a lossy technique, but always select this when you may need to restore the original file. Big Idea 2: Data

39. **A**—A good cryptographic model is easy to use in one direction, such as encrypting data, but very difficult to do in the other direction, the decryption of the data. This means that even if the information is intercepted, someone trying to exploit it will not be able to identify the correct decryption key needed. Big Idea 5: Impact of Computing

40. **D**—Many programming languages have a set limit for the integer size that can be represented. When that is exceeded, an overflow error occurs. Most languages do not display an error message. Instead, the sign bit is flipped and a positive number becomes negative and vice versa. Big Idea 2: Data

41. **A**—While models are usually on a smaller scale than the real-world feature they represent, they can be used to simulate actual events to see the result of changes to variables. These can be run without actual constraints, such as emulating an eclipse without having to wait for an actual eclipse to occur to test the hypotheses. Big Idea 3: Algorithms and Programming

42. **D**—A rogue access point on a network can capture data to save it, analyze it, or modify it. Big Idea 5: Impact of Computing

43. **A**—Each module handles functionality independently but can be combined with other modules to create new functionality. For example, if a module adds a text field to a list, it can be added to functionality to create and maintain a contact list on a smartphone. Big Idea 1: Creative Development

44. **A**—As the demand for Internet connections grows, new networks can be added along with additional routers as needed, without impacting existing services. Big Idea 4: Computing Systems and Networks

45. **A**—Your zip code, which is available in many public records, is considered part of your PII. Big Idea 5: Impact of Computing

46. **D**—A computing innovation has to have a computer program as part of its functionality. The proposed "Find my car!" app will have a program that will begin when the specified button is pushed to summon the vehicle. It will request current GPS coordinates through an API call and send them to the self-driving vehicle along with the command to turn on the car. Big Idea 5: Impact of Computing

47. **A**—The output of the app will be the longitude and latitude of the app's location. An instruction to start the vehicle will also be output from it. Big Idea 1: Creative Development

48. **B**—Tracking and storing location data is likely to occur for the app to store coordinates for frequently visited locations. This is a privacy concern because the data will be available to the organization developing the app and potentially the self-driving vehicle's manufacturer and any repair shop used. Anyone who uses the driver's smartphone can pull up the app and view the history as well. Big Idea 5: Impact of Computing

49. **A**—Any traffic congestion at the entrance to businesses and organizations is a potential harm that is due to the app itself. There could be increased air pollution anytime people leave their car idling, but that is not due to the app.

Car accidents and people parking illegally are harmful but are also not due to the app. Big Idea 5: Impact of Computing

50. **B**—The app will be activated by an event, the pressing of a button to start the program's processing. For the app to work, it will need accurate longitude and latitude coordinates accessed through an API to a GPS (Global Positioning System). If the self-driving car cannot get within a few feet of the driver, the app will not be useful and people will not continue to use it. Big Idea 1: Creative Development

51. **B**—One method of debugging involves following or tracing each line of code to determine what the program is doing versus what it should be doing based on current variable values. Big Idea 1: Creative Development

52. **C**—Metadata means "data about data." The only option that provides information about the data versus being data is information about the author. Big Idea 2: Data

53. **A**—The steps in an iterative development process are:
    • Investigate and fully define the problem to be solved.
    • Design a solution to solve the problem.
    • Prototype to code the solution.
    • Test to evaluate the solution.

These steps should be repeated as needed in additional iterations to further refine and improve the programs based on testing and feedback. Big Idea 1: Creative Development

54. **B**—Variable names should be descriptive and use "camel case" by capitalizing the first letter of the second and additional words, when two or more words are used for the variable name. Example: shoeSize. Big Idea 3: Algorithms and Programming

55. **B**—Typing in the link for the organization, such as your bank, directly in a new tab rather than clicking on the link provided will deflect a phishing attack. Big Idea 5: Impact of Computing

56. D—Using the AND and OR operators creates a compound expression. Both conditions for the AND must be true for the expression to be true, and at least one of the conditions needs to be true for an OR compound expression to be true. Big Idea 3: Algorithms and Programming

57. B—Internet redundancy means that if a path is down, then the packets can be sent via an alternate route to reach their destination. Big Idea 4: Computing Systems and Networks

58. C—Packets are same-size groupings of information to be sent over the Internet along different paths. Big Idea 4: Computing Systems and Networks

59. B—Technology tools such as spreadsheets and databases are designed to organize data and filter data through inquiries and reports to analyze it. Big Idea 2: Data

60. D—An optimization problem looks for the best solution to the problem. If someone wants to optimize their performance, they are looking to improve it. Anytime you are looking to enhance the outcome of something, you are looking for the best solution or to optimize it. Big Idea 3: Algorithms and Programming

61. D—Abstractions remove differing details to create a more general and more flexible concept. Big Idea 2: Data

62. A—Calling the RANDOM function with the correct start and stop numbers and storing it in a variable will correctly select an attendee to participate. Big Idea 3: Algorithms and Programming

63. A—A biometric indicator is something unique to the individual, such as a fingerprint or retina scan. It would be set up in advance for comparison purposes to anyone attempting to access the device.

D—A security token sent securely to a device such as a cell phone can ensure that the person is who they claim to be. The device to send the token to is set up in advance. Big Idea 5: Impact of Computing

64. A—Selection 1 is correct since it correctly tests if a number is less than 914.

B—Selection 2 is also correct because if a number is not greater than or equal to 914, then it can only be less than 914. Big Idea 3: Algorithms and Programming

65. B—Artifacts on the Internet are not necessarily free. They are someone else's intellectual property. You may not use the image without paying the licensing fee or obtaining written permission from the owner to use it.

D—The Creative Commons licensing options allow creators to make their work available for viewing, and possibly for use by others, depending on the licensing option selected. Big Idea 5: Impact of Computing

66. B—Feedback from those who will use the system is key to refining the programming solution to meet the project's requirements.

D—Reflection after each iteration of the development process also helps to ensure the program code will correctly meet the requirements. Big Idea 1: Creative Development

67. B—A sensor reading is an event. The robot's code would test for certain conditions to cause different events based on the values of the sensor.

D—A voice command is an event. Event-driven programming is when code is executed only when something occurs that the program recognizes as a valid event, such as a voice command like "Hey Google," "Siri," or "Alexa." Big Idea 1: Creative Development

68. A—Block 1 runs correctly. Each time the index reaches the last element in the list, it is reset to 1 to start displaying ads from the beginning of the list again.

C—Block 2 runs correctly. The loop is set to run one million times to keep cycling through the ads in the list, 24 hours a day, 7 days a week. The company expects the ads to change prior to reaching the one millionth time. The counter will be reset to one million each time the ads change. Big Idea 3: Algorithms and Programming

69. C—Analyzing the source of the data to identify existing bias in the data can correct the outcome of the algorithm. If historical data is used, and historically people with certain attributes were most often the managers of high-volume stores, then those people are more likely to be recommended for those high-volume stores.

D—Reviewing the data attributes, such as gender, age, income, or race, that you want the analysis to consider can help prevent or remove bias from the outcome. Big Idea 2: Data

70. A—To determine if a number is divisible by another number, the remainder must be 0. Therefore, both operations should be MOD.

C—To place the numbers at the end of the list, the APPEND command should be used rather than INSERT. Additionally, the number of parameters for the INSERT command on Line 7 are for the APPEND command rather than INSERT. Big Idea 3: Algorithms and Programming

Analyzing Your Performance on the Diagnostic Test

The exercise below will help you quickly and easily identify the chapters in Step 4 that you most need to review for the AP Computer Science Principles multiple-choice exam. Revise your study plan so that you prioritize the chapters with which you had the most difficulty.

Look at your answer sheet and mark all the questions you missed. Then shade in or mark an X in the boxes below that correspond to the question numbers that you missed. Then you will know what concepts you need to review the most.

Big Idea 1: Creative Development

23	29	35	37	43	47	50	51	53	66	67

Big Idea 2: Data

3	8	12	14	25	38	40	52	59	60	61	69

Big Idea 3: Algorithms and Programming

1	2	4	5	9	10	11	13	15	16	17	18	21	22
26	27	28	32	33	34	36	41	54	56	62	64	68	70

Big Idea 4: Computing Systems and Networks

7	24	31	44	57	58

Big Idea 5: Impact of Computing

6	19	20	30	39	42	45
46	48	49	55	63	65	

Develop Strategies for Success

CHAPTER **4**   Strategies to Help You Do Your Best
on the Exam and Create Performance
Task

CHAPTER 4

Strategies to Help You Do Your Best on the Exam and Create Performance Task

IN THIS CHAPTER

Summary: This chapter contains strategies and tips for answering the multiple-choice questions of the AP Computer Science Principles exam. You'll also find strategies to approach and master the performance task. Understanding how to most effectively and efficiently take the test and prepare the Create Performance Task (CPT) will help you get a higher score.

Key Ideas

- ✪ Practice pacing yourself on the multiple-choice exam. Don't get bogged down on questions you don't understand. Your goal is to get to the end of the exam so you get every point possible for the questions you know.
- ✪ If you don't know an answer on the multiple-choice exam, use the process of elimination to eliminate one or more answer choices and then guess. **Don't leave any questions blank**. There is no penalty for wrong answers!
- ✪ Planning, collaborating where allowed, and carefully editing your written response to conform to the scoring rubric are keys to doing well on the performance task.

Strategies and Tips for the Multiple-Choice Exam

It's safe to say that this will *not* be the first timed multiple-choice exam you've ever taken. You're familiar with how this works and have probably already developed your own style to approach this type of test. To get the highest score you are capable of, it's necessary that your method is as efficient and effective as possible. Look at the strategies below and make sure you're on the right track.

Strategy #1: Pace Yourself

Many students approach the test with the lofty goal of getting every answer correct. But this approach will get you bogged down in the difficult questions where you are not sure of the answer. You'll end up not completing the test and missing questions you could easily have gotten right. Keep in mind that you can miss a number of multiple-choice questions and still get a 5. The best strategy in approaching the test is not to worry about missing some questions; instead try to make sure you get to every question for which you know the answer.

The AP Computer Science Principles exam does *not* start out with easy questions and work its way up to the hard ones. Questions are randomly ordered so the questions that are easy for you are just as likely to be at the end as at the beginning of the test. Remember: you get the same number of points for getting an easy question right as a hard question. Don't bring down your score by not getting to all the questions to which you know the answer. If you don't know an answer, take a guess and move on. You need to get to the last question of the exam in order to maximize the number of questions you answer correctly.

Practice pacing yourself by taking the practice tests in this book and timing yourself. You have to answer 70 questions in two hours. So, you need to answer 35 questions per hour, or 17 to 18 every half hour. That's about a minute and 43 seconds per question. Keep track of your pace as you work. Ideally, you'll want to work a little faster so that at the end you have time to go back to questions you want to think more about (more about that in the next section).

The difficult questions are not the only ones that may slow you down. Don't spend time second-guessing a choice you made. This is usually a waste of valuable time. Trust your initial instincts and don't change an answer unless you are certain it needs changing.

Strategy #2: Use the Process of Elimination and Guess

You're probably familiar with this strategy from all the timed multiple-choice exams you've taken. The correct answer is right in front of you. If you don't know which one it is, immediately start eliminating answer choices you're pretty sure are wrong. If you can eliminate even one choice as incorrect, your odds of getting the question right improve. If you can eliminate two wrong answer choices, you have a good chance of guessing correctly between the two remaining choices.

Even if you can't eliminate a single wrong answer choice, you should still guess. There is no penalty for guessing incorrectly, so make sure an oval is filled in for every question.

Mark questions you want to come back to at the end if you have time. Perhaps another question will jog your memory or even offer a clue. You should try to work fast enough so that you have a little time at the end to do this. But be sure to mark the question in your test booklet, not on your answer sheet. Keep all unnecessary pencil marks off your answer sheet so that the computer that scores the test doesn't misread your marks.

Even if it's a question you want to come back to, fill in an answer choice. Don't leave it blank. You may not have time to come back. Also, marking an oval will reduce the chance that you'll mess up your answer sheet. Your worst nightmare is answering the questions correctly but getting off a row in filling in the ovals.

The process of elimination is even more powerful when used for the eight final multiple-choice questions for which you'll need to select *two* correct answers. Fill in *two* ovals for each of these questions. If you can eliminate just two wrong answers, you'll get the question right. But keep in mind that there's no partial credit; to get the question right, you'll need to have identified both correct answers.

Helpful Tips for the Multiple-Choice Exam

Reading the Question

- Read each question all the way through. Don't guess what the final question or instruction is. Note that the instruction to choose *two* answer choices is given at the end.
- Watch for words like *not, never, least, most,* and *always.* Be especially careful in selecting an answer when one of these negative words appears.
- Think of your answer before reading the choices. This can save you time and keep any distractors from making you second-guess your response.
- Read all the answer choices. Do NOT stop at the first choice you think is correct. There may be a better answer further down the choices.
- If the answer choices are not what you would expect, it's possible you misread or misunderstood the question. Read the question again and again until you understand what it is asking.

Choosing an Answer

- Guess if you do not know the answer. There is no penalty for wrong answers.
- Mark questions you want to come back to if you have time at the end. Mark them in the question booklet, not the answer sheet, where any stray pencil mark may be misread by the computer.
- Do NOT change an answer unless you are certain. Trust your initial instincts.
- Do NOT change an answer because you see there are several answers of the same letter in a row! Don't worry if you seem to be marking a lot of one letter in your answer choices.

Marking the Answer Sheet

- Fill in the bubbles on the answer sheet completely. But don't make other marks on your answer sheet.
- If you need to erase an answer, make sure it's completely erased so that the computer won't read that you filled in two ovals. Bring an eraser that won't leave smudges.
- Be sure you are filling in the answer for the correct question. Check each time you turn the page to be sure. There's nothing worse than getting the question right but putting the answer in the wrong row.

Strategies for the Performance Task

In this chapter, you'll find strategies that will give you a plan of attack for the performance task. In the next chapter (Chapter 5), you'll find a more specific step-by-step guide to the performance task. In Chapter 5, you'll find numerous tips relating to specific parts of the performance task as well as a number of pitfalls to avoid. These tips won't be repeated here; instead, this chapter focuses on broad strategies relating to how to plan for and carry out the performance task.

Strategy #1: Plan Your Project Before You Begin

Before the performance task officially begins with the required in-class time allocated to the project, be sure you think through what you will do. Your teacher has more leeway in answering questions before the project officially begins. You can ask questions about possible Create projects and get general advice. Your teacher may have your class do a practice Create project prior to the one that you will submit to the College Board. Take advantage of this to fully understand the performance task expectations. Practicing and planning before you officially begin the performance task is key to doing well.

The Create performance task requires you to develop a computer program, submit a video of the program running, and answer questions about the program you created. You should begin this task only after you have a good understanding of data abstraction and procedural abstraction, algorithms, and programming selection and iterative statements (loops), along with procedures and lists since all of these topics will be incorporated in your program and the written response.

You should choose a topic and think it through before your AP class begins the 12 official hours of class time required for the Create performance task. Be sure your programming topic is broad enough to be able to meet the criteria but not too broad so you cannot finish it on time. Before the task officially begins, you can plan what you want to do, collaborate with classmates, and ask your teacher questions about the topic or your planned methodology. But once the 12-hour time period begins, your teacher is more limited in what help can be given. After the project officially begins your teacher can only answer questions relating to the performance task in general. However, don't hesitate to ask any question you have; your teacher will decide if the question can be answered wholly, in part, or not at all.

Strategy #2: Collaborate with a Classmate

The AP Computer Science Principles assessment is unique among AP exams in that it allows you to work with another student in your class. Take advantage of this and make it part of your strategy. Creating a computer program is the central requirement for the Create performance task. Programming is almost always better if people work together on it.

Keep in mind, though, that the collaboration allowed is limited to the programming that needs to be created for the Create performance task. Each of you will need to write sections of code independently, create your own video of the program running, and work on your own to complete the written responses.

Well before the 12-hour time period in your AP class for the Create performance task, you should try to line up a partner with whom you work well. You should talk about what type of program you want to create and plan what each of you will do. Make sure you are both on the same page with all of this before you officially begin to work together during the 12-hour in-class period. Also, be sure to plan enough time to get the individual parts you each wrote integrated into the project and tested as a whole.

Don't worry if you are unable to line up a partner or simply prefer to work alone. Collaboration is not required.

Strategy #3: Evaluate and Then Edit Your Written Responses

While the AP Computer Science Principles exam is unique in that you'll find no free-response questions on the exam on test day (just multiple-choice questions), the testmakers have made up for this by including a number of free-response questions for the Create performance task. How you do on the written responses will determine most of your score on the performance task. Be sure to leave enough time to write the written response. You can have an amazing programming project, but if you do not write adequately about it, you will not receive all of the available points for it.

A key to getting a high score on the performance task is to carefully edit your written response. The next chapter contains a step-by-step guide to answering the written response prompts. As you will discover, there are strict limits on the number of words you can use for each of the free-response questions. So, first you'll need to edit your written responses to make sure they fall within the word-count limit for each question. But to really improve your score, you'll have to take the editing one step further: you'll have to evaluate your answers based on the scoring rubric the College Board has provided and then edit your responses to pick up any points you've missed.

The College Board has made public the rubric used to grade the written responses to the prompts. This rubric, which is still the current version, is included in the College Board's PDF document *AP Computer Science Principles 2021 Scoring Guidelines*. If you haven't already printed or bookmarked this document, you can find it at this link:

https://apcentral.collegeboard.org/pdf/ap-computer-science-principles-2021-create-performance-task-scoring-guidelines.pdf

This scoring rubric is complex but very specific on how points are awarded. Think of it as an "answer sheet" and use it to evaluate each of your written responses. By applying the "answer sheet" to your written responses, you can discover how many points each response would earn. More importantly, you can find out exactly what you need to add to your written response to earn any points you've missed. Edit your responses to pick up these points, being sure to remain within the word-count limit for each question.

The site also has helpful information in the form of samples of actual student responses for the Create performance task. These examples are followed by a discussion of how points were awarded based on the rubric. You can follow these examples in evaluating your own written responses. These examples with scoring explanations can be found at the bottom of this web page:

https://apcentral.collegeboard.org/courses/ap-computer-science-principles/exam

The student projects are in the left-most column labeled Create – Sample Responses. The middle column labeled Scoring Guidelines links directly to the Create performance task rubric. The right-hand column labeled Commentary has a document that explains whether points were earned based on the rubric and why or why not. The commentary for all of the sample projects is contained in the document.

Of course, evaluating your written responses based on the rubric and then editing your responses to match the rubric will take more time. You may not have time to complete this during the official 12-hour in-class time allocation. But there is no reason you can't continue working on this at home or after the official minimum time period is over. You are permitted to spend more time outside of class to complete this task. The higher score you receive will be well worth the extra time you put in.

Now you are armed with the strategies that will help you attack and master the AP Computer Science Principles assessment. The next chapter focuses on the specifics of the Create performance task.

STEP 4

Review the Knowledge You Need to Score High

CHAPTER 5

The Create Performance Task

IN THIS CHAPTER

Summary: For the Create performance task, students design and create a program, create a video showing it running, and answer prompts about the program. Make sure you are writing code and responding to the prompts for the correct year. You will have at least 12 hours of dedicated in-class time to work on the Create performance task. It must be submitted to the College Board via the digital portfolio by the published deadline, at 11:59 p.m. Eastern time.

Key Ideas

✪ The Create performance task requires you to create a computer program, record a video showing the program running, and provide a written response to questions.

✪ The Create performance task counts for 30% of your total AP score.

✪ There is not a designated programming language to use. You can choose the one you prefer. The programming language may be block code or text based.

✪ You will have a minimum of 12 hours of in-class time to complete the Create performance task.

✪ Do not make your programming project overly complicated! You can still earn all of the points with a simpler program that meets all the specified requirements.

Create Performance Task: The Basics

As you probably remember from Chapter 1, the AP Computer Science Principles exam score is comprised of two parts:

1. The two-hour multiple-choice exam of 70 questions makes up 70% of the score.
2. The Create performance task includes a program, video, and written responses to prompts and counts for 30% of the final score.

The artifacts created for the performance task must be uploaded to the College Board Digital Portfolio portal by 11:59 p.m. Eastern time on the due date. Students not attending a traditional school should contact the AP coordinator at their assigned school or at the school district level at the beginning of the school year for information on how to register for the exam and submit their performance task project. Students who are in yearlong or first-semester only AP courses must be registered with the College Board by November 15, and students in AP courses that only meet second semester must register by March 15.

The College Board's document "AP Computer Science Principles Student Handouts" provides more information about the requirements for completing the Create performance task. This PDF document was referenced in Chapter 4. If you haven't already printed or bookmarked this document, here is the link again:

> https://apcentral.collegeboard.org/pdf/ap-csp-student-task-directions.pdf

The College Board site also has examples of Create projects submitted by students along with their grading and an explanation of why each project received the scores it did (see the "Commentary" column). These projects can be viewed at the bottom of this web page:

> https://apcentral.collegeboard.org/courses/ap-computer-science-principles/exam

Be sure to look at the examples of the Create performance task that the College Board has provided online (see box above). Taking a careful look at these projects will be one of the most helpful things you can do to prepare yourself for the performance task. For each example, the Scoring Commentary document provides the score the project received and an explanation of how it was evaluated.

The Create Performance Task

The Create performance task requires you to demonstrate both your programming knowledge and your creativity. You get to design and develop a program on a topic of your choice. You also get to select the programming language to use. No other AP exam even comes close to allowing you this much choice in what you want to do!

Students are permitted to collaborate with another student on this task, but it is not required. If you do work with a partner, each student must complete some of the programming sections individually. Both students must clearly identify sections of code created individually, created by their partner, and those that were worked on together. You and your partner **must** complete your video and written responses independently.

Twelve hours of class time must be provided in class to ensure that all students have the same standard amount of time to create and document their project. You will have to turn in a video, a written response to question prompts, and the program code to the College Board using the Digital Portfolio portal.

Teachers are limited in the type of questions they can answer regarding individual projects, especially after the official in-class time to complete the task has begun. But don't hesitate to ask a question you have for the Create performance task. Your teacher will decide whether the question can be answered wholly, in part, or not at all.

You may ask your teacher about the task and submission requirements or for help identifying a topic, resolving technical issues (such as connecting to a network), or saving files.

You can also ask for help if a partner is not completing their work and for help with the correct usage of code from an application programming interface (API).

> Be sure your programming topic for the Create performance task is broad enough to be able to meet the criteria but not too broad that you cannot finish it in time.

Program Code

The program you develop needs to include several features. These are listed in a checklist in the student handout from the College Board. Use the checklist to be sure you are meeting all of the needed criteria. These are highlighted below.

Comments

You would have learned about the benefits of using comments for readability as one of the learning objectives for the course. In addition to commenting your code to explain functionality as needed, you should also use comments to indicate which section of code you created, and if you worked with a partner, which section your partner created. Since you must cite code you use that was created by anyone else, including using libraries or APIs, comments are the recommended way to do this. You can put the comment in a header at the top of your program and/or where you use the code or call it within your program. Do not use names. Use general wording, such as "my partner and I." For example, you could have comments like the following:

I independently created this code to . . .
My partner created this code that does . . .
This is a call to a module from the library . . . to do . . .

Some programming languages do not provide a way to create comments. If you happen to use one of these, you can cite code not created by you when you prepare a document of your code to turn in to the College Board. You have to submit your code to the College Board Digital Portfolio in PDF format, so you can copy or screenshot a portion of the code and paste it in a word processing document such as Microsoft Word or Google Docs. Then add a sentence in the document for citation purposes. Keep documenting the rest of your code and cite as needed. Remember to save as a PDF to turn it in. The Digital Portfolio site will only accept the file for the program code in PDF format.

Input

Your program must include input from an external source and handle the input in the code. This portion of the code must be student created. You cannot use code from another source for this in your program. The options include:

- User-provided input. This could be from data the user types on a keyboard in response to a prompt from your program. For example, if you had a guessing game, your program would prompt the user for their current guess.

  The input could also be from an event the user triggers. This could be a tap on a button, a swipe on the screen, or a shake of the device, among other types of events for event-driven programming.

- Input from a device. This could be from a sensor that feeds data to your program. Types of sensors include distance, motion, light, and sound. There are many other types of sensors that could be used.

  Another example of a device providing input is a game controller or joystick sending commands for player movement.

- Online data stream. You may immediately think of music or movies for data streaming possibilities. Those are definitely often used. Other data streams could include sensors that take constant readings. For example, apps such as step counters continually measure and record the data. Mouse clicks in a game or website are also data stream examples.

- A file. Input to a program can come from a file that was created by a different program or a person typing and saving data. Examples could include files of e-mail addresses, passwords, temperature readings, a book manuscript, grades, or items and quantities sold or returned. The possibilities are endless!

Don't forget to actually utilize the user input in your program! If you collect it, but then do nothing further with it, you will not earn credit it for it when your project is scored. We'll go over the rubric later in this chapter so you can see exactly how your work will be scored.

A list or other data collection type

Your program must include some type of data collection where you can store more than one value in a single data collection variable. You have been taught about *lists* for this course, and a list is a perfect example of a data collection! You can store more than one value in a single list variable. Other programming languages may use alternate terminology such as *array*. Some languages include other data collection types, such as dictionaries. These are acceptable to use as well.

As with the user input, be sure you use your list in the program. Don't just create one since you know you need one. If you do not use it further in your program, you will not receive credit for it during scoring.

The list is an example of data abstraction since it is much easier to manage data values of the same type in one variable name, rather than individual variables for each data element!

A procedure

You must define a procedure in your program, and the procedure must have one or more parameters. Procedures and parameters are part of the course content and are included in the Big Idea 3 chapter on algorithms and programming. Remember that procedures should be used when you have code that is needed in more than one place in your program. You can call the procedure to execute the code in it as many times as needed in your program with different values passed to it.

You must have a call to the procedure in your program, and you will need at least two calls to it for section 3d in the written response. This means you should not create a procedure that is only called once or not at all in your program. The AP readers are to check for this before awarding the point for the procedure.

Remember: values are passed to procedures using *arguments* when the procedure is called. The *parameters* in the procedure take the values from the arguments and use them in the procedure. The parameters are local to the procedure and cannot be used outside of the procedure's scope. Your procedure must use the values sent to it for further processing within the procedure. Some form of output must be created based on the input sent to the procedure. The following are some examples of output:

- Text displayed with information or a calculation result
- An image, web page, or video
- A sound file
- A tactile type output such as a vibration

Your procedure must be complex enough to include the following:

- Selection—An IF statement
- Iteration—Any type of loop is acceptable. Make sure your loop executes more than once. Students have submitted code with a loop that would only execute once by design. This will not meet the requirements in the AP rubric to earn the point!
- Sequencing—If you have selection and iteration, you also have sequencing.

The procedure you create does not have to use the RETURN statement to send data back to the calling location, but it is acceptable if it does.

While you may have built-in procedures or event handlers within your program, these will *not* count as a student-created procedure. You must write your own!

Video Requirements

You must submit a video of the program running. It must include the following features and information:

- You must show how input is entered into your program.
- At least one feature that uses the input just entered must be shown working, even if it is not working correctly. Try to show one that is key to the functioning of the program.
- The output the program produced from the input provided must also be shown.

The use of captions in your video is encouraged but not required. You may NOT narrate your video with your voice or anyone else's voice. Your name, image, or bitmoji should not be visible in your video.

The video can be no more than 60 seconds long, must be no larger than 30 MB, and must be in one of the accepted file formats. If your video is too large, there are many tools available to compress it to the 30 MB or less size requirement. Check your video after compression to be sure that it is still viewable! Sometimes files become corrupt or are too blurry to view.

Check the College Board's document "AP Computer Science Principles Student Handouts" for the most current list of acceptable file formats. As of this writing, these are .mp4, .wmv, .avi, or .mov. (If you haven't already printed or bookmarked this PDF document, see the box earlier in this chapter for information on accessing it.)

> **PITFALL TO AVOID:** Even if you work with a partner, you each must create your own video.

Rubric Readiness

To earn this point, you must have a video that shows input to your program, program functionality, and output. You cannot show screenshots or other images of your program or just the code in the video. You must show the program running. You must *also* have a written response in section 3a. See the Rubric Readiness checklist under 3a below.

Written Response Requirements

You have a maximum of 750 words total to answer the prompts. Be sure to clearly label each prompt, and be direct about answering the question asked. That is not many words to get your ideas across, so ensure your writing is succinct and clear. Make sure you are working from prompts labeled 3a, 3b, 3c, and 3d. Those are the new prompts. If you are using prompts labeled 2a–2d, then you have the old prompts! Do *not* use the old ones, as you will not earn many points after all of your hard work. The new prompts are very different! To help avoid this, the College Board will have you upload your written responses to a template, but you don't want to find out you used the wrong prompts after you've finished!

Your program code is not included in the 750-word-count limit. Remember that you must work independently on your written responses to the following prompts. Collaboration is not allowed on these!

Be sure to leave plenty of time to complete the written response. You can write an amazing program, but if you do not write adequately about it to answer all the questions, you will not receive many points for it. The scoring focuses mostly on your written responses, not on how cool your program is.

Section 3a

There are three parts for the first prompt. You have to answer each part to be able to earn the credit, and partial credit is not given. You have roughly 150 words to answer this prompt in total.

3.a.i. Describe the overall purpose of the program.
This is *what* the program is supposed to do. For example:

The purpose of my program is to play a guessing game of numbers between 1–100.

You don't need many words for this section. Be specific and use the word "purpose." It makes it very clear when it is being scored.

3.a.ii. Describe the functionality you presented in your video.
This is where you describe what the program is doing in your video. Even if you used captions in your video, you must complete this response. Expand on your captions to provide more detail or provide the details if you did not caption.

- Describe what the program code in the video does.

For example: The program shows instructions for how to play the game. It then starts the game and asks the user to try and guess a number from 1 to 100. The player types in a number. The program then compares the guess to the secret number to see if it is correct.

3.a.iii. Describe the input and output of the section of code you showed in the video.

- Describe the input and how it is sent to the section of code you showed.

For example: The user types in a number that is their current guess using a real or virtual keyboard.

- Describe the output produced from the input provided after the code completes.

For example: If the guess is correct, a "Congratulations!" screen is displayed. If the guess is greater than the number, then the words "too high" are displayed on the screen.

If the guess is less than the actual number, then the words "too low" are displayed. The number of remaining guesses is also displayed on the screen along with an encouraging message to keep trying if the player did not guess correctly.

Rubric Readiness

To earn this point, you must have a video showing the following:

- Input to your program
- The program functioning using that input
- Output from the input shown

AND your written response to section 3.a describing the following:

- The purpose of your program (what it's supposed to do)
- The functionality shown in the video
- The input and output as shown in the video

Remember, you cannot show screenshots or other images of your program or only the code in the video. You must show the program running. This should be an easy point to earn. Use the video to show off your hard work and creativity! Just make sure you also meet the written criteria listed above.

Section 3b List data type

This section is all about the list or other data collection type you used in your program. You have to include parts of your actual code and answer the prompts. You should plan to use about 200 words for all of this section. The program code does ***not*** count in the total word count. Just as with section 3a, you must answer all five sections of this prompt to earn the points. You do not get partial credit—it's all or nothing.

3.b.i. Paste the code segment showing data stored in the list (or other data collection type). If you declare the list and load it with values, you can show that statement. If the list is initially empty, paste the line of code where you define it and also include the code where you add elements to the list.

3.b.ii. Paste the code that shows the data in the list being used.
This will vary depending on the purpose of your overall program. You can show elements of the list being used, such as using a loop to traverse the list and checking list elements for some purpose. You can show new data being created based on the list values. There are many possibilities that are acceptable. However, do not include your entire program and expect the person scoring your project to find the list being used. You will not earn the point if you do this.

3.b.iii. Name the list you are using in this section.
Some programs use multiple lists, so make sure you name the list you included in your snippets of code in 3.b.i and 3.b.ii. All you need to write is the list name.

3.b.iv. Describe what the data in the list represent in your program.
Be sure to describe the list data you are referencing in the above sections of this prompt! For example: This list holds the various tools, potions, and spells that the player's character gains during the game. These are added to the list when earned and removed when the player uses them in the game to stay alive or advance.

3.b.v. Explain how the list manages complexity in your program.
This is the section where you'll use most of your 200 words. Lists are examples of data abstractions that you learned about during the course. Without a list, your program

would need multiple variables to hold the different values that are stored in your list. Keeping up with multiple variables is more complex, introduces more room for a variety of errors, is less readable, and is harder to maintain.

Rubric Readiness

Section 3b can earn two of the six points on the rubric. This may be a little confusing, as only the first four parts of section 3b are considered to earn the first point. Section 3.b.v is considered, along with a closer look at the code showing the list being used, for another point.

First point for this section:
The following items must be in section 3b of the written response to earn this point.

- Check to be sure you have code that shows how elements were stored in the list.
- Include a separate section of code showing the same list being used in the program. Do not include your entire program.
- Provide the name of the list.
- Describe what the data in the list represent for your program.

Second point for this section:
To earn this point, the code segment provided in 3.b.ii must show the list managing complexity in your program. The first point considers how the list is being used in the code to achieve the program's purpose. This point looks at the list and how it handles complexity. Students must also write about how the list is used in their program to manage complexity, including how the code could either not be written without a list or how it would have to be written differently without using a list. Be sure to reference the list you highlighted.

Section 3c Procedure

This section requires you to paste or screenshot two sections of code related to a procedure that you wrote. Students often lose points here by using a built-in procedure, such as *random()*, or an event handler. Be sure to use a procedure that you wrote or you and your partner wrote together. You then write about the procedure in 200 words or less for the combined writing. Program code does ***not*** count toward the 200-word count.

3.c.i. Student written procedure code segment
Copy and paste or screenshot a procedure that you or you and your partner created. The procedure must have at least one parameter and implement an algorithm with sequencing, selection, and iteration. You learned about these features throughout the course and should have included them in your procedure. Now write about your knowledge!

3.c.ii. Procedure call code segment

This section of code has to show that your procedure was used in your program by the call to invoke it. Paste just the call to the procedure, including the argument(s).

3.c.iii. Describe what the procedure does
Describe the functionality of the procedure. This is how the procedure works. Then write about how the procedure impacts the overall program functionality. For example: This procedure takes in two numbers that represent scores for each player and determines which number is higher. The higher number means that player won the game. Without this procedure, the game would end without indicating who won and without giving positive reinforcement for the users to want to play again.

3.c.iv. Algorithm

This is where you describe in detail how the procedure's algorithm works. Remember that an algorithm is a set of steps to complete a task. Be sure to include how it shows the following:

- Selection with an IF around the / (condition)
- Iteration with any type of loop
- Sequencing—The steps running in a particular order for the needed functionality. If you have selection and iteration, then you have sequencing. Just don't forget to describe it.

You have to write in sufficient detail so that someone else could recreate the algorithm from your words. Therefore, don't just say you have an IF statement. Describe what the condition tests and what happens if it is true. If you also have an ELSE IF or ELSE, be sure to describe those as well. The same holds true for the iteration description. Don't simply say you have a loop. Describe what code is repeating with each iteration and when the loop stops. With sequencing, describe how the steps have to be in a particular order for the algorithm to work correctly.

Rubric Readiness

Section 3c can earn two of the six points on the rubric. The first three parts of section 3c are considered to earn the first point. Section 3.c.iv is considered for an additional point along with a closer look at the code for the procedure that you included.

First point for this section:
The following items must be in section 3c of the written response to earn this point.

- Check to be sure you have code that shows a procedure that you or you and your partner developed. The procedure must have at least one parameter. Do not use a built-in procedure or an event handler. Those will not be considered student-developed and you will not earn the point.
- Include a separate section of code showing the procedure you referenced being called. Do not include your entire program.
- Describe *what* the procedure does AND *how* it works within the overall program. If you only write about one of these, you will not earn the point.

Second point for this section:
- To earn this point, the code for the procedure is reviewed to ensure it includes sequencing, selection, and iteration.
- You must provide a detailed description of what the algorithm is AND how it works in your procedure. It has to be detailed enough that someone else could reconstruct it based on your description. Don't rewrite the code—just describe it.

PITFALL TO AVOID: The algorithm chosen can use an API or library call you imported into your program, but cannot be *only* the API code. It also must be longer than one instruction (e.g., DISPLAY or PRINT would not be acceptable).

PITFALL TO AVOID: Be sure to write about what the algorithm does **and** how it does it.

Section 3d

This section is where you show two calls to the same procedure you've been writing about in section 3c, and each call must cause a different section of the code to be executed. You have up to 200 words for all of the sections in 3d combined. Program code is **not** included in your word count.

3.d.i. Two procedure calls

You will document two calls to your procedure using two different arguments or sets of arguments if you have more than one parameter. The arguments in each call *must* cause a different section of code in the procedure to run. For example, if your procedure tests if a number is positive, have one call to it use a positive number as the argument and the second call should use a negative number.

First call: numPositive(50)
Second call: numPositive(–4)

3.d.ii. Condition being tested

Here you need to document the condition being tested in each call to the procedure using the values in section 3.d.i.

First call: The code tests to see if a number is positive using a selection statement. It checks if the value passed to the procedure is greater than or equal to 0. Since 50 is greater than 0, the condition is true.

Second call: The code tests to see if the number is greater than or equal to 0. It is not, so the condition evaluates to be false.

3.d.iii. Results of the call

Describe what happens in the code with each call. Be sure you used an example that has at least two branches, one for each case you used.

First call: Since the argument, 50, is positive, the count of positive numbers is increased by one. The number is then added to a calculation of the sum of the positive values entered by the user.

Second call: The argument, –4, is not positive, so an error message is displayed on the screen telling the user that the number was invalid and to enter a new number that is a positive integer.

Rubric Readiness

Section 3d can earn one point. All three sections of the written response must be included to earn the point AND the procedure you included in section 3c is used here. Be sure you write about the same procedure in your response!

- Provide two calls to the procedure with two different values for the argument(s). Each argument needs to branch to a different result of a condition in the code.
- Describe the condition(s) being tested by the different arguments.
- Describe the result of each call. The results should be different because the arguments you use are supposed to execute different sections of your code.

Program Code

This section includes your **entire** code in PDF format. Be sure to acknowledge who wrote sections of code that you did not, whether it was your partner or through use of an imported library. You can show comments in your code that indicate this or write the statement in a document before saving it in PDF format. Be sure your code is legible!

Keeping programming notes to document design decisions and programming structures as you implement algorithms and incorporate abstraction will help in writing the written response for this section.

You are allowed to work with a partner on this project, even though you both must also independently create sections of code and you each must work independently to create your own video and written responses. Remember that you cannot submit a project you have worked on in class as a practice Create project.

Always refer to the College Board's document "AP Computer Science Principles Student Handouts" for specific details on the code and written response expectations. If you haven't already bookmarked or printed this document, here is the link again:

https://apcentral.collegeboard.org/pdf/ap-csp-student-task-directions.pdf

Submitting Your Performance Task to the College Board

To submit your Create performance task, you must first be registered for the AP exam by November 15 if you are in a yearlong or first-semester-only course or March 15 for courses that only meet second semester. Once you register with the College Board, you can then join your class with a code your teacher will provide.

If you took an AP class in a prior year, you will already have an AP account. Be sure to use this same account. If you cannot remember your username or password, you can click the "Forgot username or password" option, and a message will be sent to the e-mail address you registered with.

Once you have logged in, you will have information to confirm or enter for the first time. You may then request to join the class your teacher has set up. You must be registered in an approved AP Computer Science Principles course to be able to access the digital portfolio. Your teacher will then approve your request and your account will be ready to accept the performance task files.

Independent study students must contact the AP coordinator at their assigned school or their school district. Students must be registered in an approved class to be able to access the digital portfolio website. This is where the Create performance task is uploaded. If you do not have a local school to contact, please call the College Board at 1-877-274-6474.

You can then access the Digital Portfolio site from your College Board "MyAP" account or using the link:

https://digitalportfolio.collegeboard.org/

The performance task is broken down into separate parts you must upload individually.

Create Performance Task
This performance task has three components:

- Individual Video—labeled IV
- Individual Written Response—labeled IWR
- Program Code—labeled PC

Until you load a submission, the components are labelled with a gray square □.

After you submit a section, the shape will show an orange triangle, which means *draft* mode. △ You may still upload new versions that will overlay the existing version in draft mode. When you are ready for the final submission of your project components, you'll be prompted to confirm that each file is in the correct section, your name is not included in any of the documents or the file name, and that you did not plagiarize. After you submit as *final*, you cannot overlay a new version anymore and a green check mark shows ✔. However, your instructor may return a file to you after final submission. The teacher has to indicate one of the valid reasons for returning the final submission, such as a corrupt file or the wrong file. No files can be returned after the submission date passes.

PITFALL TO AVOID: You cannot have a file with the same name in multiple sections of the Create components. The portfolio portal will not allow you to upload a file with the same name as one you already submitted in a different section. You can use the same file name to overwrite a file in the same section.

 Be sure to check that you plan to take the multiple-choice exam while you are in the digital portfolio.

 To avoid delay in the event the site slows down or becomes unavailable due to high demand, plan to finish and submit your project before the due date. This date is set by the College Board each year and can be found on their website.

If you cannot complete all aspects of the Create performance task before the submission deadline, you may still submit the sections you have completed to the College Board portal. They will be graded. You will only receive points for the sections that were submitted.

› Rapid Review

The Create performance task requires you to create a computer program, record a video showing the program running, and provide a written response to questions.

You will have a minimum of 12 hours of in-class time to complete the Create performance task.

The Create performance task must be uploaded to the College Board Digital Portfolio site by 11:59 p.m. Eastern time on the due date set by the College Board each year.

Review the examples and rubrics on the College Board site. Grade your own project based on the rubric and modify as needed before your final submission to the College Board.

Be aware of the maximum word counts for each section of your written responses for the performance task.

The Create performance task counts for 30% of your total AP score.

Do not make your programming project overly complicated! You can still earn all of the points with a simpler program that meets all the specified requirements.

CHAPTER 6

The Explore Curricular Requirement

IN THIS CHAPTER

Summary: The Explore curricular requirement is in its second year. You will do at least three activities during the school year to learn how to recognize a computing innovation and analyze it in specified ways. In conjunction, there will be a stimulus-type scenario. It will have a reading passage and potentially graphs and charts for you to review. There will be five multiple-choice questions requiring you to analyze the information in the passage to be able to select the best answer for the questions. To prepare, make sure you are working with the Explore Curricular Requirement document and NOT the Explore performance task, which is no longer required.

Key Ideas

KEY IDEA

✪ A computing innovation has a computer program that is essential to its operation.

✪ Computing innovations have data as input, process the input, and create output in some form.

✪ Computing innovations can be used in unintended ways.

✪ Computing innovations may have privacy, security, or storage concerns.

✪ Computing innovations can have beneficial or harmful effects and an effect could be considered either, depending on your perspective.

✪ There will be one Explore stimulus reading passage with five multiple-choice questions relating to the passage on the AP exam.

Key Terms

Computing innovation
Beneficial effects
Harmful effects

Privacy concern
Security concern
Storage concern

Explore Curricular Requirement: The Basics

Now in its second year, the Explore curricular requirement replaces the Explore performance task. Be sure you are using information from the College Board for the 2022–2023 AP exam. The focus of the Explore curricular requirement is identifying and analyzing computing innovations. There are three different activities that should be covered during your course with your teacher to help you prepare and practice this analysis. If you are preparing for the exam independently, don't forget to include these activities.

In addition, the AP Computer Science Principles exam will have a stimulus-prompt-type scenario. It provides information, such as a paragraph to read and charts to review, about a made-up computing innovation. There will be five multiple-choice questions associated with the stimulus material on the exam. These questions will be grouped together with the passage.

The three activities done during the course are designed to prepare students for the stimulus questions. They build knowledge about the following:

- What makes an innovation a "computing" innovation
- Identifying and analyzing the data that feed into the computing innovation
- Potential risks to privacy, security, and storage of data collected and used by the computing innovation
- Intended and unintended effects of the computing innovation that could result in either beneficial or harmful impacts

Computing Innovations

A computing innovation is one that has a computer program that is essential to the innovation being able to operate. You should be able to describe the program and what it does for an innovation. If you can classify an innovation as any of the following, then it is a computing innovation.

- A physical innovation—such as a GPS
- Nonphysical computing software—such as an app
- Nonphysical computing concept—such as social networking

Input/Processing/Output

Another key topic you will see in the stimulus questions deals with the data used by the computing innovation. With the program you developed for your Create performance task, you had to demonstrate and write about input to your program and output from your program and how the program or a procedure within the program used the data to produce the output. This is the same idea, so you've had some experience with the concept!

A key concept is being able to distinguish the data from the device that collects the data. A lot of students have trouble with this, so be sure you've got it. For example, a sensor is a data collection device. It sends the data it collects to the program. The data would be values for distance, temperature, motion, among many others, and it is *input* to the computer program in the innovation.

The innovation's program then processes the data and produces some type of *output*. With our example of sensor data, if the temperature is above a certain limit, an alert message may be sent or the air conditioner may be turned on. The message and "turn on" signal are examples of output.

Analyzing Data

You could also see questions about other important concepts related to analyzing a computing innovation's data. These include the following:

- How the data collected could be traced to an individual (privacy)
- Who can access the data (security)
- Where the data is warehoused (storage)

Many students have difficulty with the difference between privacy and security. Be sure you can describe this.

Privacy is protecting our identity. If someone accesses partial data, could they piece together who we are through that data and other publicly available data? Similarly, if our data is supposed to be combined with a lot of other data in a way to mask our identities, is it possible to drill down and identify an individual? These are privacy issues.

Security deals with who can access our data. Organizations are supposed to limit who can see or update our data. Schools have to maintain a lot of data about students and teachers. Keeping your data secure includes ensuring another student will not be able to see your grades nor will you be able to see other students' grades in an online gradebook. It also means that your science teacher may be able to *view* all of your grades but can only *change* your science grades, not your English or math grades.

Data storage concerns center around where the data is located. If your school data is stored on a local server, the data should be protected so only authorized people are able to access it. However, all organizations should keep backup copies of their data in case a disaster, like a burst water pipe, destroys their local server. If the backup data is stored in the cloud, is it encrypted while it is sent to the location in case it is intercepted? Who keeps it private and secure at the backup location?

Impact of Computing Innovations

The effects of any innovation, including computing innovations, are the results or outcomes from its *intended* use. These effects can be beneficial or harmful, and sometimes the same effect can be both to different people. When you are analyzing information in one of the stimulus questions, try to look at the effects from different viewpoints to help you see potential impacts and whether they would be considered a positive or a negative.

It is also important to recognize when computing innovations are used in ways they were not intended. Sometimes this can be great, such as when the World Wide Web branched out from its original intention of sharing scientific papers. The World Wide Web has had many beneficial impacts on society, giving us the ability to communicate with anyone in the world who has access in real time, on the economy through e-commerce and the ability to make purchases online, and on culture because we are able to view and learn about other cultures or see and set new trends.

There are also harmful effects related to the web. It's not all unicorns and rainbows. People harass and cyberbully using the web. They commit fraud with online purchases, and they spew biased and inaccurate information about other cultures.

As you can see, it all depends. You need to be able to identify these aspects, and the three projects you did during your class would help you develop and practice these skills.

❯ Analyzing a Stimulus Question

Let's try a practice question and analyze it as we go.

A food delivery company is developing an app to optimize the number of delivery personnel on duty for faster delivery. It is tracking historical data to use to predict future staffing needs. The historical data includes zip code, time of day, and order information.

To be able to streamline their weekly food order, the company started collecting orders per address. After collecting data, they noticed patterns with certain homes and concluded the homeowners are out of town during those weeks. They decide to offer a targeted ad to send to people who appear to be out of town in a regular pattern to order food for delivery when they return.

1. Predicting that homes could be empty on certain dates is an example of:
   (A) A security concern since the regular drivers would know which homes did not order on a given week
   (B) An economic impact to the company due to lost sales while regular customers are out of town
   (C) A storage concern since that is extra data to be stored and tracked but is not likely to result in additional revenue
   (D) A privacy concern since anyone with access to the data could identify the home

Let's look at each option and see what it is asking. A security concern is one where people who should not be able to view or update our information have that capability. If our address is included in a list of those to receive a special ad, and anyone can see it, it is a security concern. However, the response goes on to state that the regular drivers would know which homes were potentially unoccupied. The drivers could know that without viewing the data. Also, the question is asking about *predicting* which homes could be unoccupied, which is not related to the security of the data. So option (A) is out.

Option (B) deals with lost revenue to the organization since regular customers did not order. While is it an economic impact, it is not due to predicting which homes will not be ordering in a particular

week. It's going to occur regardless, and could occur even if people are in town. So (B) is not the answer.

(C) is looking at the amount of data the company is collecting and storing for analysis. While that could be a concern, it is not due to the analysis that led to this prediction. Those are two separate events. (C) is also not the correct response.

Remember that a privacy concern is one where our identity could be exposed. The question references "predicting" that homes could be empty. If software is predicting that no one is home and our address is reasonably tied to that prediction, then it is a privacy concern for us. (D) is the correct answer.

2. Which potential harm is most likely to occur due to the new marketing program?
   (A) Lost sales due to people traveling
   (B) Lost sales due to public perception of the targeted ad
   (C) Higher spoilage rate of food inventory that cannot be sold
   (D) Fewer delivery drivers available for unexpected orders due to lower projected sales during certain weeks

There will be lost sales due to people traveling, but it's only because they are out of town, not due to the new marketing program. Option (A) is not the correct answer.

In this option, (B), the lost sales are due to the public perception of those receiving the ad (and whomever they tell). Since it indicates their travel schedule is known, most people would not be happy about receiving an advertisement about that. When people feel exposed and the data is out of their control, they are more likely to stop using the service completely to feel like they are doing something to protect their data. (B) is the correct answer.

While food that goes bad is a cost and a harm to the restaurant, it is not related to the marketing program. (C) is not the answer.

Trying to schedule delivery drivers when sales are not known in advance is always difficult and an ongoing problem for any business doing deliveries. However, this potential issue is not related to the marketing program. (D) is not the correct answer.

3. The data in the chart shows the average distance a driver has to travel during a typical evening shift. What data is needed to schedule driver routes that is not provided in the chart?

Data needed ?	Driver #	Average miles per driver	Zip code for delivery	Type of driver vehicle	Driver phone #	Number of orders to deliver	Customer address	Deliver food warm or cold?
	14	100	11111	Car	123-456-7890	15		W
	15	85	11112	Truck	234-567-8901	22		W
	29	92	11110	Hybrid	345-678-9012	35		C

(A) Data with the next closest address
(B) Time of day
(C) If food needs to be kept warm or cold—to keep the food quality intact
(D) Toll roads on the route to the delivery location

To be able to schedule the routes for the drivers, we'll need the number of orders, which is available in the chart, and zip code, which is also available. We would also need to know the next closest address to be able to schedule the route. A heuristic approach will be used to determine this using the next closest neighbor approach. Calculating the optimized route would run in an unreasonable amount of time. The correct answer is (A), as the next closest address is needed to plan the route. This can be accessed through a GPS program.

In option (B), the time of day is useful because traffic patterns do change, but it's better to get the traffic patterns for the day of the week rather than the time of day.

Option (C) is important to delivering quality food, but with portable devices to keep food cool or hot, it is not a consideration in planning the driver route.

Option (D) can also impact the time it takes between locations, but with fast-pass cards that allow drivers to drive through toll booths and be counted electronically, it is not a significant factor. Without the next closest address, it would not be possible to know if a toll road is even on the route yet.

4. What is the most helpful expected output after processing the time of the order as input to the program?
(A) Ingredients needed to order to restock for next week's order
(B) Approximate cooking time
(C) Driver name for the delivery
(D) Estimated delivery time

If the order time is added as input, there are several available outputs. The question asks for the most helpful expected output, so keep that in mind as you evaluate possible answers.

Option (A) is needed by the business, but it is not an expected output of this program, which is to plan the number of delivery drivers needed. (A) is not the correct answer.

Option (B) uses the approximate cooking time, which helps to know when the order will be ready, but that would be another useful input to have rather than an output. (B) is not the answer.

Option (C) would be an output to know who will take the order, but it is not the most helpful. (C) is not the answer.

Option (D) is the best option. With the input data available, the best output will be the estimated delivery time. That's also what the customer wants to know!

5. What is a potential unintended use of this program?
- (A) Employees placing fake orders to be scheduled to work
- (B) As a route planning app in addition to an employee scheduling app
- (C) Crime watch usage of neighborhoods where people are out of town
- (D) Increased crime at empty homes based on the data stored by the company

While some employees may place fake orders, there is no guarantee that they will be called in to work. If caught, they would probably be fired, so it's not worth the risk. (A) is not the correct answer.

While the company planned for the app to schedule delivery drivers, with the information available to it, it can also be used for route planning. Option (B) is the best answer.

Since the pattern emerged about people being out of town, the data may not be accurate in all cases, and this would not be helpful to the company's main line of business. Option (C) is not correct.

If increased crime occurred due to the company's data being available to others who commit the crimes, the company would probably end up out of business. (D) is not correct.

› Stimulus Practice Questions

A city has placed ramp metering lights, which are traffic lights on entrance ramps, to help improve the flow of traffic. A camera records data at the location and transmits it to the city's data center.

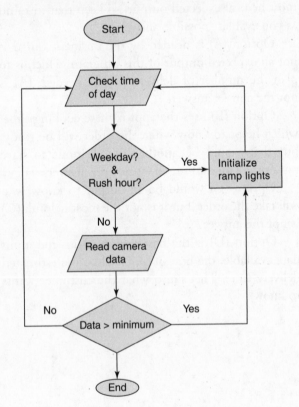

1. Which of the following data cannot be captured at the ramp entrance?
- (A) Number of cars on the highway
- (B) Date
- (C) Location of the ramp meter
- (D) Number of cars that pass through the entrance ramp each hour

2. What type of concern is most realistic?
- (A) Privacy concern through capture of vehicle information
- (B) Security concern if Department of Motor Vehicle employees can view the data
- (C) Storage concern for the high amount of data collected due to high volume of vehicles that use the entrance ramp
- (D) Personal protection concern due to potential sharing of data with other government agencies

3. If you are responsible for writing the code to activate values for the ramp light on and off cycles, what data could you use?
- (A) Camera data
- (B) Typical traffic patterns for weekdays
- (C) Number of red/green cycles in an hour
- (D) Pressure sensor data as cars enter the ramp

4. What is the least likely potential benefit to society from this innovation?
   (A) People will change their routes to access the highway at less congested entrance ramps, improving the overall traffic flow.
   (B) The air quality could improve with fewer traffic jams.
   (C) There will be fewer accidents due to safer merging onto the highway.
   (D) The better flow of traffic leads to decreased fuel consumption.

5. Now you've been asked to add code to your program to allow the activation signal to automatically turn off if traffic on the entrance ramp backs up and blocks side roads. What data is needed to do this?
   (A) Sensors
   (B) Cameras
   (C) Average number of vehicles that fit on the ramp
   (D) When side streets are blocked by the entrance ramp traffic

› Answers and Explanations

1. **A**—The number of cars on the highway cannot be determined by the data that is available at the entrance ramp. The date and location of the entrance ramp and the number of cars that have used the entrance ramp hourly are available data.

2. **A**—With the camera taking photos of cars on the entrance ramp along with date, time, and location, the privacy of your information is a concern. The combination of the data can be used to identify the owner of the car, if not who was actually driving it. Your whereabouts can be tracked and you can be identified through it if the data is not adequately protected.

3. **B**—The typical traffic patterns will provide you with reasonable values to initialize the timing for the ramp lights. The camera and sensor are devices, not data. They provide data, but the specific data is not listed. The number of red/green cycles will vary per hour based on the amount of traffic. Knowing how many cycles could occur an hour is not useful data as it may change based on the input.

4. **B**—All of the options list a possible benefit. However, decreased air pollution is the least likely to occur since cars are still on the highway. It would also be difficult to prove that the improved air quality was exclusively a result of the ramp lights.

5. **D**—The data from sensors located on side streets would be needed as input to allow the shut-off feature to be programmed. Sensors and cameras alone are devices, not data. The average number of vehicles that fit on the ramp could help, but comparing the average to actual vehicles may not indicate that side streets are blocked. The current data from side street sensors is needed. Of course, the program would also need to turn the ramp lights back on once the side street traffic cleared.

CHAPTER 7

Big Idea 1: Creative Development

IN THIS CHAPTER

Summary: People are creative! We may develop something just for us and our family or friends or an app to share with the world, for free or for a fee. There are processes in place to create well-developed and tested programs that include multiple stages of designing, coding, and testing. Collaboration, feedback, and iteration are key aspects of software development.

Key Ideas

✪ Collaboration on projects with a diverse team who represent a variety of backgrounds, experience, and perspectives can develop a better computing product.

✪ A development process to design, code, and implement a software application using feedback, testing, and reflection should be used to create software applications.

✪ Documentation should be developed that includes the requirements, constraints, and each program's purpose. Internal comments in programs should also be included.

✪ Programs must be adequately tested before releasing them to others to use. Debugging is the process of finding and correcting errors in programs.

Key Terms

Code segment
Collaboration
Comments
Debugging
Event-driven
  programming
Incremental development
  process
Iterative development
  process
Logic error
Overflow error

Program
Program behavior
Program documentation
Program input
Program output
Prototype
Requirements
Runtime error
Syntax error
Testing
User interface

Creativity in Computer Science

Computer Science is full of opportunities to be creative! Creativity is a way to express your personal ideas, color combinations, fonts, wording, and images, among countless other options. There are numerous design decisions needed for a programming application to be easy to use and interesting to view. For example, there is a great deal of software written for entertainment purposes. Creativity is essential for these so that people will want to use their time and possibly money to view or play them. Similarly, there is a great deal of software available to use to develop your own creation, from audio and visual files to mobile apps and everything in between. These software programs allow the creation and continued refinement from lower levels of detail or "rough sketches" to highly precise, "polished" ones. Depending on the ultimate planned outcome, software tools can provide an opportunity to create a sample or working prototype to obtain suggestions for improvement prior to investing the time and money required to create a "ready to sell" version.

Computing Innovations

Computer artifacts are anything created by a person using a computer. These include, but are not limited to, apps, games, images, videos, audio files, 3D-printed objects, and websites. Sometimes learning a new software tool and experimenting with the different features the software provides can result in a creative and unexpected result leading to a new innovation.

There are many types of innovations, but computing innovations have to include a computer program as part of its functionality. For example, a map was an innovation in its day, but maps are not computing innovations. However, GPS (Global Positioning System) driving instructions, one of my favorite innovations, and digital maps such as MapQuest and Google Maps, rely on computer code to provide their functionality.

Computing innovations can be a physical device, such as the GPS, or a virtual one, such as MapQuest or Google Earth. A computing innovation's purpose can be to solve a problem, such as needing directions on how to get somewhere or something that is entirely new. Understanding the purpose of the innovation helps developers create the solution to implement it.

Think of the first rocket ships designed to travel into orbit and then the moon. It had never been done, so it was truly innovative! The team members may not have known how they were going to do it initially, but they at least understood what their ultimate goal was. And they succeeded!

Collaboration

Collaboration has many benefits in the software development world. From the start, by working with sponsors of the project to identify its purpose, and then closely working with those who will actually use the software to understand the functionality needed, collaborative efforts consistently prove to save time and result in a better outcome by providing differing views and ideas in the development process. It can make for occasional lively meetings as team members share their views and negotiate design decisions too! A more homogeneous development team may inadvertently include bias in their software. The variety of views and experiences in a more diverse project team helps identify bias or prevent it in the first place. This is generally true in any field, and computer science is no exception. It also helps to have more than one person listening to the users to provide a clear understanding of the goals to meet or issues to solve. We hear and process information based on our experiences, so multiple perspectives can better identify and clarify what the application should provide early in the process. I once worked with a project team that used color to indicate crucial information. Red was an alert, yellow was cautionary, and green represented normal processing. The colors were not in a particular order like a traffic light was. It wasn't until someone who was color-blind tested the software that anyone realized that it couldn't be based on color alone. Text had to be added along with the color indicators.

With team members with different backgrounds, experiences, talents, and locations, effective team dynamics are essential to ensuring they work well together. This includes communicating with each other, both during agreements and disagreements, in a productive manner. Effective teams are able to negotiate and resolve conflicts to the betterment of the project, leaving the team working relationships intact. Consensus building is an important process and skill, and newly formed teams often go to workshops to develop or improve their communication and consensus building skill set.

Professional programmers seldom work in isolation. Teams are formed to complete the project. Collaboration among the team members and with their customers is instrumental to creating a quality solution. Programmers work with teams to design a solution, and may work individually to create sections of code, similar to designers, writers, composers, and artists of all types when they are producing something. They then come together for testing and feedback.

Communication among team members is crucial as they program separate modules that will need to work together for the total solution. Pair programming is one commonly used method to help facilitate collaboration as well as create correct code. One person types in the program while the other reviews the program, states what to type in, and watches for errors. It also helps to have someone other than the developer test the program code to identify problems and help find solutions. It is always good to have more than one person understand the problem and solutions in the event a key team member leaves the project team before the work is finished.

Many companies have a national if not international presence or vendors in other locations. Technology makes it possible to collaborate with people in a variety of locations even if you are programming for yourself or a smaller organization. Many tools provide a way to share documents via the cloud for people to work on together, regardless of their time zone or location.

Online tools such as shared documents to record progress, problems, and solutions can aid in collaboration, especially when team members are in different locations from each other.

Development Process

Projects are all around us, whether it's writing a research paper for school, completing a science lab, producing a graduation ceremony, or planning a celebration. Computer science also has projects where teams or individuals write code to create solutions for their user or customer.

So you have a great idea for an app, or you have a project to complete for school or a part-time job you have. How do you get started to get the great idea out of your head and ready for someone to use? People over many years have faced this same dilemma. Fortunately, development processes have been created for individuals and teams to use to get us moving in the right direction.

A development process helps individuals and teams bring their ideas to fruition. Many people have a method or their own process to follow to get their creative juices flowing. This can be a traditional process, similar to an outline or timeline a person might follow, or an approach that is more "trial and error" or exploratory in nature. Both methods can create entirely new software applications or create a new use from combining all or parts of existing applications. It usually takes an iterative or incremental process to get from an idea to the actual creation in whatever form it takes. These processes can be used to find new solutions to problems as well as to create something of the creator's choosing.

The following steps are considered the key steps for successful project development.

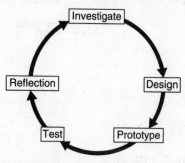

Software Development Process

Investigation

 This step involves investigating the problem or idea to fully understand it. You really cannot create a good and complete solution without fully understanding what you are supposed to accomplish and any limitations involved. It's highly unlikely that you will have unlimited time and money to create something, so the earlier you learn of any constraints, the better you can plan for them. This step also involves defining what the project needs to solve. All users with a stake in the program solution must be interviewed to document and understand what they need the project to do. You will have a much better product if you thoroughly understand the problem that needs to be solved before beginning to write the code.

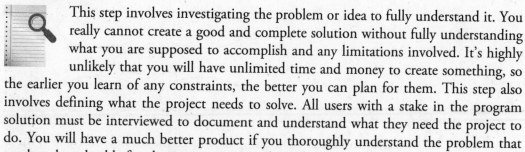 Ask lots of questions of those who will or could use your program. Use surveys and questionnaires to collect data about what needs to happen. Shadow several people to find out what they currently do and how they do it. Document it in some form, and then confirm your understanding with all of them. It's amazing sometimes that things seemed so clear, but when you show them to someone, they say that's not at all what they meant!

It is also important to survey a variety of designated or potential users of the software. Just like the software development team, a variety of user perspectives and backgrounds and locations, if applicable, will help you create a better product that reflects and incorporates their various viewpoints.

All the details and specifications that you identify through investigation are included in the project requirements. This document also includes constraints identified and the user interactions that need to occur. All of this information feeds into the design.

Design

This phase involves taking the requirements identified and creating some form and functionality around them. The investigative phase provides information about *what* the project should do. The design determines *how* the requirements will be met. Ongoing communication with the users is important in creating a successful programming solution. There are several common ways individuals or teams work to create a good design. These include:

Brainstorming—This is a process of identifying as many ideas as possible without commenting or evaluating them until the process is done. Often one seemingly "out there" idea can trigger another idea that is workable. No judgment on ideas is allowed!

Storyboarding—This process is used in many fields, such as making videos as well as game design. There are layouts available for use, and you identify the functionality that goes together and identify the data and where it comes from, how it is processed, and where it goes next. Place the design decisions related to these in the panel of the storyboard. Then repeat the stages for the next section until all the requirements have been included.

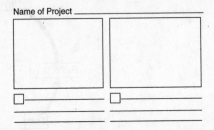

Modules—Designers will often group features of an application that belong together into a module or component. For example, starting a new game includes resetting scores to 0, refreshing or clearing the screen, and moving players to their starting positions, among others. All of these requirements could be grouped in a module.

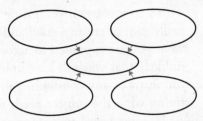

User interface—Designing how someone uses the software is the key to its success and the speed with which it may be adopted. All of the interactions both into and out from each step that people will see and use are considered the "user interface." People evaluating and recommending software usually comment on how easy to use, how visually appealing, how useful the user interface, and how the overall "user experience" is. Designers use anything from paper diagrams to transparencies, overlaying them with new interactions based on selections, to fully designed screen images to create and test user interfaces.

Testing strategy—It may sound strange to think of testing this early in the process. There isn't any code written yet, but this is when the testing strategy should be identified. You already know the functions the software needs to do based on the requirements documented in the investigative phase. Make sure the testing strategy addresses each requirement.

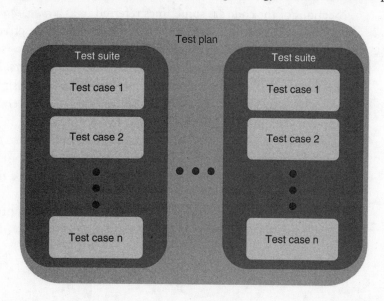

Prototyping

Prototyping is a very effective process, especially when working with users on design or a new technology they will use. It can be a mockup of the user interface screens to give users a starting point for suggestions. Many times people have a hard time describing what they want, but they know it when they see it! Design often works like this.

Prototypes can also include small simulations of working code to give a realistic view of how the process will work. Feedback is critical to getting well-designed software, and prototypes are inexpensive ways to get a start on the feedback cycle.

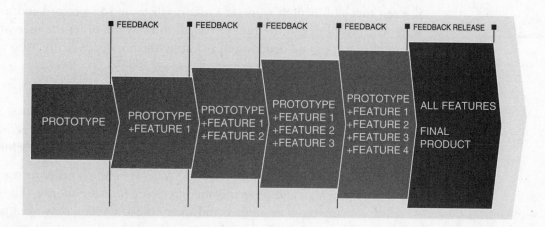

Testing

Program Basics

Let's talk programming basics. Lines of code written in a programming language make up a software program. The code can run or "execute" its specified instructions on a computer. Sections of the code are sometimes referred to as a *code segment*. Segments work together to perform a certain function. How a program *behaves* describes how it runs during execution and how anyone using it interacts with it. This includes screens and messages displayed, buttons to press, menu options to select, and many others. Programs are described by their overall purpose as well as how they perform to accomplish the purpose.

The program will have some way to request or receive *input* and react to the input. Input is data provided to the program by someone using it, through a sensor, a file of data, a microphone, an image, or some other method. *Event-driven programming* relies on an event to occur to trigger code to run. These events are input to the program. Examples of events include finger swipes or taps, a message coming through via a text, a mouse click, or a timing event.

Through processing the input, programs generally produce some form of *output*. Output can include writing to a file for use by another program, displaying a message or image on a device, playing a song or video, or printing a 3D object, among others.

Test Plans

You have to thoroughly understand what the program should do, produce, and display to **effectively** test a project and find any errors. All features, using expected data and unexpected data, should be tested to determine if the programs work and if they provide the functionality as intended. Using the testing strategy defined in the investigative phase, a good test plan will have the test cases and expected results identified for all the requirements. When the code is executed, the actual results are compared to the expected results to determine if the code is working or not. The expected and actual test results can be used by a programmer to prove a program runs correctly.

All program functionality must be adequately tested as well to ensure program correctness. This includes testing with valid and invalid data as well as "boundary" cases, which are those on the edge of program limitations.

> **Example:** If something should happen when a value is less than 32, also check 31 and 33 as the boundary cases.

Testing should also ensure that all features work in the way the user needs them to. Do not just test that all functions work. If a user needs to update a record and uses three different ways to accomplish this, be sure to test all three in the order the user would use them to ensure they work as needed, as well as testing them independently. Also test what happens if they are used in the wrong order.

Debugging

Debugging means finding and correcting errors in your program. There are steps you can take when creating your code to help with later troubleshooting. Remember that test cases with expected results should be set up to evaluate each requirement before testing begins.

- Use procedures rather than duplicating code. It is much easier to read and understand a shorter program, and programs that use procedures are shorter. The procedure can be called as many times as needed, and then needed updates only need to be made in one location in your code. See the chapter on Big Idea 3 for more on procedures.

- Another step is to use well-named variables and procedures. If they are descriptive names that communicate what they do, it is easier to trace through a program and understand what it is supposed to do. See Big Idea 3 for more information on variables. For example: *amtDue* is much clearer as a variable name than *ad*.
- Hand-tracing the flow of the program line-by-line is also an effective debugging tool. This is often the best way to find a logic error. You write down the variable names and values as they change along with iteration numbers of loops and check the code line-by-line.
- Many IDEs (integrated development environments) where you can write and test your code include coding visualizations. These show the code structure and each line that executes to help track where errors are occurring.
- Debuggers are programs written to test and debug other programs. Many IDEs include debuggers. These are like automated versions of hand-tracing and show your code step by step as it executes.
- The use of temporary print or DISPLAY statements inside a program help with debugging. By printing out intermediate values to the screen or on paper, or to indicate when a program reaches a certain section of code, the programmer can more easily identify the error. These extra print statements are removed after the error is resolved.

There are several types of errors that can occur when testing. The types you must know for this course are described below.

Types of Errors

Syntax errors deal with things like punctuation or missing parentheses ( ) and typos. These are identified when you try to compile your program and must be corrected before the program will run. Each programming language has its own syntax, or rules, that must be followed.

Runtime errors do not cause an error at compile time but occur when the program is executing. A common example is when a variable has a value of zero and the program tries to divide by it. The program may run successfully many times when the value is not zero, but will crash when it is zero.

Logic errors occur when the program produces unexpected results. These errors are typically harder to identify. You may think your program ran correctly, because there were no identified errors. The program can run, but the actual results would be different than expected.

The test cases with expected results can really help identify these. If you have a table of expected test results, and the program does not produce the expected value, you need to carefully check your code to find and correct the problem and be sure you understand what the program is supposed to do. The problem could be as simple as using "+" rather than "–" in a calculation, or you may have used the wrong variable name in a program statement.

Overflow errors occur in computers when an integer is larger than the programming language can hold. A fixed number of bits are assigned to hold integers in many programming languages. When the limit is reached, an overflow error occurs. This varies for different computers, and you are not expected to know this value for each computer for the AP exam. See the Big Idea 2 chapter about data for more information about overflow errors.

Reflection

There are two development processes you need to know for this course. Each involves reflection of results before moving on in the development process.

An *iterative* development process is a repetitive one. The steps are repeated several times throughout the project as new information is gathered or clarified, testing is performed and revisions are needed, or customers change their mind about what they need. Each iteration produces a better result. After working through the investigation and design phases, often the coding/prototyping, testing, and reflection steps are repeated multiple times until the code works. Sometimes you do have to go back to other phases to work through those steps again. Feedback is a significant step in this process. You can create a working program, but if it is difficult to use or confusing, then people will not use it. Ask them! Ask a variety of people. You can ask your friends, but make sure to ask others as well. Friends may think too similarly to you or not want to tell you the truth.

An *incremental* development process breaks the pieces of the program into smaller sections. A section is coded, tested, modified, tested, and so on until it is working. Then work begins on another section. Once it is working, it is also tested for any interactions with sections of code already completed. Then work begins on the next module, and the cycle continues. The overall software system is built piece by piece, or incrementally, until completed. For example, if you are writing an app for a game, you might break it into the following sections:

- Instructions
- Game play
- Keeping score
- Determining the highest score
- Starting a new game

These all work together to create the complete game. Each section can be worked on independently, even by different people, until it is working correctly, and then it will be tested with the rest of the modules already written.

Be sure you understand these steps and follow them when you are working on your Create performance task. You will have a better product as a result!

Documentation

Program documentation is the "guide" to how the program is designed to work. The requirements document created in the investigation phase is the start of the program documentation. Programmers should also add to the program documentation, explaining the program features and how it should be used to meet the functionality originally identified in the specifications. This also could be in the form of a user guide to use in training those who will use the programs as well as "help" text. Ideally, documentation will be created as the program is being developed by the programmers to accurately record what a program is intended to do.

Well-named variables and procedures can be somewhat "self documenting" by describing their purpose, but do not take the place of additional documentation. Documentation is so useful when you either return later to modify the code or a team member has to pick up your code and understand what it is doing to successfully make modifications.

Programmers should comment blocks of code inside the program to indicate the functionality of those sections. Remember that comments are ignored when the program is translated into machine code and are to help people understand what is going on in a program. Comments should also be used in a program to explain complex or confusing sections of code. Note that not all programming IDEs allow comments, so the program documentation becomes even more important in these cases.

Another important topic to include both in your code as a comment and in the project documentation is crediting any code used from another source. This can be a program library imported into the program or through an API (Application Programming Interface) that allows connectivity to an external program. This is important for giving credit to the author as well as stating where the code originated if changes need to be made that will impact the use of the code.

› Review Questions

Concepts

1. Collaboration can provide which of the following?
   (A) Several points of failure
   (B) Clean data
   (C) Duplication of effort
   (D) Better products resulting from different perspectives

2. What is a benefit of using a software development design process?
   (A) By following the process, the code will work the first time.
   (B) Using the process, the code will be efficient regardless of a programmer's experience.
   (C) The code will be developed in 50% less time using a development/design process.
   (D) The process is iterative, resulting in a better program.

3. Which of the following is not a common step in many software development processes?
   (A) Designing
   (B) Investigating
   (C) Identifying patterns
   (D) Testing

4. What do using surveys, interviews, and observations identify?
   (A) Device specifications
   (B) Program errors
   (C) User requirements
   (D) Valid program input

5. Why is documentation important?
   (A) To explain a program's purpose and functionality
   (B) To make it easier to understand and modify the code later
   (C) To be useful for training people on how to use the program
   (D) All of the above

6. Why should boundary values be tested?
   (A) Testing boundary values is not necessary.
   (B) To ensure they are identified as errors
   (C) To ensure warning messages are sent about the boundaries
   (D) To ensure the program does not include too few or too many elements

7. What is a crucial step in an iterative development process?
   (A) Feedback
   (B) Preparing prototypes
   (C) Meeting deadlines
   (D) Meeting budget constraints

8. What is a benefit of understanding a problem before coding?
   (A) A better designed program is created to handle all the needed functionality.
   (B) Less testing is required.
   (C) Little or no documentation is then needed.
   (D) Users will not need training to use the program.

9. Which phase in the development process determines how to meet the application requirements?
   (A) Analysis
   (B) Design
   (C) Programming
   (D) Testing

10. How do event-driven programs progress?
    (A) They run in a linear fashion from start to end.
    (B) The code executes sequentially.
    (C) The code executes when an action occurs that it is programmed to recognize.
    (D) The code runs iteratively.

Application of Concepts

11. What is one way to debug a program?
    (A) Add temporary print messages to determine program values.
    (B) Test with different data values each time.
    (C) Document the error in the user guide and online help text.
    (D) Override the error with the correct value.

12. Which development process breaks the requirements down into small modules and adds the code, once working, to the project as a whole?
    (A) Additive
    (B) Incremental
    (C) Iterative
    (D) Spiral

13. What is one way to ensure testing is thorough?
(A) Create expected results prior to testing.
(B) Create a diagram of the program's processing.
(C) Execute the code to ensure it runs.
(D) Add temporary DISPLAY statements to see intermediate results in the program.

14. What type of error breaks the rules of the programming language, like a grammatical error?
(A) Logic error
(B) Overflow error
(C) Runtime error
(D) Syntax error

15. If your program executes without errors, but the results are incorrect, what type of error do you likely have?
(A) Logic error
(B) Round-off error
(C) Runtime error
(D) Syntax error

16. Which method of finding errors is most useful to identify logic errors?
(A) Creating new test cases
(B) Hand-tracing
(C) Rerunning the program with different inputs to see the impact on outputs
(D) Running a simulation

17. Attempting to access an invalid index in a list results in what type of error?
(A) Logic error
(B) Overflow error
(C) Runtime error
(D) Syntax error

18. What is an example of event-driven programming?
(A) Prompting a user to type in a response
(B) Using constants for data values in place of variables
(C) A mobile device that orients to a new position
(D) A microphone transmitting audio data to a program

› Answers and Explanations

1. D—Collaboration can provide the possibility of insights we may never get otherwise by having team members with different backgrounds and perspectives create, design, and evaluate data, documents, products, and so on.

2. D—The steps in the software development design process are iterative, causing the developer to reevaluate after testing to fix and improve the program. No process can ensure that the code will be correct the first time, nor be efficient, nor decrease the development time by 50%, making D the correct answer.

3. C—Finding patterns is not a common step in the software development processes. The other options are key steps in developing a well-designed and working program.

4. C—These are investigative tools used to determine user requirements for the application.

5. D—Documentation is important to:
- Explain a program's purpose and functionality
- Make it easier to understand and modify the code later
- Train people on how to use the program

6. D—Boundary values should be tested to ensure the program does not process too few or too many elements. These are common errors in programs.

7. A—Feedback from users on the proposed design and programs is a key aspect of an iterative development process.

8. A—One benefit of understanding a problem before coding is creating a better designed program to handle all the needed functionality.

9. B—The design phase determines how the application requirements will be achieved.

10. C—An event-driven program is one that waits for an event, such as a swipe or mouse click, to trigger the code to run.

11. A—One way to debug a program is to add temporary print messages to determine program values.

12. B—The incremental development process breaks the requirements down into small modules. Once coded and tested, the module is added to the overall application.

13. **A**—Creating expected results for the data you are testing prior to testing allows you to compare the actual results to the expected ones to ensure the program is functioning correctly.

14. **D**—A syntax error keeps the code from executing until it is corrected. These errors include things like missing punctuation, unmatched parentheses, and typos.

15. **A**—A logic error is the likely culprit. These can occur if you use the wrong variable name for a calculation or use the wrong operation, such as subtraction rather than addition.

16. **B**—Hand-tracing the code can help identify where a logic error occurs. (There are other debugging tools that are also useful for finding logic errors.)

17. **C**—This will result in a runtime error. The program may run accurately many times or through most of the program until the index position becomes too large or too small for the list you are using. The program will end with an error.

18. **C**—A mobile device that orients to a new position is an event that a gyroscope in the device will recognize. The gyroscope recognizes orientation so code will be initialized to redisplay information on your screen with the new orientation.

› Rapid Review

Advances in technology provide the ability to share programs or their output with users worldwide. They can become popular with widespread use very quickly. These advances have spread the development of new programs and technologies and have expanded use of existing program applications to other businesses and organizations. Software that is developed by teams with different skill sets and perspectives results in better designed and programmed solutions. Collaboration by the team has many benefits, including sharing the workload, creating better solutions than an individual probably would, and testing of each other's work.

Software development should use an iterative developmental process, an incremental development approach, or both. An iterative process is a repeating process that continues with feedback, rework, and testing until the users' requirements have been met. An incremental process keeps breaking down the requirements into smaller chunks. Modules of code can be developed and tested, and once they are working correctly through using an iterative approach, can then be incorporated into the larger application.

Both processes include consulting with users, analyzing and designing a solution, coding the solution, and then testing. Documenting the programs and providing external documentation for those using the system are very important to make it easier to use, maintain, and modify the code as the users' needs change.

Documenting the requirements is important to identify what the program application needs to accomplish and to get sign-off when it is complete and working. Commenting the code is needed to document what the code does along with explaining complicated sections of code for the person that updates the code in the future.

Program input can be from a variety of sources such as from the user, files, other programs, or from events, which include taps or swipes to trigger the execution of code. Program output can be sent from a program to another program, written to a file, or sent to a device such as a printer or speakers.

Thorough testing of software is critical before releasing it for general use, although programs developed for personal use do not need the same level of testing and documentation.

Expected test results should be identified early in the design process for testing the code. Actual results should be compared to the expected ones to determine if the program is working correctly for all possible conditions. Syntax errors must be corrected before the program will run and are specific to the programming language. Runtime errors occur when the program is executing. It may run fine sometimes, but certain conditions cause it to end with an error. Logic errors do not prevent the program from running but produce incorrect results. The expected test results help find these errors. Overflow errors occur when a number is too large for the computer to handle with its architecture. Debugging is the process of finding and fixing errors in the code.

CHAPTER 8

Big Idea 2: Data

IN THIS CHAPTER

Summary: This chapter focuses on how data is represented in the computer. To identify new information through data, it may need to be labeled to make it easier to find, sometimes compressed for ease of sharing, and stored, secured, and processed to make sense of it for solving problems or for identifying new findings.

Key Ideas
- ✪ Abstractions including numbers, colors, text, and instructions can be represented by binary data.
- ✪ Numbers can be converted from one number system to another. Computers use the binary number system.
- ✪ Metadata helps us find and organize data.
- ✪ Computers can clean, process, and classify data more accurately and faster than people can.
- ✪ Using computer programs to sift through data to look for patterns and trends can lead to new insights and knowledge.
- ✪ Searching for bias in the data collection process is important.
- ✪ Communicating information visually helps get the message across.
- ✪ Scalability is key to processing large datasets effectively and efficiently.
- ✪ Storage needs led to the creation of lossy and lossless compression techniques.

Key Terms

Abstraction
Analog data
Bias
Binary number system
Bit
Byte
Classifying data
Cleaning data
Digital data
Filtering data
Information
Lossless data
  compression
Lossy data compression
Metadata
Overflow error
Patterns in data
Round-off or rounding
  error
Scalability

Number Systems

Data. It comes from everything we do. Someone or some organization is interested in our data. This data can be stored in variables or lists and can be input to programs or output from them. Let's go into depth about how this data can be represented and analyzed.

Binary is the number system used in computer science. Computers read machine code, which at the lowest level, is made up of 0s and 1s. This is the binary number system. A "0" represents no electrical charge, and a "1" represents a charge. "Current" and "no current" are easy conditions to detect. These binary digits are referred to as *bits*. Eight bits make up a byte.

Numbers as Abstractions

Abstraction is a concept that is a little hard for many students to grasp. The basic idea is that we remove details to make something more general. This makes it easier to use the process for multiple purposes versus one specific purpose. One benefit is that we do not have to know what goes on behind the scenes, meaning how something works. We only need to know that it works. Let's apply this concept to numbers.

Think of several ways you can represent the number of marbles in the pile in the image.

8, eight, ocho
VIII (Roman numerals)

Each of these is a simplified way to represent how many marbles are in the pile. Each numeric representation is an abstraction, because they simplify the details of what we have, and we know that we have "eight" of them. Each of the different number systems represents the same amount. Other number systems can also be used.

Since this is a digital document, the image of the marbles is also represented by binary digits, 0s and 1s. We see the image of the marbles and do not need to know how the shapes and colors are represented by the bits. The words on this page are also represented by bits, 0s and 1s. All digital data are represented by binary digits.

Binary Number Conversions

All number systems use the same principles.

Our base 10 decimal system uses 10 numbers from 0 to 9.

Here's a quick review of first- or second-grade math, because you probably don't look at numbers this way anymore. When you need to represent the number 10, you have to carry over to a new column, the "tens" column, and use two numbers. Your number represents how many "tens" you have and how many "ones" you have. When you need to represent the number "100," you have to carry over to a third column, the "hundreds" column. (The concept of "carrying over" is now often termed "regrouping.")

Each new column represents the next power of 10.

10^3	10^2	10^1	10^0
Thousands	Hundreds	Tens	Ones
1000	100	10	1

Base 2, binary, uses two numbers, 0 and 1.

When you need the number 2, you have to carry over to a new column, the "twos," and use two numbers to represent it. Your number represents how many "twos" you have and how many "ones" you have. For the number "4," you carry over to a third column, the "fours." The next column is the "eights."

Each new column to the left represents the next power of 2.

2^3	2^2	2^1	2^0
Eights	Fours	Twos	Ones
8	4	2	1

Converting Decimal Numbers to Binary

When you need to convert a decimal number to binary, create the following table on your paper. We will use a byte (8 bits), but the table can keep going to the left with 2 raised to the next power. Today, most personal computers are 64-bit machines, so the table can get quite large!

2^7	2^6	2^5	2^4	2^3	2^2	2^1	2^0
128	64	32	16	8	4	2	1

Notice that each column to the left represents an increasing power of 2 that **doubles** the column to the right of it.

To convert a decimal number to binary, use the following algorithm with the above table.

1. Write down the decimal number.
2. Subtract the largest number from the binary table that is the same or less. (When you subtract, you cannot have a negative number.)
3. Mark a 1 in the column on the table for the power of 2 you subtracted.
4. Mark an 0 in the columns that could not be subtracted and were skipped.
5. Repeat steps 2 to 4 until your decimal value reaches zero.
6. Note: Use leading 0's on the left to make a byte (8 bits).

Example 1: Convert 21 to binary.

Starting from the left-most column, the first number you can subtract without having a negative result is 16. Place a 0 in each column to the left of 2^4 and a 1 in the column for 2^4.

$$\begin{array}{r} 21 \\ -16 \\ \hline 5 \end{array}$$

Take the number remaining after subtracting and find the next number in the table that can be subtracted without resulting in a negative number.

You cannot subtract 8, so place a 0 in the 2^3 column.
You can subtract 4, so place a 1 in the 2^2 column.

$$\begin{array}{r} 5 \\ -4 \\ \hline 1 \end{array}$$

The result is now 1, so place a 0 in the 2^1 column and 1 in the 2^0 column.

$$\begin{array}{r} 1 \\ -1 \\ \hline 0 \end{array}$$

Answer: $21_{10} = 00010101_2$
The subscript 10 means base 10 (decimal) and the subscript 2 means base 2 (binary).

2^7	2^6	2^5	2^4	2^3	2^2	2^1	2^0
128	64	32	16	8	4	2	1
0	0	0	1	0	1	0	1

Example 2: Convert 119 to binary.

Create your table of powers of 2 from 2^0 to 2^7.

Starting from the left-most column, the first number you can subtract without having a negative result is 64. Place a 0 in the 2^7 column to the left of 2^6 and a 1 in the column for 2^6. Subtract the value of 2^6, which is 64, from 119.

$$\begin{array}{r} 119 \\ -\ 64 \\ \hline 55 \end{array}$$

The next power of 2 is 2^5, which is 32. This can be subtracted without a negative result, so place a 1 in the 2^5 column.

$$\begin{array}{r} 55 \\ -32 \\ \hline 23 \end{array}$$

The next power of 2 is 2^4, which is 16. This can be subtracted without a negative result, so place a 1 in the 2^4 column.

$$\begin{array}{r} 23 \\ -16 \\ \hline 7 \end{array}$$

We cannot subtract 8 and have a positive result, so place a 0 in the 2^3 column. We can subtract 4, so place a 1 in the 2^2 column.

$$\begin{array}{r} 7 \\ -4 \\ \hline 3 \end{array}$$

We can subtract 2 from 3, so place a 1 in the 2^1 column.

$$\begin{array}{r} 3 \\ -2 \\ \hline 1 \end{array}$$

The result is now 1, so place a 1 in the 2^0 column.

$$\begin{array}{r} 1 \\ -1 \\ \hline 0 \end{array}$$

The result of the conversion is:
$$119_{10} = 01110111_2$$

2^7	2^6	2^5	2^4	2^3	2^2	2^1	2^0
128	64	32	16	8	4	2	1
0	1	1	1	0	1	1	1

Converting Binary Numbers to Decimal

To convert a binary number to decimal:

1. Write the binary table as we did in the examples above with each bit of the binary number in the appropriate column.
2. For columns that have a 1 in them, add the values of the power of 2.
   (You are multiplying 0 or 1 times the value of the power of 2 in each column.)
3. The total of all columns with a 1 in them equals the decimal value equivalent.

Example 1: Convert 00011011 to decimal.

2^7	2^6	2^5	2^4	2^3	2^2	2^1	2^0
128	64	32	16	8	4	2	1
0	0	0	1	1	0	1	1
0 * 128 +	0 * 64 +	0 * 32 +	1 * 16 +	1 * 8 +	0 * 4 +	1 * 2 +	1 * 1 =

16 + 8 + 2 + 1 = 27

Example 2: Convert 11011001 to decimal.

2^7	2^6	2^5	2^4	2^3	2^2	2^1	2^0
128	64	32	16	8	4	2	1
1	1	0	1	1	0	0	1
128 * 1+	64 * 1 +	0 * 32 +	1 * 16 +	1 * 8 +	0 * 4 +	0 * 2 +	1 * 1 =

128 + 64 + 16 + 8 + 1 = 217

Anytime you have a binary number that is all 1s to the right, the number in decimal is always 1 less than the next power of 2. Logically this makes sense, since you cannot have the number 2 in binary. The next value would need a new column and would be the next power of 2. For example:

$00000111_2 = 7_{10}$ because the next value in the chart would be $2^3 = 8$ or 1000_2

$00011111_2 = 31_{10}$ because the next column is 2^5 or 32

$01111111_2 = 127$ because the next column is 2^7 or 128

How Binary Numbers Can Be Interpreted

Letters

In addition to the numbers we just reviewed, binary numbers can also represent letters for text fields. Each letter has a binary value mapped to it. The software for the particular application knows when it sees a binary number whether it is looking for a number or a letter and interprets it accordingly.

Colors

Binary numbers are also used to represent colors. The human eye primarily detects red, green, and blue. Other colors are a combination of these three colors in different amounts. Computer monitors work the same way and add differing amounts of red, green, and blue to create the colors that are displayed. That is where RGB, for red, green, and blue, came to be known and can still be seen as a label for monitor and projector connections.

Earlier color representations used a byte (8 bits) for colors using three bits for red, three for green, and two for blue: RRRGGGBB. Only 256 colors could be represented using 1 byte. The retro arcade games and old video games you may have seen used 256 colors.

Now computers use one byte for each color. RRRRRRRRGGGGGGGGBBBBBBBB. With eight numbers for each color, we can create 256 possible shades of red times 256 possible green shades times 256 possible blue shades:

$$256 * 256 * 256 = 16,777,216 \text{ possible colors}$$

Notice in the table below:

Blue has the full amount of blue, but no other color.

Black is zero amounts of red, green, and blue.

Silver has equal amounts of red, green, and blue.

Color Chart Examples

Color name	RGB (red green blue) triplet
Blue	(0, 0, 255)
Silver	(192, 192, 192)
Purple	(128, 0, 128)
Ruby	(224, 17, 95)
Emerald	(80, 200, 120)
Black	(0, 0, 0)
White	(255, 255, 255)

The software program takes in the binary value and interprets it as a color, text value, or number, based on what the program is expecting.

Machine Instructions

When your code is converted from the natural language type command, such as: print("Error!"), to machine language, it is converted to binary. Just as with numbers, text, and colors, the compiler or interpreter is software that knows how to convert the values and what they represent in binary.

```
print("Error!")
```

The text "Error!" is converted to binary as below.

01000101 01110010 01110010 01110010 01110010 00100001

The "print" command is also converted to binary along with the instructions in binary that tell the program how to print text.

In summary, if we simply had a binary number: 00101001, we would not know what it represented. It could be a number, text, color, instruction, or other representation. However, the software using it knows what it is and how to interpret it.

Overflow Errors

Overflow errors occur in computers when the integer to be represented needs more bits than the programming language can represent. A fixed number of bits are assigned to hold integers in many programming languages. When the limit is reached, an overflow error occurs. This varies for different computers, and you are not expected to know this value for each computer for the AP exam.

Think of it like a car odometer when it is at the highest value it can show.

When you travel one more mile or kilometer, the odometer can roll over to 000001. A computer does not roll over to 1 when it reaches the maximum value it can hold. Instead, the bit that represents the number's sign (positive or negative) is flipped. The overflow error for an expected positive number as the result is a negative number and the result indicating an overflow error for an expected negative number is a positive number.

Example: Assume 999 is the largest number that can be represented even though we know it would be in binary. If you add 1 to it, you would expect the result to be 1000. Since the computer cannot process this number, it produces -000 as the result, which is the smallest number our example here can represent. It does the addition, but 1 is now in the sign position, which flips our value to be negative. Your program will not produce an error when this occurs. Be sure to test for this condition, especially when you know very large or small numbers may be used with the program.

Sign bit 1 = on	9	9	9
		+	1
1	0	0	0

It takes the same number of digits to represent a positive number as the negative of it. You can think of it as needing the same number of digits if you took the absolute value of a negative number. Both the positive and negative numbers have a sign digit included.

Other programming languages represent integers based on the size of the computer's memory rather than being set by the programming language. On the AP exam, this is how numbers will be represented. You will not need to calculate a value that would create an overflow error, but you might see a question about the concept.

Rounding or Round-off Errors

Rounding errors occur because of the way numbers with decimal points are stored in the computer. They are imprecise and are stored as a whole number + the decimal point + the fractional part of the number. This imprecise nature can cause rounding errors and possibly inaccurate results in your programs.

Example: 1.0 could be stored as 0.999999998

You are not responsible for knowing the ranges for real numbers on the AP exam. Whole numbers are stored precisely as the integer they represent.

Analog Data

Analog data is a continuous stream of data values. Think of the sound a train whistle makes as it nears and then leaves a crossing. It changes pitch (higher and lower tones) and gets louder and softer as it nears and leaves the crossing. It can be represented by a continuous wave representing the sound. Analog data can represent anything, including colors. Back in the predigital days, music was on albums and cassettes in analog format. When we made a copy of the recording, it was not an exact duplicate, and we lost some of the sound quality.

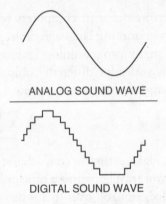

ANALOG SOUND WAVE

DIGITAL SOUND WAVE

As we know, digital data is just 0s and 1s. It approximates the continuous stream of analog data by taking *samples* or measured values of it at defined intervals such as each millisecond. The digital data plays these values back and it appears continuous due to the sampling rate. The conversion of analog data to digital is an abstraction, because we don't know or need to know what happens in between each digital value taken at its point in time. We just know that it sounds or appears the same as it did when it was in analog format.

With today's digital data, a master version of a recording or image is just 0s and 1s, so you can easily make an exact match with no loss of quality. This has an impact on the ethics and legality of sharing perfect digital copies of music, videos, games, and books.

Data Compression: Lossless and Lossy

There are considerations and trade-offs that have to be constantly evaluated when it comes to storing data. Image files become large very quickly. Therefore, compression techniques were developed to decrease their size. Some images store data by *pixel* (picture element).

If you had an image that was 300 × 400 pixels = 120,000 *pixels*, with 3 bytes per pixel for color as described previously, it would take approximately 120000 * 3 = 360,000 *bytes* for one picture. Depending on the bandwidth, this image could take up to a minute to download, which is quite slow for one image.

We can reduce the amount of space needed to represent the image or other file through *data compression*:

- Lossless compression techniques allow the original image to be restored. No data is lost, but the file size cannot be as compressed as with lossy techniques.
- Lossy compression techniques lose some data in the compression process. The original can never be restored, but the compression is greater than with lossless techniques.

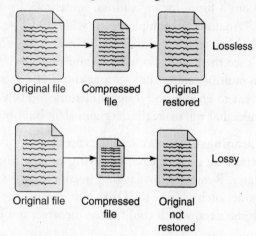

Many compression techniques assign a code to each character, including numbers and special characters. Characters that appear more frequently get a shorter code; those that appear less frequently get a longer code. The larger the file, the greater the opportunity for a greater savings on file size. To illustrate, think of a song with verses and a refrain. The verses are usually unique while the refrain is the same and repeats after each verse. The refrain provides an opportunity for compression with fewer symbols needed to represent it.

If full file restoration is not required, then a lossy compression algorithm is best, especially when the data is quite large and will take a long time to transmit. If you need the file restored to its original resolution, then you must use a lossless compression program. For example, medical and financial data would need to use a lossless compression technique.

JPEG (Joint Photographic Experts Group) images reduce file sizes up to 90% by replacing similar colors with the same color in large parts of the image. The replacements generally cannot be detected by the human eye.

The same concepts apply for music and video files. There are lossy and lossless compression programs that can be used with these files. As with image files, the original file can be restored with the lossless technique but not with a lossy one.

Processing Data to Get Information

Computers and Data

So much raw data is being collected constantly in all fields. Every purchase you make, those you return, websites you visit—all involve data that businesses collect. But what does it mean? Computers enable us to process data to turn it into information for decision making and research. Computers can often identify patterns in data that individuals would not be able to detect. As is often the case, there are also trade-offs to consider with large amounts of data.

Data collected from all types of events—such as visits, searches, inquiries, orders, returns, temperatures, scores, attendees, acres planted, acres harvested, fish, birds, photos, videos, and audio files—are considered to be raw data. These are all just values and descriptions until we make sense of it. While humans can usually do an adequate job on small amounts of data, there is no way we could process the vast amounts of data now collected in many raw datasets. We get tired, distracted, and bored, and then errors occur or opportunities are missed. Computers were made for this!

How Computers Help Process Data

People often enter data differently. This is almost a given if different people enter it. When I fill out a form, for my address, sometimes I use "Road" and other times I abbreviate it as "Rd." Atlanta has multiple streets with "Peachtree" in the name. If someone leaves off street, road, drive, and so on, the data is incomplete and inaccurate. Sometimes I make typos but don't see them until I've already hit "Enter"—if I see them at all. Sometimes data comes in from multiple sources or locations and needs to be combined. Data needs to be consistent for patterns to emerge and insights identified. There are programs created to make these minor changes that will make the data consistent but not change the meaning of it for future analysis.

- **Cleaning:** One area computers are very helpful with is "cleaning" the data. This includes removing corrupt data, removing or repairing incomplete data, and verifying ranges or dates. Removing or flagging invalid data is very useful. Cleaning data can also change values such as "dr." to "Drive" for consistency. Again, individuals could easily miss errors in the data, which could cause incorrect results in later processing.

- **Filtering:** Computers are also able to easily "filter" data. This means that different subsets can be identified and extracted to help people make meaning of the data. For example, all temperature values greater than 98.6 could be meaningful and need further processing or perhaps just a count of how many there are in the entire dataset might be useful.

- **Classifying:** Additionally, computers can help make meaning of large datasets by grouping data with common features and values. These groupings or classifications would be based on criteria provided by people who need to work with the data. There could be single or multiple criteria used for these groupings. These would depend on the reason that the data was collected.

- **Bias:** This can unintentionally be present in data. It occurs when the data collected does not represent all the possibilities in the pool of available options. For example, the census used to not have an option to check for multiracial individuals, so people had to choose one. This would potentially overrepresent the population of some races and underrepresent others. Prior data was biased with no way to identify when it occurred or a way to correct it. Bias in data does not go away by collecting larger amounts of data to analyze.

- **Patterns:** The data analysis starts with a hypothesis or question to check. The data is then processed using this criteria to see if patterns emerge. Computers are able to identify patterns in data that people are either unable to recognize or cannot process enough data to see the pattern. This process is known as "data mining." New discoveries and understandings are often made this way. When new or unexpected patterns emerge, the data has been transformed into information for people to begin to interpret. Computers make processing huge amounts of data possible so people can make sense of it. Machine learning is related to data mining, but it uses the data to make predictions. Through these predictions, actions can be programmed to occur when certain criteria are met, making it appear that the device has "learned" how to react or perform. This is how artificial intelligence (AI) works.

Correlations

Be cautious about *correlations* between data values. A correlation may not mean one thing caused the other. Always do further research with data from additional sources, not just more data from the same source, to prove the relationship exists. There is a website where the author, Tyler Vigen, correlates margarine consumption with the divorce rate in Maine and civil engineering degrees with mozzarella cheese consumption. These make the point—they may correlate, but one is not caused by the other! Take a few minutes and explore some of the funny examples.

Scalability

Scalability is the ability to increase the capacity of a resource without having to go to a completely new solution, and for that resource to continue to operate at acceptable levels when the increased capacity is being added. This means you do not have to bring the entire system down to add new resources. Everything already in place keeps operating normally, and new resources are added without impacting routine processing. The increase should be transparent to anyone using the resource. For example, processing should not slow down as the amount of data increases when solutions are scalable. In the case of data, the resource would be additional servers to store and process the data. Scalability is an important aspect to be able to store and process large datasets. These files cannot fit on our computers or most organizations' servers. Parallel computing systems may be needed to process these large datasets. See the Big Idea 4 chapter on computing systems and networks for more information about parallel systems.

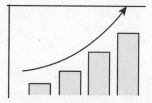

The "cloud" is considered a scalable resource. People connect, store, share, and communicate across the Internet. As traffic or demand for resources increases, the cloud service manages the demand by providing additional resources such as servers. Networks can also provide scalability. As more devices are added to the network, network managers increase access points and other devices to accommodate the additional network devices and traffic.

Note that scalability also includes the ability to downsize as needed, again without impacting the storage or processing.

Larger datasets have the potential for more patterns and information to ultimately be identified. While smaller datasets can still yield valuable information, often larger datasets are needed for patterns to begin to emerge. Many companies offer services including platforms for data storage and processing.

Metadata

Metadata is data that describes data and can help others find the data and use it more effectively. It is not the content of the data, but includes information about the data such as:

- Date
- Time stamp
- Author/owner
- File size
- File type

Changing, adding, or deleting metadata does not impact or change the actual data in any way. It allows us to organize and add structure to our data in addition to making it easier to find. Metadata includes "tags" that are used to identify the content. These tags enable web searches to find the data more easily. Multiple tags about a file are useful to help people find it with their search criteria. When you are adding anything to the web, think carefully about the tags you provide. Think about ways you would search for information like yours. The more tags the better, because we all think in different ways and our search criteria will be different, but we all are looking for the best outcomes to our searches.

How People Work with Computers to Process Data

We have the data cleaned and organized. Now it's time to process it! Software tools such as spreadsheets and databases can be used to filter, organize, and search the data. Search tools and filtering systems are needed to help analyze the data and recognize patterns. You are not required to know details about a specific tool. Programs can repeat and reframe data in the search for patterns. Sometimes data may be transformed, which might be extracting specific sections from data, such as age, or doubling values to see if a trend occurs. It could mean eliminating negative values from a subset used for analysis. Sometimes it's a calculation such as averages. For example, clothing businesses can get an awareness of what colors and sleeve lengths to order and sell in certain parts of the country during certain times of the year.

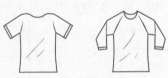

Sharing and Communicating Information

What did your analysis find? All of the work collecting and processing the data leads to this! Sharing the results and effectively communicating them is the next step. After data has been cleaned and organized, it needs to be reported and represented in ways so people can easily view it. There are many tools available to aid in communicating the insights identified from the data to others. Graphics in the form of charts, tables, and other designs are useful to present data in a visual format and in a summary format. Remember the phrase, "A picture paints a thousand words"? Use it. The human brain is wired to process information visually, so the use of images and other visual tools are effective ways to convey a message to help others understand it. Offering ways for others to interact with the data, such as providing sound files or videos when someone selects an option, is also useful. There are many apps and digital tools to present the information in an inviting and engaging format.

Identifying patterns and insights is a lot like sifting through the sand and dirt and then finding gold flakes or nuggets. To an organization, data converted to knowledge or information is like gold!

› Review Questions

Concepts

1. Which data compression technique provides the most compression?
   - (A) Lossy
   - (B) Lossless
   - (C) Filtering
   - (D) Classification

2. Which of the following best describes abstraction?
   - (A) Adding complexity so the concept can apply to more uses
   - (B) Simplifying complexity to make the concept more general
   - (C) Combining procedures to make a new one
   - (D) A set of instructions to do a task

3. Why is cleaning data important?
   - (A) It ensures incomplete data does not hide or skew results.
   - (B) It removes bad data.
   - (C) It repairs incomplete data.
   - (D) All of the above.

4. If analyzing data indicates a company should only hire people with a college degree because they stay at the company longer, what is this a potential indication of?
   - (A) Good data management practices leading to good hiring practices
   - (B) Frequency analysis to identify commonalities in the data
   - (C) Bias in collecting the data
   - (D) Data assessment and inquiry of hiring practices

5. What is one way in which number systems are abstract?
   - (A) The same amount can be represented by different number representations.
   - (B) A number can be best represented by one number system.
   - (C) Symbols can not be used to add, subtract, multiply, or divide them in their abstract form.
   - (D) They use constants.

6. Why is analyzing data with computers important?
   - (A) To identify patterns that humans cannot see
   - (B) To increase the viability of server farms
   - (C) To verify existing solutions to problems
   - (D) To test due diligence

7. What is the number system used by computers?
   - (A) Base 10 (decimal)
   - (B) Base 8 (octal)
   - (C) Base 2 (binary)
   - (D) Base 16 (hexadecimal)

8. When does an overflow error occur?
   - (A) When the computer runs out of memory to store program instructions
   - (B) When the flow of binary digits reaches a broken pathway and cannot arrive at its destination
   - (C) When an integer requires more bits to represent it than the programming language provides
   - (D) When the numerator in a calculation is larger than the denominator

9. What is information about the author of a document considered to be?
   - (A) Metadata
   - (B) Content
   - (C) Context
   - (D) Mididata

10. What is the amount of data compression an algorithm can produce reliant upon?
    - (A) No repeating parts of the file being compressed
    - (B) Several patterns in the data
    - (C) A large file size
    - (D) A small file size

11. How can an organization begin the process of analyzing data?
    (A) By following an iterative development process
    (B) By establishing measurements the data should show
    (C) By developing hypotheses and questions to test
    (D) By checking to see if the data matches previously collected data

12. What is 214_{10} in binary?
    (A) 11010100
    (B) 11010110
    (C) 11010111
    (D) 01101011

13. What is a reason to perform additional research on correlations found through data analysis?
    (A) There may not be an actual cause-and-effect relationship between the correlation variables.
    (B) A single source may not provide enough data for a conclusion.
    (C) To understand the relationship between the variables.
    (D) All of the above.

14. The letter "M" is represented by 01001101 in binary. What is this in decimal?
    (A) 414
    (B) 76
    (C) 77
    (D) 1101

15. Metadata is used to
    (A) provide updates to the data.
    (B) help find and organize data.
    (C) brand the data.
    (D) sort the data.

16. Which number type is stored imprecisely in memory?
    (A) Integers
    (B) Numbers with decimals
    (C) Both
    (D) Neither

17. When is *sampling* needed?
    (A) Sampling is used to store analog data.
    (B) Sampling is used to approximate real-world data.
    (C) Sampling is used when converting from digital data to analog data.
    (D) Sampling is used when converting from analog data to digital data.

18. An example of metadata about sea turtle nests could be
    (A) number of eggs in the nest.
    (B) location of the nest.
    (C) number of incubation days.
    (D) tracking number assigned to the nest.

19. Being able to add or remove resources to store large datasets is called
    (A) scalability.
    (B) filtering.
    (C) efficiency.
    (D) routing.

Application of Concepts

20. Data compression algorithms are used when the data
    (A) needs to be shared with a large number of people.
    (B) needs to be kept secure.
    (C) is too large to send in a timely manner.
    (D) needs to be sent a large physical distance away.

21. How many more bits are available if you go from a 32-bit computer to a 64-bit machine?
    (A) Twice as many
    (B) 32 more
    (C) 2^{32} more
    (D) 32^2 more

22. Your program is comparing temperatures to determine how many patients have a fever. Your selection statement's condition is not working correctly when the variable *patient_temp* is 98.6. What could be one reason why?

    ```
    IF (patient_temp = 98.6)
    ```

    (A) The format is incorrect for this condition.
    (B) A round-off error occurred.
    (C) An overflow error occurred.
    (D) The test condition is invalid.

23. Given a table of lunchroom leftovers, what can be determined from the data?

Date	Total meals	Total meals left over
1/29/18	800	25
1/30/18	750	5
1/31/18	800	42

    (A) Most popular items
    (B) Days of field trips when classes missed lunch
    (C) Days with high absenteeism
    (D) Amount of wasted budget dollars

24. A company purchases a large block of data from a social media site. If they want to analyze the data to learn more about potential customers, what techniques should they use?

    (A) Simulations to test different hypotheses about what data could be present
    (B) Data analysis to identify patterns and relationships in the data for further analysis
    (C) Maximization to get the highest return on their purchase of the data
    (D) Data processing to use the data with existing company software to see if it will run on their systems or if new ones will need to be developed

25. What order should these be in to go from smallest to largest?

    1. Binary—01110111
    2. Decimal—111
    3. Binary—01111011

    (A) 1, 2, 3
    (B) 2, 1, 3
    (C) 3, 1, 2
    (D) 3, 2, 1

26. A magnet school wants to advertise its students' success taking AP exams to prospective families. What's the best method to share the summarized data?

    (A) Post an image of student results on social media sites.
    (B) Create an interactive pie chart that can drill down to topics and overall scores posted on the school's website.
    (C) Write a report for a marketing pamphlet.
    (D) Send an e-mail to families with middle-school-age children.

27. Which topic needs the use of programs to analyze the data to identify insights?

    (A) The average number of students who drive to school each day
    (B) The record of wins and losses for all sports teams under their current coaches compared to prior years' win/loss records
    (C) The number of library books in a school district that need to be replaced each year
    (D) The standardized test scores for current students compared to test scores across the country for the past decade

28. A school district wants to analyze the data about their high school graduates who attend local community colleges. What information can the school district obtain from the following data that the school has available?

    Student name
    Number of students in the graduating class by high school
    High school graduation year
    Student self-reported plans for after high school
    Total numbers from local community colleges of enrolled students and their high school
    Total number of local community college students enrolled in each degree program

    (A) Average number of in-state students who enrolled in a local community college
    (B) If the number of local graduates who enroll in a local community college is increasing, decreasing, or stable
    (C) Number of local high school students who graduate from a local community college
    (D) Popular degree programs in the community colleges

❯ Answers and Explanations

1. **A**—Lossy data compression provides the most compression. Filtering and classification are not data compression techniques.

2. **B**—Abstraction means simplifying and taking away details to make something more general and flexible.

3. **D**—Data needs to be cleaned to remove or repair corrupt or incomplete data to ensure valid data is used for research and analysis.

4. **C**—This represents bias in that if a company historically mainly hired people with college degrees, then the data being analyzed would show that they stayed with the company longer because of higher numbers overall.

5. **A**—Number systems are abstract because the same amount can be represented by different number representations, such as binary, decimal, or hexadecimal.

6. **A**—Analyzing data allows us to identify patterns that could help solve problems or identify new possibilities that people likely could not process.

7. **C**—Computers use the binary or base 2 number system consisting of 0s and 1s.

8. **C**—An overflow error occurs when a number needs more bits to hold it than the programming language provides. Think of it like a three-position odometer reaching 999. At the next mile, it should read 1,000, but it cannot store a number that large. Instead, it rolls over to 1, which is an invalid representation of the mileage.

9. **A**—Information about the author of a document is metadata or data about the data.

10. **B**—Algorithms can provide a larger percentage of compression when there is repetition in the data, such as sections with repeating patterns. The entire pattern can be represented by one character or symbol in the compressed result. While larger data files are more likely to have these patterns, it's not a guarantee, and smaller datasets can also have repeating sequences.

11. **C**—Developing hypotheses and questions and testing these with the data helps gain insight and knowledge about it.

12. **B**—214_{10} is 11010110 in binary.

13. **D**—Each of these is a reason to perform additional research and analysis to validate the correlation.

14. **C**—$01001101_2 = 77$

    $(01001101)_2 = (0 \times 2^8) + (1 \times 2^7) + (0 \times 2^6) + (0 \times 2^5) + (1 \times 2^4) + (1 \times 2^3) + (0 \times 2^2) + (1 \times 2^1) + (1 \times 2^0) = (77)_{10}$

15. **B**—Metadata helps organize and tag data so that it can more easily be found.

16. **B**—Integers, or whole numbers, are stored precisely. Real numbers with a decimal and fractional part are stored imprecisely in computer memory.

17. **D**—Sampling is used to convert analog data to digital by taking samples of the analog data at intervals to create a digital representation of those values.

18. **D**—Data about the data would be the tracking number for the nest. The other values are details about the nest itself.

19. **A**—Scalability is adding or removing resources to store and process large datasets.

20. **C**—Compression techniques are used when data is too large to send in ways such as an attachment to an e-mail or when it would take too long to send it in its original, expanded form.

21. **C**—The computer increases from 2^{32} to 2^{64} bits. Therefore, the increase is 2^{32} bits.

22. **B**—A round-off error occurred. If the variable *patient_temp* contained 98.6, it could be stored in memory imprecisely as 98.5555559. The selection statement is then comparing 98.5555559 to 98.6, so the condition is false, when it is expected to be true.

23. **D**—While answers B and C hint at the cause, you cannot tell for sure from the table data. You can take the number of meals left over and multiply it by the cost of each meal to determine the budget dollars lost.

24. **B**—Data analysis is the transformation of data to identify patterns and connections. Companies can then use the data to identify business opportunities to take advantage of or threats to avoid.

25. **B**—The binary number 01110111 converts to 119 in decimal. The binary number 01111011 converts to 123. Therefore, the decimal number is smallest, then the first binary number in #1, then the second binary number in #3.

26. **B**—Prospective families will likely check the school's website for additional information. Therefore, an interactive pie chart can provide high-level information and drill down to more information when sections of the pie are selected. Social media accounts may not reach all families, and a marketing pamphlet cannot provide as much information or the drill-down ability. Sending a mass e-mail may be flagged as spam, and families may not open an e-mail from an unexpected source.

27. **D**—The test scores compared to all other scores for the prior decade will be a large dataset. Searching for correlations between current student data and prior data is a task that needs programs to process the data. The other options will have exact numbers on manageable-sized datasets that a person could identify manually or by using a local computer for processing.

28. **B**—With the high school graduation year along with the community college enrollment numbers plus the students' high schools, the school district can determine if the number of their high school graduates who enroll in local community colleges is increasing, decreasing, or stable over time.

› Rapid Review

Data is being generated all the time, around us and by us, through sensors, mouse clicks, camera clicks, recordings, buttons pressed, and screens swiped, among many other ways. This data can provide valuable information to various interested parties but only after it has been processed by computers. Then, the data can be analyzed to see what new information can be extracted.

Computers, at their lowest level, use binary numbers, 0 and 1, to represent everything. Therefore, a sequence of binary numbers could represent an object such a number, color, sound, image, or instruction. Computer programs are written to interpret the sequence based on what they need.

Numbers are an abstraction to represent "how many." Different number systems such as decimal and binary, express "how many" in different representations. These number representations can be converted to other number systems. Round-off errors can occur due to how the decimal portion of numbers are stored in computers. Real numbers are not stored precisely in computer memory. This means 1.0 could be stored as 0.9999998, resulting in round-off errors. Programming languages may have a set number of bits that can represent integers. Attempts to use more bits to represent a number result in an overflow error.

Analog data has continuous values and creates a smooth curve as values change. Digital data uses only 0s and 1s and approximates analog data by using samplings of the analog values.

Transmitting data to and from locations creates a concern around how to send such large amounts of data. Compression techniques, both lossy and lossless, were created and use algorithms to decrease the original file size to make transmission and storage easier. Lossless techniques enable the original file to be restored, while lossy techniques create smaller files, but the original file cannot be restored.

Metadata is identifying data about data, such as date and time created and owner of the data. When metadata is used effectively to organize and tag data, searches can successfully find what the person needs.

Humans cannot process large datasets manually. Computers must be used to help find the patterns, trends, and connections the data provide. There are tools, such as spreadsheets and databases, to store the data and then run queries to identify features of the data. Big data is too large to use standard processing tools and needs scalable solutions that can seamlessly add more resources as the data grows to store and process it.

Processing raw data includes activities such as cleaning and filtering data. It can also include classifying the data into various groupings. These activities can help identify patterns in the data that can then provide valuable information. Once data has been processed and analyzed into information, it needs to be communicated to other interested groups. Visual representations can effectively communicate the findings and can be done through tables, diagrams, charts, summary representations, or interactive displays.

CHAPTER 9

Big Idea 3: Algorithms and Programming

IN THIS CHAPTER

Summary: Algorithms are solutions designed to create something new or solve problems. They are fundamental to programming. Programs implement algorithms and can be developed for any reason, personal or professional; can utilize a variety of input and output; and can be easily shared.

This course does not require students to use a particular programming language. Therefore, the format of questions on the exam will use a standard format. There are some key differences from most programming languages. **One difference is that lists start at index position 1**, which is different than many programming languages. Students must be familiar with this format to ensure they are not slowed down or confused when reading the exam questions!

Students will have a copy of the Exam Reference Sheet (see the Appendix) during the exam.

Key Ideas

✪ Abstractions are created by removing details and making concepts more general. Programs use data abstraction and procedural abstraction to manage complexity.

✪ All algorithms can be written using a combination of sequential, selection, and iterative statements.

✪ Variables hold values in programs. Assignment statements change the value stored in a variable.

✪ Procedures are reusable blocks of code.

✪ Parameters accept values that can differ each time the procedure is used.

✪ Return statements exit a procedure and can send values back from the procedure to the calling program.

✪ Lists are collections of data stored in one variable. FOR EACH loops traverse each item in a list.

✪ Some algorithms cannot run in a reasonable amount of time, usually for large datasets. Heuristics can sometimes be used to find a solution that is close enough. Undecidable problems have no solution for all instances.

✪ Simulations are abstractions to test theories in a safer, controlled, and faster environment.

Key Terms

Algorithm	Lists
API	Logical operators
Argument	Modularity
Arithmetic operators	Modulus
Assignment statement	Optimization problem
Binary search	Parameter
Boolean values	Procedural abstraction
Clarity	Procedure
Code statement	Pseudocode
Concatenation	Readability
Condition	Relational operators
Data abstraction	RETURN statement
Decidable problem	Selection statement
Decision problem	Sequential statement
Efficiency	Simulation
Element	String
Expression	Substring
Heuristic	Traverse
Iterative	Undecidable problem
Library	Variable
Linear search	

Algorithms: The Building Blocks of Programming

Computers run the world! Or so it seems, more and more. Therefore, we should all have an idea of what programming is about. Computer programs can be written for a multitude of reasons, such as for businesses, scientific research, the entertainment industry, and personal use. Programs can include video, audio, images, text, buttons to push, and items to drag and swipe.

Algorithms

An algorithm is a set of steps to do a task. Recipes are algorithms. They are a set of steps to prepare food. Instructions for taking medicine make up an algorithm. Directions to get from one location to another are an algorithm.

In computer science, algorithms are the set of steps to solve a problem or complete a task. Algorithms are implemented with software. Examples are programs to:

- Calculate grade averages
- Run the air conditioner when the room temperature reaches 78°F
- Calculate the shortest route from home to school on your GPS

Algorithms have the potential to solve many problems once the programs are written for them to run. For example, a sorting algorithm is simple conceptually. Once it is programmed, an indefinite number of datasets can be sorted using it. As improvements are made to software and hardware, additional programming implementations are now feasible. For example, large datasets can now be handled by distributing the data over multiple programs or multiple devices, each processing a section of the code or data at the same time.

A section of code may work independently or can be used with other programming modules. These program modules read in values, make computations as needed, and produce output to automate processes. Programs may have a variety of data coming in (input) and going out (output). Input or output data could be in the form of text, video or images, audio files, or other formats, depending on the needs of the programming solution.

Languages for Algorithms

Algorithms can be written in several ways. Natural language is our native speaking and writing language, so it is much easier for people to use and understand.

Programming languages are very strict with their syntax, which is like their grammar and structure. This includes both block-style programming languages and textual programming languages. These are written for the computer to execute and may be more difficult for beginning programmers to understand. Pseudocode is used to map out a program's structure before beginning to write the code and uses a combination of natural and programming languages. As you first start out designing algorithms, you will likely use more natural language features. As you learn more about a programming language, your pseudocode may begin to include more coding-like features. Pseudocode cannot run on computers and needs to be translated to a programming language to do so. While most programming languages are fairly equitable in being able to implement an algorithm in the code, some were written for specific uses in a particular subject area, such as physics, and are better suited for these uses.

Flowcharts

Diagramming an algorithm before programming it is another way, like pseudocode, to plan out your program prior to starting to code it. Flowcharting helps to visualize how the program will be structured. You may see places for loops and procedures at this early stage. In some ways, it's like doing a puzzle. You can see how requirements are met with the flowchart, and how some may work better in a certain order or combination in your future code.

There are predefined shapes used by programmers for creating flowcharts. While there are many shapes, the basics are as shown in the following chart.

Symbol	Name
	Start/End
	Arrows to show relationships between shapes
	Input/Output
	Process
	Decision

Many software programs, including word processing software, include flowcharting shapes. There are other programs written specifically for creating flowcharts. While you won't have to create a flowchart on the AP exam, you might have to view one and answer questions about the content of it.

Using Algorithms

Algorithm Readability and Clarity

An important feature of any algorithm and program is how easy it is to read and follow. Hand in hand with readability is clarity. Clarity refers to how easy it is to understand. Generally, a program that is readable is clear. Readability is important to help programmers understand a program. The original programmer may not be the person who makes changes to it later. Even if it is the original author, if a period of time exists between writing it and modifying it, readability and clarity will impact the time and ability of the programmer to revisit and remember the details about the program before modifying or correcting the code. Features of readability and clarity include variables and procedures that are named according to their use and effective documentation of the program with comments in the code along with blank lines to separate sections of code.

Always be aware that there is more than one correct algorithm to solve a problem at hand or to create something new. Finding different algorithmic solutions can be helpful in identifying new insights about the problem. Different algorithms may also have different levels of efficiency or clarity.

Foundations of Computer Programming

Variables

Variables are placeholders for values a program needs to use. A program may need variables for numbers, both integers and real numbers, as well as text fields and Boolean values. Programs can assign values to variables as well as update the value to be a new one.

Variables can be used in expressions, both mathematical and textual. An important aspect of variables is naming them well. As discussed earlier, a good name for a variable is one that is descriptive. This makes it "self documenting" in that it describes the value or values that the variable holds, such as age, name, temperature, or score.

Variables are data abstractions because we do not need to know the details of how and where the values are stored in memory. We can reference the data value using the variable name, managing the complexity of programs and making them much easier to create, update, and understand. The variable can hold a single data value or a collection of values, if it is a list.

Data Types

The computer stores everything as 0s and 1s. Data types are the way computers assign some meaning to these binary digits. Doing this allows us to use those values in particular ways, such as numbers and text. There are four main data types you should understand for the exam: strings, integers, real (fractional) numbers, and Booleans.

Strings

Strings are text fields that are just a series of characters and are denoted with quotation marks around the string field. Any character, number, or symbol can be part of a string. When numbers are part of a string, then they will be considered to be text, like in a street address. In this case, you cannot use them in calculations because they are text fields, not numbers. There are many processes that are commonly done with strings, and most programming languages include prewritten procedures providing this functionality.

- *Concatenating* strings means "adding" them or "gluing" them together.
  For example, suppose we have the following two strings stored in the variables *msg1* and *msg2*.

  ```
  msg1 ← "Coding"
  msg2 ← "is great!"
  ```

  Concatenating them would produce: `Coding is great!`
  Exam questions may use a procedure format and pass the two strings to be concatenated as parameters. The concatenated value would be returned by the procedure.

  ```
  Concatenate(firstName, lastName)
  ```

  A procedure such as the one above would take two strings and return the concatenated version as one string holding a person's full name.

- *Substrings* are sections of strings.
  You can reference a character in a string using its index, or position in the string. The first letter is the index 1, the second character is the index 2, and so on. Using the example above, the substring of *msg2*, "is great!", starting at index 6 and going to the end would be:
  eat!

Character	i	s		g	r	e	a	t	!
Index	1	2	3	4	5	6	7	8	9

Notice the space between "is" and "great!" gets its own index value. A space is a valid character!

You may see questions about substrings on the AP exam in the format:
ProcedureName(string, start, length)

ProcedureName would be the name, such as Substring, given in the question for the procedure.

As the first parameter, *string* would be the variable to use in the substring operation.
The second parameter, *start*, is a parameter that tells us the first index position of our new substring.

The last parameter, *length*, represents how many index positions to include in the new substring.

For example, if a variable *msg1* holds the value "Coding ", then calling the procedure Substring with the following start and length would give us:

```
msg1 ← "Coding "

Substring(msg1, 1, 3) would return: "Cod"
```

Integers

Integers are whole numbers. (They do not have a decimal point.) Integers can be used in mathematical operations and expressions, whereas strings (text fields) cannot.

"Fractional" Numbers

These are numbers with a decimal point, even if a number has 0 (zero) for the decimal value, such as 52.0. These numbers can also be used in mathematical operations and expressions.

Mathematical Processes

Most programming languages include mathematical operations. For the AP exam, you need to understand the basic math functions of:

+ add
− subtract
* multiply This is an asterisk and is found above the number 8 on your keyboard.
/ divide   Watch the direction of the slash for division. This key is beside the right *Shift* key.

MOD modulus math   Returns only the remainder after dividing

Modulus math uses division but only provides the *remainder* as the answer, not the quotient.

MOD is the symbol used for modulus math in many programming languages and is how you will see it on the AP exam for this course.

20 MOD 4 = 0   The quotient is 5 with a remainder of 0, so the answer is 0.
21 MOD 4 = 1   The quotient is 5 with a remainder of 1. The answer is 1.
 3 MOD 7 = 3   Anytime the first number is smaller than the second, the quotient is 0 and the remainder will always be the first number. Here, the answer is 3.

A common use for "MOD math" in programming is to find even or odd numbers. A number that is divisible by 2 with a remainder of 0 is even. An IF statement could use this test in its condition:

IF num MOD 2 = 0   The condition is true if the current value of the variable *num* is even.

Assignment Statements

To assign a value to a variable, the assignment operator is used. In many programming languages, a single equals sign, =, is used as the assignment operator. For this AP exam, the left-facing arrow, ←, is used. The variable name is always on the **left** of the ← sign.

The programming language will evaluate the right-hand side of the assignment operator and then place the value into the variable on the left-hand side of it. The format to assign a value to a variable for text and block coding on the AP exam is:

Text:

```
        variable ← expression
```

Block:

```
variable ← expression
```

The previous value stored in a variable is overwritten by a new assignment statement. In this example, a variable named *score* is assigned the value 10. It is then assigned the value 11. The value 10 is gone and no longer available.

```
score ← 10
score ← 11
```

Just like in your math class, expressions are calculations to be evaluated to an answer or single value. In computer science, the value is then assigned to a variable if the value will be needed later. It also could be displayed on a screen or printed.

```
x ← 3.14 * 5            Multiply 3.14 by 5 and store it in the variable x.
PI ← 3.14               Assign a variable named PI the value 3.14.
area ← PI * radius * radius  Assign the variable area the result of PI
                        times radius².
```

You will get an error if you write:

```
5/9 * (fahr - 32) ← celsius
```

The variable must be on the left and the assignment arrow points left.

```
celsius ← 5/9 * (fahr - 32)    This is the correct way to set up the
                               calculation.
```

The expression will be evaluated and loaded into the variable *celsius*.

P Parentheses
E Exponents
M Multiplication
D Division
A Addition
S Subtraction

NOTE: MOD has the same precedence as multiplication and division.

The order of operations PEMDAS (see above) used in math is followed by programming languages. It is always better to use parentheses to ensure the correct order of processing for a mathematical expression.

$f - 32 * 5 / 9$ does not provide the same value as $(f - 32) * (5 / 9)$.

Boolean Values

Boolean values are one of the foundations of computer code. Understanding Boolean is important for writing correct, readable, and efficient code. Boolean values can only be true or false, needing only one bit to represent its value. Relational operators are used with Boolean values. These are just like in your math class:

= equal
≠ not equal

>   greater than
<   less than
≥   greater than or equal to
≤   less than or equal to

Two values are compared based on the relational operator and determined to be true or false. For example, if we assign values to variables *num1* and *num2*:

```
num1 ← 5
num2 ← 10
```

num1 > num2 evaluates to *false* because at this moment, num1 is 5 and num2 is 10. Five is not greater than 10.

Compound Conditional Statements Using Logical Operators: AND, OR, NOT

Boolean expressions can be simple or compound. Multiple expressions can be combined using the logical operators AND, OR, and NOT. These also evaluate to either true or false.

AND LOGICAL OPERATOR   To be true, both of the operands on either side of the AND operator must be true when evaluated individually. In the example below, "licenseEligible" will be set to true only when the age is greater than or equal to 16 *and* the Boolean variable "learnersPermit" is true. Otherwise, "licenseEligible" will be set to false.

```
licenseEligible ← (age ≥ 16) AND (learnersPermit = true)
```

These will be on the AP exam and are on the Exam Reference Sheet as:

```
Text:

        condition1 AND condition2


Block:
```

$$\boxed{\text{condition1}} \text{ AND } \boxed{\text{condition2}}$$

OR LOGICAL OPERATOR   For the OR operator, either or both of the operands can be true for the condition to be true. In this example, if the day is a Saturday OR the month is July, then the sleepLate variable will be true. The day can be any day as long as the month is July, and the month can be any month as long as the day is Saturday for sleepLate to be true.

```
sleepLate ← day = "Saturday" OR month = "July"
```

These will be on the AP exam and are on the Exam Reference Sheet as:

```
Text:

        condition1 OR condition2


Block:
```

$$\boxed{\text{condition1}} \text{ AND } \boxed{\text{condition2}}$$

NOT LOGICAL OPERATOR   With the NOT operator, if a condition was true, then NOT makes it false. If a condition was false, then NOT makes it true.

This will be on the AP exam and is on the Exam Reference Sheet as:

Text:

```
NOT condition
```

Block:

You can have a single Boolean value or a Boolean expression as either operand using the logical operators AND and OR. For example:

```
(time = 1800) AND (dog = true AND currentTemp < 80)
```

time = 1800 evaluates to true or false as a single Boolean value

dog = true AND currentTemp < 80 both have to be evaluated first and compared with AND. The result of that as a Boolean is then used as the right-side operand of the first AND.

Let's assume the time is 1800 (6:00 p.m.), so that is true.

Let's assume we do have a dog, so that is true.

The currentTemp is 82, so (currentTemp < 80) is false.

Our Boolean expression evaluates to:

```
true AND (true AND false)
```

The right-hand side (true AND false) must be evaluated and is false. Remember, both operands must be true for an AND to be true.

```
true AND false
```

Finally, the overall condition is evaluated with AND. Both sides are not true, so it evaluates to:

```
false
```

I have a dog, and we usually walk at 6:00 p.m., but if it is too hot for her paws on the asphalt, we'll go later!

Program Statements

Here's some great news! All programs can be written using a combination of only three types of statements. These statements are used over and over and can be combined for more complex needs, but there are only three! They are:

- Sequential
- Selection
- Iterative

Sequential

These are statements that are executed as written in order in the program. As we start writing our programs, a *code statement* has an action that will be executed when the program is run. Once a statement is complete, the next statement is run. Naturally, they have to be in the correct order to accurately complete the algorithm. Think of the result if the steps for a recipe or solving an equation were out of order! And if you have the other two types of statements, selection and iteration, then you also have sequential statements.

Selection Statements

These are a key component to many programs. They use the "if (condition)" structure, and the evaluation of the condition uses Boolean values. As we know, Booleans can only be either true or false, so the program statements associated with the condition only run when the condition at that moment evaluates to "true." This changes the flow of the program from every statement running sequentially to filtering out some of the code that will execute, based on the Boolean value.

These are written on the AP exam as:

```
Text:
        IF(condition)
        {
            <block of statements>
        }

Block:
```

Notice that the code to be executed when the condition is true is surrounded by the curly braces, { }, in the "Text" version. The code within the braces is indented, which helps with readability. It also makes it easier to see if you are missing a closing brace }!

For example:

```
IF grade_point_average ≥ 90
{
    grade ← "A"
}
```

When the condition evaluates to false, the code within the braces is skipped. Sometimes we want to execute different code when the condition is false. We have a way to do that! Each IF statement can also have an ELSE statement. The ELSE is optional, but when included, it must be part of an IF statement's structure. The statements associated with the ELSE will only run when the IF condition is "false." Notice that the code to run for the ELSE is included in its own set of curly braces { }. The code within the braces is also indented, which helps with readability.

These are written on the AP exam as:

```
Text:
        IF(condition)
        {
            <first block of statements>
        }
        ELSE
        {
            <second block of statements>
        }
Block:
```

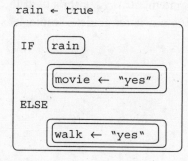

Example 1:

```
rain ← true
```

This is read as "if true" and since *rain* is currently true, it is true.

Example 2:

```
IF (season = "Summer")
{
    alarmClock ← false
}
ELSE
{
    alarmClock ← true
}
```

Example 3:

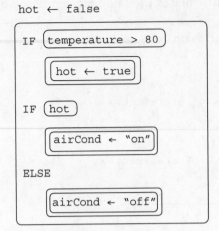

```
hot ← false
```

Read as "if true."

This could also be written as:

```
IF (hot = true)
    airCond ← "on"
```

There are often cases where there are multiple possibilities in a condition. One example is converting a number grade to a letter grade. Depending on the student's number average, the letter grade could be an "A," "B," "C," "D," or "F." An IF condition can handle all those possibilities using *nested* conditional statements. ELSE IF is used in conjunction with an IF when there are multiple options. Using our letter grade example, let's set up the conditions.

```
IF (average ≥ 90)
{
    DISPLAY ("Grade: A")
}
ELSE IF (average ≥ 80)
{
    DISPLAY ("Grade: B")
}
ELSE IF (average ≥ 75)
{
    DISPLAY ("Grade: C")
}
ELSE IF (average ≥ 70)
{
    DISPLAY ("Grade: D")
}
ELSE
{
    DISPLAY ("Grade: F")
}
```

There is no limit on the number of "ELSE IF" statements you can have in a program. Notice that each "ELSE IF" has a condition to evaluate. Only the "ELSE" statement does not have a condition. The braces and indentation are also used to identify the code that will be run when a particular condition is true.

Once a condition evaluates to be true in the nested IF structure, the code associated with that condition is run and the rest of the ELSE IF conditions are not tested. The IF statement is over at that point. The program continues with the next line of code after the complete IF statement or terminates the program if there are no other lines of code.

You could write multiple IF statements rather than use an IF/ELSE IF structure. However, each individual IF statement's condition would be evaluated. Every condition that is true would then run the code associated with it. This is less efficient, especially if you have large datasets to process. It could also produce unexpected results. For example, let's rewrite our letter grade code to use multiple IF statements and see what happens.

```
IF (average ≥ 90)
{
    DISPLAY ("Grade: A")
}
IF (average ≥ 80)
{
    DISPLAY ("Grade: B")
}
IF (average ≥ 75)
{
    DISPLAY ("Grade: C")
}
IF (average ≥ 70)
{
    DISPLAY ("Grade: D")
}
IF (average < 70)
{
    DISPLAY ("Grade: F")
}
```

We would need to add another condition to test for less than 70 that the ELSE would not have had.

In this case, if our average was 92, then each letter grade except "F" would print because each condition would be true. The algorithms appear very similar, but this version provides different as well as incorrect results. To get the correct results, we need to modify the structure and use a range in our condition.

```
IF (average ≥ 90)
{
    DISPLAY ("Grade: A")
}
IF (average ≥ 80 AND average < 90)
{
    DISPLAY ("Grade: B")
}
IF (average ≥ 75 AND average < 80)
{
    DISPLAY ("Grade: C")
}
IF (average ≥ 70 AND average < 75)
{
    DISPLAY ("Grade: D")
}
IF (average < 70)
{
    DISPLAY ("Grade: F")
}
```

The condition now includes the upper and lower values.

The condition now includes the upper and lower values.

The condition now includes the upper and lower values.

Only the lower condition is needed.

You can write the same algorithm in different ways and each can still be correct. Similarly, different algorithms can be written to solve the same problem, just in different ways.

In your Create project, you may have had ELSE IF statements. These will not be tested on the multiple-choice questions on the AP exam.

Iterative

Iterative statements are also referred to as repetitive statements or loops. This type of programming statement also changes the sequence of lines of code that are executed. Code that is associated with these statements repeats as many times as specified before continuing with the rest of the program.

Among several benefits of loops is that the code will be shorter because we can avoid duplication. This also makes the code more readable and easier to understand. Also, if we need to correct an error or make an update, we only have to do this in one place.

You are responsible for understanding three types of loops for the AP exam. The "REPEAT n TIMES" and "REPEAT UNTIL (condition)" are covered here. The FOR EACH loop is covered in a future section in this chapter.

REPEAT n TIMES Loop

This loop will repeat a specified number of times: "n" is a variable that must be set to a positive integer for the loop to run. The code that is repeated is indented underneath the REPEAT statement and within the braces, { }, just like with the IF/ELSE statements. The braces, { }, are required for loops in this course. The indentation is good programming practice.

```
num ← 5
REPEAT num TIMES    num is currently 5, so the code within the braces will repeat 5 times
{
    < code within the loop >
}
```

This is the format you will see on the AP exam.

```
Text:

        REPEAT n TIMES
        {
            <block of statements>
        }

Block:
```

```
REPEAT n TIMES
    block of statements
```

This example repeats for each player and displays the player's name and jersey number. In this case, the display screen could be the large screen in a stadium.

```
numOfPlayers ← 25
REPEAT numOfPlayers TIMES
{
        DISPLAY (playerName, jerseyNum)
}
```

REPEAT UNTIL (Condition) Loop   The REPEAT UNTIL loop has a condition to evaluate at each iteration of the loop.

The loop will continue to run while the condition evaluates to "false." This is similar to how an IF statement works except the condition for the IF statement must evaluate to true for it's code to execute. However, remember that IF statements execute once. REPEAT UNTIL loops can execute multiple times or not at all, depending on how the condition evaluates.

Each iteration or pass through the loop must change the condition. If we did not have this, we would end up with an *infinite* loop. With an infinite loop, the condition never has a chance to change to "true," so it continually repeats. Eventually your computer's resources are used up and it crashes. (A restart of your computer will free up the resources.)

This is the format you will see on the AP exam.

```
Text:
        REPEAT UNTIL (condition)
        {
            <block of statements>
        }

Block:
```

```
        REPEAT UNTIL ( condition )

            block of statements
```

Example:

```
num ← 0
REPEAT UNTIL (num > 5)
{
        < code within the loop >
        num ← num + 1

}
```

num must increase with each iteration so it will eventually be greater than 5.

This statement adds 1 to the current value of num and stores it back into the variable.

If the condition is initially true, the code in the loop will not execute at all. In the following example, num is initialized to the value 10. When the REPEAT UNTIL condition is evaluated, num > 5 is true, so the loop will never be run. The program will skip the loop and continue with the next line of code after the closing brace, }.

```
num ← 10
REPEAT UNTIL (num > 5)
{
        < code within the loop >
}
```

Note that you can also have a loop of any type within another loop.

```
REPEAT UNTIL (time = 1500)
{
        REPEAT 7 TIMES
        {
            <code>
        }
}
```

Combining Algorithms

One of the key features of algorithms is that once they are created, you can use them over and over, combine them for more complex problem solving, or modify them for a new use.

For example, you can create an algorithm to ask a user to select a menu option by typing in the number.

- To ensure the user typed in a correct number, you could call a different algorithm to check for a valid number.
- If the number is not valid, call a third algorithm to display an error message.
- If the number is valid, call the algorithm to process the selected option.

Each of these algorithms can work in a variety of different scenarios. By creating them and ensuring they are accurate, using them to solve a different problem in a new algorithm saves time and helps ensure the new algorithm produces accurate results.

Common Algorithms

There are common algorithms that are helpful to know. You can easily implement one when needed, which can help speed up development of the program. These include:

Determining the **maximum** or **minimum** number from two or more numbers.

The pseudocode for the maximum of two numbers is:

> Compare the numbers.
> Store the larger number as the maximum.

For the minimum of two numbers:

> Compare the numbers.
> Store the smaller number as the minimum.

If you have more than two numbers, a computer can still only compare two at a time. One number would be the current largest (or smallest), and the other would be the next number to compare it to.

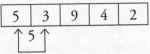

largest = 5 after first comparison

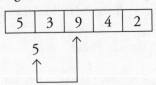

largest = 9 after second comparison

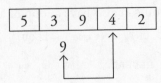

largest = 9 after third comparison

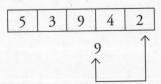

largest = 9 after last comparison

Another common algorithm is calculating the **sum** and **average** of a group of numbers. This is fairly straightforward since it is a concept you have already learned in math class. One key element to remember is that you need to keep count of how many numbers you have added together so you will be able to calculate the average. The pseudocode for this algorithm is:

1. Set counter and sum to 0.
2. Get the current number.
3. Add it to the existing sum and store the new value back into the variable sum.
4. Add 1 to the counter.
5. Repeat steps 2–4 until all numbers have been added and counted.
6. Divide the sum by the counter to calculate the average.
7. Display the sum and average.

A frequent use for "MOD math" in programming is to find if **one number is divisible by another**. For example, a number that is divisible by 2 with a remainder of 0 is even.

```
IF (num MOD 2 = 0)
{
        DISPLAY ("Number is even")
}
```

Robots

This course and exam also cover the movements of robots through a grid. There are four commands you are responsible for understanding and using. These are included in the Exam Reference Sheet, which you will have a copy of during the exam. The triangle represents the robot's starting point and the direction it is facing.

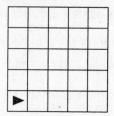

One command the robot can follow is MOVE_FORWARD. The robot moves one step forward in the direction it is already facing. If the command would place the robot in a blacked-out box or past the border of the maze, the command cannot be executed. This is how the command will appear on the exam.

```
Text:
        MOVE_FORWARD
```
```
Block:
    MOVE_FORWARD()
```

The robot can also rotate left or right. The robot only changes the direction in the square it is already in. It does NOT move forward. Many students forget that and also move the robot forward.

```
Text:
        ROTATE_LEFT ()
        ROTATE_RIGHT()
```
```
Block:
    ROTATE_LEFT
    ROTATE_RIGHT
```

Finally, there is a command, CAN_MOVE, that we can use to determine if the robot can make a valid move forward before moving. It returns a Boolean value, true or false. The mazes often have boxes blacked out. This means that the robot cannot land on or pass through those.

CAN_MOVE can be used in an IF statement in your code to navigate through the maze. This command takes a parameter that indicates the direction to test. Valid values for the direction parameter are:

- left
- right
- forward
- backward. Remember that to go backward, you can turn left or right twice. Each turn is 90 degrees, so two commands would be 180 degrees, or back toward the direction the robot came.

Text:

    CAN_MOVE(direction)

Block:

CAN_MOVE [direction]

Example to solve the grid above:

```
REPEAT UNTIL (end)
{
    MOVE_FORWARD()
    MOVE_FORWARD()
    IF (CAN_MOVE (right))
    {
        ROTATE_RIGHT()
    }
    REPEAT 4 TIMES
    {
        MCVE_FORWARD()
    }
    ROTATE_LEFT()
    MOVE_FORWARD()
    MOVE_FORWARD()
}
```

You can expect to see questions in a couple of different formats. One way is to provide the code and a starting point for the robot. The question asks where the robot would end up after the code executes. You would have four possible solutions to select from. Don't forget to consider which direction the robot would be facing at the end! That is one "gotcha" for many students.

Another common format is to provide a maze with the starting and ending points marked. The solutions provide different chunks of code. You are asked which set of code would correctly move the robot through the maze.

Lists

Lists are a collection of items, such as a grocery list or a playlist of music. A list in a program can be a collection of numbers, words, phrases, or a combination of these. Usually a list only contains one type of data in a single list, but some programming languages do allow different types of data in the same list. Lists provide the ability to store more than one value in the same variable, separated by commas, when the variable is defined as a list. This makes designing a solution and processing items in a list much easier! The list is a generalization (or abstraction) of a group of values, numbers, or strings that can be used in certain ways. Lists are also called arrays in some programming languages.

On the AP exam, you will see these notations for lists.

Create a new list that is empty:

Text

```
listName ← [ ]
```

Block

```
listName ← ( )
```

Create a new list and initialize it to the values listed.

value1 will be the first item in the list, value2 is the second item, and so on.

Text

```
listName ← [value1, value2, value3, . . . ]
```

Block

```
listName ← (value1, value2, value3)
```

Copy all the values from list1 to list2. If list1 contains the values [5, 10, 15], then after the statement is executed, list2 will exist and contain the values [5, 10, 15].

Text

```
list2 ← list1
```

Block

```
list2 ← list1
```

List Indices

Individual items in a list are called *elements* and are accessed by position using an index. Index positions are always integers and are enclosed within square brackets [index]. **For the AP Computer Science Principles exam, the list index starts at 1.** This is different from many programming languages, so be alert to this on questions!

On the AP exam, the format to access an element of a list will look like:

Text:

```
listName[i]
```

Block:

```
listName i
```

You can assign a value directly to a list position using the index. This code assigns the string "popcorn" to index position 1 of the list *snacks* and the value in the variable *fruit,* which holds the string "grapes" to index position 2.

```
fruit ← "grapes"
snacks[1] ← "popcorn"
snacks[2] ← fruit
```

The list *snacks* will look like this: ["popcorn", "grapes"]

The AP exam format to assign a value to a list element is:

```
Text:
    listName [i] ← variable
```

```
Block:
    listName i ← variable
```

You can also assign the value stored in a list to another variable. Here the variable *favFruit* will be assigned the value currently in the second element of the list, which is "grapes."

```
favFruit ← snacks[2]
```

The exam format for assigning a list element to a variable looks like:

```
Text:
    variable ← listName[i]
```

```
Block:
    variable ← listName i
```

If you attempt to reference a position in the list that does not exist, your program will end with an "index out of bounds" error. It could be an index value less than 1 or an index value higher than the length of your list. If our list of snacks is:

```
snacks ← ["popcorn", "grapes", "chips", "cheese", "nuts"]
```
snacks[9] does not exist.
snacks[0] does not exist.

To assign the value of one list element to another list element, use the same format where the element indicated is through the index position. The current value in the list element is overwritten with the new one. The element in the index position you are writing from does not change!

```
Text:
    listName[i] ← listName[j]
```

```
Block:
    listName i ← listName j
```
Example:
```
    snacks[1] ← snacks[4]
```
Our list now becomes: ["cheese", "grapes", "chips", "cheese", "nuts"]

Built-in Methods

Most programming languages will have built-in procedures, or "methods," of common functionality to use with lists. These generally include functionality such as:

- Adding an item to a specific position in a list. The INSERT command causes elements to the right of the indicated index position, i, to shift right one position to make room for the new element. Nothing is overwritten. The new value is inserted into the given index position, and the size of the list is now one element longer.

```
Text:
    INSERT (listName, i, value)
```

```
Block:
    INSERT listName, i, value
```
Example:
If we have a list:
```
    numbers ← [1, 3, 14, 15]
```

The command:

```
INSERT (numbers, 3, 5)
```

Will change our list to be:

```
numbers ← [1, 3, 5, 14, 15]
```

- Appending an item to the end of the list. The APPEND command will add the new element to the end of the list, so no index position is needed. The size of the list increases by one.

```
Text:
    APPEND (listName, value)
```

```
Block:
```

```
APPEND  listName, value
```

Example—using our same list of numbers:

```
numbers ← [1, 3, 5, 14, 15]
```

The command:

```
APPEND(numbers, 29)
```

Changes our list to be:

```
numbers ← [1, 3, 5, 14, 15, 29]
```

- Removing an item from a list. The REMOVE command deletes the element at the provided index position and shifts the remaining elements one position to the left. The size of the list decreases by one.

```
Text:
    REMOVE (listName, i)
```

```
Block:
```

```
REMOVE  listName, i
```

Example—using our list of numbers:

```
numbers ← [1, 3, 5, 14, 15, 29]
```

The command:

```
REMOVE (numbers, 2)
```

Changes our list to be:

```
numbers ← [1, 5, 14, 15, 29]
```

- Length. The length of a list is the number of elements in the list.

```
Text:
    LENGTH (listName)
```

```
Block:
    LENGTH  listName
```

Example—using our list of numbers:

```
numbers ← [1, 5, 14, 15, 29]
```

The command:

```
LENGTH (numbers)
```

Returns the value 5 because there are five elements currently in the list.

This number can be useful in processing items in a list. You can use references such as:

```
snacks[LENGTH(snacks)]
```

to access the last item in the list without having to know the length in advance. First, the value LENGTH(snacks) is evaluated and returns the number 5 for our current list. Our statement now looks like: snacks[5], which is the value "nuts".

With thousands or millions of elements in a list, we can't count them all. Even with a few dozen, people would occasionally make mistakes, and it would take so much longer than the split millisecond a computer would take. Write the code and let a computer do it!

There are many other built-in methods, and you should become comfortable with looking these up along with their format for programming languages you use in the programming language documentation.

Checking Each Item in a List

The FOR EACH loop is the third type of iterative statement you must know for the AP exam.

```
FOR EACH item IN list
```

The above statement is a loop that will automatically repeat the code for each element in the list. This is called *traversing* a list. The programmer chooses the name for the iteration variable "item". Each pass of the loop will assign the value of the next element in the list to the variable "item". Processing lists with a FOR EACH loop takes advantage of features of both structures.

The format for the AP exam is:

Text:
```
FOR EACH item IN listName
{
    <block of statements>
}
```

Block:

```
FOR EACH item IN listName
    block of statements
```

For example, let's define a list and initialize it to various fruits.

```
fruit ← ["kiwi", "grapes", "peach", "pineapple", "orange"]
```

We can set up a FOR EACH loop to process each element in our list. This FOR EACH loop will repeat once for each element in our *fruit* list, in this case, 5 times.

```
FOR EACH food IN fruit
{
  IF (food = "watermelon" OR food = "pineapple")
  {
      DISPLAY("A great-tasting fruit is", food,"!")
  }
}
```

Pass	food	IF condition
1	kiwi	False
2	grapes	False
3	peach	False
4	pineapple	True
5	orange	False

With each pass, the variable *food* will take on the next element in the list. We can then add "IF" conditions or other statements to process the elements. When the list element stored in *food* is "watermelon" or "pineapple", the condition in the IF statement is true and a message will be displayed. The table shows each numbered pass through the loop, the value of the variable *food* with each pass, and the Boolean result of evaluating the condition.

The FOR EACH loop stops after the last element in the list has been processed. You will *not* get an "index out of bounds" error nor will you have an infinite loop when processing a list with the FOR EACH loop.

NOTE: The Exam Reference Sheet that you will be given for the exam has information about lists and the FOR EACH loop.

Common Algorithms

There are algorithms that are frequently needed for processing lists with iteration. These include finding the **largest or smallest number in a list**. Here is an example using a REPEAT UNTIL loop with a list of grades.

`index ← 2`	This variable represents the index position for a list element.
`largest ← gradeList[1]`	This sets the largest number to be the first list element.
`REPEAT UNTIL (LENGTH(gradeList) = index)` `{`	This loop will process each element in the list. Our condition checks to see if our index variable equals the length of the list.
`    IF (largest < gradeList[index])`	This checks each list element to see if it is larger than the current value of the variable *largest*.
`    {`	
`        largest ← gradeList[index]`	This sets a new value for the variable *largest*.
`    }`	
`    index ← index + 1`	This updates the index by 1.
`}`	

Another common algorithm is finding the **sum and average** of the values in a list. This example uses block programming like you would see on the AP exam.

```
sum ← 0
    FOR EACH grade IN gradeList
        sum ← sum + grade

DISPLAY "The sum is: ", sum

DISPLAY "The average is: ", sum/LENGTH gradeList
```

Notice that we did not have to count the number of items in the list. We used the LENGTH() method to count for us!

Searching

Searching deals with finding the needed element from everything in the dataset or determining that it is not there. There are several common algorithms that have been written to search for items in a list. You are responsible for understanding two of them: linear and binary searches.

LINEAR SEARCH Linear searches, also called sequential searches, check each individual record, starting at the beginning and going to the end, one after the other in order to either find the desired data or to determine it is not in the dataset. Such a search is easy to understand and simple to implement, and it does not matter if the data is sorted. With a linear search, the best case is if the item is first in the list; the worst case is if it is not in the list at all. It is easily implemented using the FOR EACH loop.

Search for 10

| 8 | 65 | 42 | 29 | 14 | 5 | 2 | 15 | 10 | 9 |

```
FOR EACH num in list
    {
        IF (num = 10)
        {
            DISPLAY ("Found 10!")
        }
    }
```

BINARY SEARCH Binary searches are far more efficient than linear searches. However, data must be *sorted* to use a binary search. The binary search is considered a "divide and conquer" algorithm because it divides the dataset into two equal parts. Feedback about whether the value in question is higher or lower than the midpoint of the list determines which half to discard and which half to continue searching. The dividing and searching steps are repeated until the value is found or determined to not be in the list.

For example, if we are looking for a number in a list of integers from 1 to 100, we can find it within 7 searches. The binary search method is that efficient! Let's look for the number 42, and remember our list has to be sorted for the binary search to work.

Our first guess would be 50, the midpoint of the list.

| 1 | 2 | 3 | . . . | **50** | 51 | . . . | 98 | 99 | 100 |

The feedback would be that our number is lower, so we throw away numbers from 50 to 100.

Our second guess would be 25, the midpoint between 1 and 49.

| 1 | 2 | 3 | . . . | **25** | 26 | . . . | 47 | 48 | 49 |

The feedback would be that our number is higher, so we throw away numbers between 1 and 25.

Our third guess would be halfway between 26 and 49, or 37.

| 26 | 27 | 27 | . . . | **37** | 38 | . . . | 47 | 48 | 49 |

The feedback is that the number is higher, so 26–37 is gone.

Our fourth guess is halfway between 38 and 49, or 43.

| 38 | 39 | 40 | . . . | **43** | 44 | . . . | 47 | 48 | 49 |

The feedback is lower, so our fifth guess is halfway between 38 and 42, or 40.

| 38 | 39 | **40** | 41 | 42 |

The feedback is higher this time, so we know our number is either 41 or 42.

| **41** | 42 |

If we guessed 41, the feedback is higher, and on the seventh guess, we get the correct number, 42!

| **42** |

Since our first guess is in the middle of the list, a REPEAT UNTIL (item is found) loop works better for the binary search. The binary search is so efficient that you can find a number within 10 guesses in a list of 1,000 numbers. Make sure you follow the binary search algorithm for it to work!

You will not have to analyze algorithms on the AP exam but you will need to recognize the common ones included in this course.

Procedures

Procedures are also called functions in some programming languages. These are sections of code that will be executed only when they are called by the main program or another procedure. They must be defined in a program before they can be used in the program.

There are several benefits of using procedures.

- Reuse of code reduces the length and complexity of programs by not duplicating code.
- Procedures increase the ease of maintaining or fixing programs because you only have one place to update code rather than several.
- Use of shorter blocks of code that do only a few tasks makes the code more readable and easier to understand.

When you find yourself needing the same section of code more than once in a program, that is a clue that you should put the code in a procedure. You can then use it as many times as needed in your program by calling it. Procedures should have descriptive names to help identify their purpose.

The format for defining a procedure on the AP exam is:

Text: The code for the procedure goes between the braces { }.

```
PROCEDURE procedureName(parameter1, parameter2, . . . )
{
    <block of statements>
}
```

Block:

```
PROCEDURE procedureName  parameter1, parameter2, . . .

    block of statements
```

Parameters/Arguments

The use of *parameters* can make procedures more flexible. Parameters allow the calling program to send values to the procedure. They are passed to the procedure as *arguments* when the procedure is called. The values sent to the procedure can be different each time, making the procedure more flexible through the ability for multiple calls to the same section of code.

The values sent to the procedure must be sent in the same order that the parameters are defined, if there are multiple parameters. They also must be of the same data type (number or text field) that the procedure is expecting. If a number is expected and the procedure receives a string, then an error will occur. The number and type of parameters are identified when the function is defined.

For example, if we define a procedure to calculate the amount owed for a purchase, we would need to know the item name, represented by a string field, the price, which would be a decimal number, and the quantity, an integer. These are parameters because this information would need to be passed to the procedure each time it is used as the quantity and price would vary for each item.

```
PROCEDURE checkOut (item, price, quantity)
```

The parameters are: *item*, *price*, and *quantity*.

Calling a Procedure

When the procedure is "called," the program will pause at that location and execute the code in the procedure. When the procedure finishes, control returns back to the line of code where the call occurred. This is another programming structure that modifies the sequential flow of the program.

You call a procedure by its name and include parentheses. Any arguments are passed in the parentheses, separated by commas. The AP exam will show procedures being called with arguments using the format:

```
procedureName(arg1, arg2, . . . )
```

The call to the procedure *checkOut* for 5 cookies at $1.19 each would be:

```
checkOut(cookie, 1.19, 5)
```

The **arguments** are: *cookie*, *1.19*, and *5*.

Recall that abstraction is the removal of details to make something more general and therefore more flexible. This is exactly what procedures do in programs. Details are abstracted away so the procedure is more general and can be used multiple times. Once a procedure is working, you don't need to worry about how it works, just that it does. The details of how it works are abstracted away. You only need to know the name of the procedure, the number and type of parameters, and the output to expect. This is called procedural abstraction.

Return

Procedures have an optional feature called a *return* statement. The *return* statement has two uses. One purpose is to end a procedure before the end of the code is reached. No other code in the procedure will be executed after the *return* statement. The other use is to send a value back to the calling program.

The format for the RETURN statement on the AP exam is:

```
Text:
      RETURN(expression)

Block:
```

```
RETURN expression
```

Procedures may perform a calculation or collect data in the procedure and need to send it back to the calling program. To do this, the data value or variable name is included in the RETURN statement. The procedure can also use an expression in the RETURN statement. The expression will be calculated prior to the RETURN being executed and only the value will be sent back to the calling program. When the RETURN statement is run, the procedure ends and control is returned to the calling program along with the value sent back, if any.

This RETURN statement calculates the area of a circle but does not store it in a variable. It sends the value calculated back to the code where it was called.

```
RETURN 3.14 * radius * radius
```

The RETURN statement in this example sends back the value currently stored in the variable, *area*.

```
area ← 3.14 * (radius * radius)
RETURN (area)
```

When a procedure is called expecting a value to be returned, that value must be stored in a variable so it will be available to use elsewhere in the program. Otherwise, it is lost in cyberspace and cannot be retrieved. Just as we can execute a calculation with an assignment statement and store the end result in the variable, we can use the same format with a call to a procedure. The program will see the call to the procedure, pause the program to execute the procedure's code, and then store the returned value in the variable.

```
variable ← procedureName(arg1, arg2, . . . )
```

Using our checkOut procedure, we would store the amount due for the item in a variable.

```
toPay ← checkOut(cookie, 1.19, 5)
```

The format for defining a procedure with a RETURN statement on the AP exam is:

Text: The code for the procedure goes between the braces { }.

```
PROCEDURE procedureName(parameter1, parameter2, . . . )
{
    <block of statements>
    RETURN(expression)
}
```

Block:

```
PROCEDURE procedureName  parameter1, parameter2, . . .
    block of statements
    RETURN  expression
```

Built-in Procedures

Built-in procedures are prewritten and tested code that are included with the programming language.

DISPLAY()

DISPLAY() is a built-in procedure used for this course on the exam. We do not know how this procedure is coded, only that we can use it multiple times, pass it different types and values to print, and that it works.

The AP exam will show the DISPLAY built-in procedure in the format:

Text:

```
DISPLAY(expression)
```

Block:

```
DISPLAY  expression
```

INPUT()

INPUT() is another built-in procedure that you will see on the AP exam. It accepts data from the user, usually from the keyboard. When the programming language sees this command, it will pause the program and wait for something to be typed on the keyboard. As soon as it detects that the "Enter" key has been pressed, it will capture the keystrokes up to that point.

The AP exam format is:

Text:

```
INPUT()
```

Block:

```
┌─────────┐
│ INPUT   │
└─────────┘
```

We need to store the user input in a variable to use in our program. Otherwise, whatever was typed is not saved and is lost in cyberspace. It would therefore not be available to make decisions, select options, display messages, or for other features of your program. For example, this INPUT() statement will assign what the user types to a variable called *name*.

```
name ← INPUT()
```

APIs AND "LIBRARIES"   For each programming language, there are prewritten programs to provide commonly needed functionality, and these programs are stored in libraries, which are folders with several programs. These could be written by you to reuse in other programs, shared by a friend or classmate, or posted on a trusted website and saved for others to use. The "INPUT" procedure is an example of a built-in program in a library. You have to use it in the way specified, but you do not have to write the "behind the scenes" code to use it in your program, greatly simplifying your program and the time it would take to write it.

Some of these built-in programs are already included in the programming language. There are others that you can *import* into your program when needed. You will need the exact name of the library to import, and you must import it before using any of the programs in the library to let your program know where to find them. *API* stands for "Application Programming Interface." The API documentation provides the information needed to set up the interface and use the newly connected software.

You can always look up the APIs/libraries for the programming language you are using in the program documentation. Documenting the procedures in an API and how to use them is important so others can use them successfully. Some APIs connect various software components. For example, including Google Maps in an app can be accomplished using an API that allows the user of the app to use Google Maps without leaving the original app. This is how businesses provide directions to their location from your location on their website.

RANDOM   Generating random numbers is a frequently needed feature in programs. Most programming languages have a library of prewritten code for a variety of random number generators.

```
num ← RANDOM(1,10)
```

RANDOM needs two values passed to it using arguments, the beginning and ending range for the selected random number. In this example, the program generates a random number between 1 and 10 inclusive and stores it in the variable *num*. Inclusive means both the starting and ending numbers are included in the pool of possible numbers. Each time the code is executed, a random number will be generated. Sometimes it could repeat the prior number since it is randomly generated each time, and sometimes it will be different, but it will always be within the given range.

The AP exam format for using RANDOM is:

Text:

```
RANDOM(a, b)
```

Block:

```
RANDOM a, b
```

Simulations

Simulations are designed to represent and mirror the real world for testing. This is an example of abstraction at a very high level. The details are removed to focus on the impact of the conditions to be measured or evaluated during the simulation. The tests and results enable insights, knowledge, and discoveries to be made without constraints that would exist in the real world. For example, flight simulators let pilots test without lives being lost or aircraft destroyed. Anyone working with simulators needs to watch for bias that could be included because of the choices of elements from the real environment that were included or excluded. Different simulations with different elements included or excluded can help determine if bias is present.

Hypotheses can be evaluated and then refined with the use of simulations without real-world impact or constraints. For example, scientific phenomena can be tested in the laboratory, simplifying the environment and functionality tested rather than having to wait for the next real-world occurrence. This reduces cost and saves time. Simulations can be used to test potentially dangerous situations without putting anyone at risk. The simulations can also be modified based on the results of tests and then retested. In a simulated environment, many more tests can be performed and evaluated, leading to new findings, insights, and solutions. To introduce the variability of the real world, simulations often use a random number generator as a factor.

For example, Google Earth is a model of the planet Earth, with topography, borders, roads, cities, and some buildings represented. Simulations could determine the shortest distance to travel between two locations as well as the fastest travel time based on the landscape and infrastructure.

Analyzing Algorithms

To review some vocabulary, a *problem* is a task that can or cannot be solved with an algorithm. An *instance* of a problem is a specific example. A *decision problem* has a yes or no answer. An *optimization* problem is one that should find the best solution for the problem. We use these terms in determining an algorithm's efficiency.

Algorithm Efficiency

The *efficiency* of algorithms deals with resources needed to run it in terms of how long it will take and how much memory will be needed. This becomes especially important with extremely large datasets, and efficiency is usually stated in terms of the size of the input. While the time will vary based on the computer used, general rules are used to determine the efficiency of these algorithms.

You will not be asked about the formal analysis (Big-O) of algorithm efficiency on the AP exam.

Efficiency can be determined by mathematically proving it and informally measured by actually running it on datasets of different sizes and measuring how long it took and the memory resources needed. It checks these based on the number of times the statements execute for the input size.

We have talked about how there can be more than one right solution to a problem in computer science. These different algorithms may all be correct and readable but could have different efficiencies. Sometimes more complex algorithms can be more efficient, and more efficient algorithms may be able to better handle larger datasets. Algorithms that run with a linear, squared, cubed, or other polynomial efficiency run in a reasonable amount of time. In the chart below, notice how rapidly the exponential line becomes almost vertical even while the size of the dataset is quite small. This shows how quickly algorithms with exponential efficiency may not run in a reasonable amount of time.

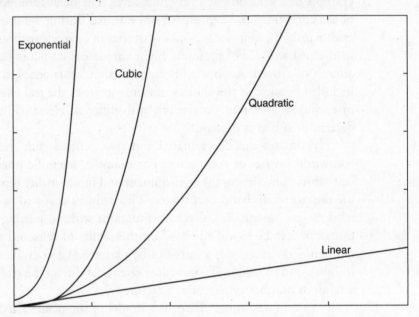

Limits of Algorithms

Algorithms have limits, and there are some problems for which we do not have efficient enough algorithms to solve. These algorithms can't run in a reasonable amount of time with our current technology. As the dataset grows large, the algorithm is too inefficient to process the data. The algorithm could work for smaller datasets but needs exponential or factorial time or resources to run for large amounts of data. This can be good, as this is an aspect of cryptography that keeps our personal information private. There are too many options to check each one. We couldn't have online shopping without it! However, the day may come when these problems can be solved as advances continue to be made in computers.

Often these problems that do not run in a reasonable amount of time can use a *heuristic* approach. This is an approach that may not be optimal or the best but is close enough to use as a solution. One common example is the traveling salesman problem. Given a list of cities, the goal is to find the shortest path between them all. The algorithm to make a list of every possible path and then choose the shortest one becomes unwieldly very quickly. The heuristic approach is to find the nearest neighbor to a city and take that path. Then find the nearest neighbor to that city and so on. This modified algorithm is achievable in a reasonable amount of time and resource usage, so it is a viable solution.

You will not have to find heuristic solutions on the AP exam. Just be sure you understand the concept.

Undecidable/Unsolvable Problems

A *decidable* problem is one where an algorithm can be written that results in a correct "yes" or "no" answer for all inputs. Determining if a number is prime is an example of a decidable problem.

In contrast, an *undecidable* problem does not have an algorithm that can give a correct "yes" or "no" for all cases of the problem. An algorithm may work for some cases, but not all. The halting problem is one famous example of an unsolvable problem. It states that "given an arbitrary computer program, with an arbitrary input, decide whether it has an infinite loop." (It sounds simple but can make your head spin!)

You will not have to determine whether a problem is undecidable on the AP exam. Just be sure you understand the concept!

› Review Questions

Concepts

1. What term describes values that can only be either true or false?
   (A) Decidable
   (B) Algorithmic
   (C) Boolean
   (D) Sequential

2. What is/are used to determine whether code should be run for both "IF" statements and "REPEAT UNTIL" loops?
   (A) Pseudocode
   (B) Iterations
   (C) Conditions
   (D) Events

3. Which combination of statements can be used to express algorithms?
   (A) Iterative, sequential, and selection
   (B) Correctness, efficiency, and clarity
   (C) Readable, iterative, and efficient
   (D) Selection, conditional, and Boolean

4. What type of problem cannot currently be determined or explained by an algorithm?
   (A) Indefinite problem
   (B) Undecidable problem
   (C) Tractable problem
   (D) Unreasonable problem

5. When is a compound condition using the logical operator AND true?
   (A) When either of the conditions are true
   (B) When both conditions are false
   (C) When both conditions are true
   (D) When the NOT operator is also used

6. Which type of loop runs a set number of times?
   (A) Indefinite
   (B) REPEAT UNTIL
   (C) Infinite
   (D) REPEAT n TIMES

7. Why is a "divide and conquer" search more efficient than a linear search?
   (A) You only look at half the dataset.
   (B) You eliminate half the dataset with each iteration.
   (C) You search all the values.
   (D) It divides the data into two sections based on even and odd index values.

8. Sequential statements
   (A) run one after the other in the order given.
   (B) run only when the condition is true.
   (C) run until a loop finishes.
   (D) run until the user enters "done."

9. Else statements
   (A) run each time an "if" condition is true.
   (B) run when an "if" condition is false.
   (C) run every time an "if" statement runs.
   (D) do not need an "if" statement to run.

10. With a problem that cannot be solved for all cases, what can sometimes be used as a close approximation?
    (A) A travelling solution
    (B) A solvable solution
    (C) A heuristic solution
    (D) A tractable solution

11. What are variables used for in programs?
    (A) They hold values: numbers, Booleans, or strings.
    (B) They link libraries of programs to the current program.
    (C) They indicate how long the fraction part of a real number is.
    (D) They hold the indices for a list name.

12. How can an individual element in a list be identified?
    (A) Use the index or number of the element's position in the list.
    (B) Use the built-in procedures for lists.
    (C) Use the full list name.
    (D) Use the list name plus the value in the list at the needed position.

13. How do parameters and arguments differ?
    (A) The words can be used interchangeably.
    (B) Parameters are sent to procedures where they are then used as arguments.
    (C) Arguments are sent to procedures where they are then used as parameters.
    (D) Arguments are the intermediate values in a calculation until the calculation is complete and then stored in the parameter.

14. What is a reason to use a procedure?
    (A) When you need a section of code once in a program
    (B) To avoid duplicating code
    (C) To avoid a loop
    (D) To use with a condition

15. How are assignment statements processed?
    (A) The left side of the ← is processed and then assigned to the variable on the right.
    (B) The right side of the ← is processed and then assigned to the variable on the left.
    (C) Strings are processed first and then numbers.
    (D) Numbers are processed first and then strings.

16. What helps manage complexity in a program by abstracting out the details and allowing programmers to use variable names?
    (A) Data abstraction
    (B) Element abstraction
    (C) Memory abstraction
    (D) Procedural abstraction

17. What is string1 concatenated with string2 when:

    ```
    string1 ← "Tik"
    string2 ← "Tok"
    ```

    (A) Tik Tok
    (B) "Tik" "Tok"
    (C) Tik
        Tok
    (D) "TikTok"

18. If the variable *name* has the value "Hannah", what is the value if we take the substring of *name* starting at position 4 and going to the end?
    (A) "ah"
    (B) "Hann"
    (C) "nana"
    (D) "nah"

19. With Boolean, what does "A OR B" mean?
    (A) Neither A or B can be true for the condition to be true.
    (B) If A is true, then the condition is true.
    (C) If B is not true, then the condition is true.
    (D) Both A and B must be true for the condition to be true.

20. Which are more abstract: high-level or low-level programming languages?
    (A) High-level
    (B) Low-level
    (C) Both have the same level of abstraction.
    (D) Neither are abstract.

21. Procedures are abstract:
    (A) By the use of parameters
    (B) By being easier to manage
    (C) Through reuse
    (D) All of the above

22. How are simulations useful?
    (A) They allow the modification of multiple variables at a time to determine what changes make the most impact.
    (B) They provide the freedom of testing all possibilities without interference.
    (C) They can test the impact of a dangerous situation on a pilot test group of people prior to a real-world event.
    (D) They allow testing of hypotheses without impacting or being impacted by the real world.

23. What does an API provide?
    (A) The pseudocode for commonly used algorithms
    (B) A way for apps or programs to communicate with each other
    (C) The arguments and parameters for a procedure
    (D) The program code for commonly used modules

Application of Concepts

24. How can a smaller representation of something, such as an event or process, be used to determine what could happen in the real world?
    (A) Through simulations
    (B) Through planning
    (C) Through imaging
    (D) Through the use of lab work

25. What is the output of the algorithm written in pseudocode below at 7:00 a.m. Friday?

    If Monday–Friday at 8:00 a.m.
        Set thermostat to 62
    If Saturday or Sunday
        Set thermostat to 70
    If time is 5:00 p.m.
        Set thermostat to 68

    (A) 62
    (B) 68
    (C) 70
    (D) Unknown

26. The algorithm below is not working correctly. Which line of code will make it work as intended?

    (Compare cars to available parking spots)

    ```
    availSlots ← 180
    parkingLot ← [ ]
    REPEAT UNTIL (availSlots = 0)
    {
        availSlots ← availSlots - 1
    }
    DISPLAY (parkingLot)
    ```

    (A) APPEND(parkingLot, availSlot)
    (B) REMOVE(parkingLot, availSlot)
    (C) INSERT(parkingLot, availSlot, name)
    (D) REPEAT UNTIL (LENGTH(parkingLot) = LENGTH(availSlots))

27. Which line of code can be placed inside the braces { } to fix the following loop so it will not be an infinite loop?

    ```
    name ← " "
    REPEAT UNTIL (name = "done")
    {
        DISPLAY ("Student name is: ", name)
    }
    ```

    (A) IF name ≠ "done")
    (B) count = count + 1
    (C) name ← INPUT( )
    (D) name ← studentRoster

28. Below is a flowchart of an alarm clock snooze process. What value does the variable "count" have after tracing through the flowchart?

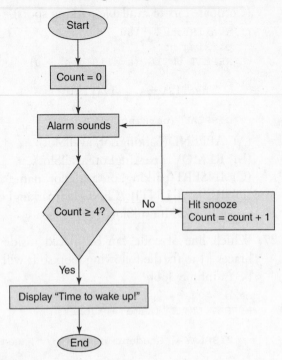

(A) 0
(B) 4
(C) 5
(D) Count = count + 1

29. Are the two conditional statements equivalent?

```
age > 42    NOT (age < 42)
```

(A) Yes
(B) No
(C) Only when age is a positive number
(D) Only when age is 0

30. What are the elements in the list "fruit" after the code below?

```
fruit ← ["grapes"]
APPEND (fruit, "bananas")
APPEND (fruit, "oranges")
APPEND (fruit, "apples")
REMOVE (fruit, 2)
INSERT (fruit, 3, "mango")
APPEND (fruit, "kiwi")
INSERT (fruit, 5, "blueberries")
REMOVE (fruit, 1)
```

(A) grapes, mango, apples, blueberries, kiwi
(B) oranges, mango, apples, blueberries, kiwi
(C) apples, mango, kiwi, blueberries
(D) bananas, mango, apples, kiwi, grapes

31. What is the result of executing the following code when called with LeapYear(3004)?

```
PROCEDURE LeapYear(year)
  IF (year MOD 400 = 0)
  {
      DISPLAY (year, "is a leap year!")
  }
  ELSE IF (year MOD 100 = 0)
  {
      DISPLAY (year, "is not a leap year.")
  }
  ELSE IF (year MOD 4 = 0)
  {
      DISPLAY (year, "is a leap year!")
  }
  ELSE
  {
      DISPLAY ("Invalid year entered.")
  }

DISPLAY ("Enter a year:")
yr ← INPUT( )
LeapYear(yr)
```

(A) 3004 is not a leap year.
(B) 304 is not a leap year.
(C) 3004 is a leap year!
(D) Invalid year entered.

32. Which block of code sets the alarm for each day of the week?

Block 1:
```
IF (day = "Wed")
{
    setAlarm ← 8
}
ELSE IF (day = "Sat" OR day = "Sun")
{
    setAlarm ← 11
}
ELSE
{
    setAlarm ← 9
}
```

Block 2:
```
IF (day NOT("Sat") OR day NOT("Sun"))
{
    setAlarm ← 9
}
IF (day = "Wed")
{
    setAlarm ← 8
}
```

(A) Block 1
(B) Block 2
(C) Block 1 and Block 2
(D) Neither Block 1 nor Block 2

33. What is returned from the procedure below after the call: weight (9, 10, 11)?

```
PROCEDURE weight(wt1, wt2, wt3)
{
   IF (wt1 ≥ wt2 AND wt1 ≥ wt3)
   {
       RETURN wt1
   }
   ELSE IF (wt2 > wt3 OR wt2 > wt1)
   {
       RETURN wt2
   }
   ELSE
   {
       RETURN wt3
   }
}
```

(A) 9

(B) 10

(C) 11

(D) 1011

34. What type of algorithm is the following code using?

```
nums ← [5, 14, 42, 29, 2523, 1898, 15,
737, 42, 5910, 60, 1023]
count ← 0
FOR EACH number in nums
   IF (number = 42)
   {
       DISPLAY("Found!")
       count ← count + 1
   }
DISPLAY ("The number was found", count,
"times")
```

(A) Binary search

(B) Bubble sort

(C) Linear search

(D) Merge sort

35. How are procedures a form of abstraction?

(A) By being able to use a procedure without knowing how it works

(B) By understanding the code in a procedure to use it correctly

(C) Through the ability to modify the code in a procedure for a particular use

(D) Through eliminating the use of comments to make the code more abstract

36. At which ending location does the code place the robot?

```
REPEAT UNTIL (END)
{
   IF (CAN_MOVE(forward))
   {
       MOVE_FORWARD()
   }
   ELSE
   {
       ROTATE_LEFT()
   }
}
```

(A)

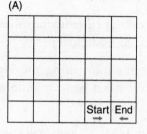

(B)

(C)

(D)

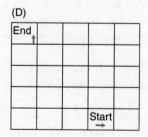

› Answers and Explanations

1. **C**—Boolean values can only be either true or false.

2. **C**—Conditions can be used to determine whether code should be run for both "IF" statements or "REPEAT UNTIL" loops. The conditions evaluate to True or False and processing continues based on the Boolean value.

3. **A**—Algorithms can be expressed using a combination of iterative (loops), sequential, and selection (IF) statements.

4. **B**—Problems that cannot currently be solved by an algorithm are called undecidable.

5. **C**—A compound condition using the logical operator AND is true when both conditions are true.

6. **D**—A "REPEAT n TIMES" loop will run "n" times, where "n" must be a positive integer.

7. **B**—A "divide and conquer" search is more efficient than a linear search because you eliminate half of the dataset with each iteration.

8. **A**—Sequential statements run one after the other in the order given.

9. **B**—"Else" statements run when an "IF" condition is false. They are skipped when the IF condition is true.

10. **C**—A heuristic solution can be used with an unreasonable problem that cannot be solved for all cases. It provides a "close enough" solution.

11. **A**—Variables are used to hold values, which can be numbers, Booleans, or strings in programs.

12. **A**—An individual element in a list can be identified using the index, which is the number of the element's position in the list.

13. **C**—Arguments are sent to procedures, where the values are then passed to the parameters that are local to the procedure.

14. **B**—One reason to use a procedure is to avoid duplicating code, because the procedure can be resused as many times as needed in a program.

15. **B**—Assignment statements process the right side of the ←, which is then assigned to the variable on the left.

16. **A**—Data abstraction manages complexity with the use of variable names and lists to reference and update data values without needing to know the details of computer memory and addresses.

17. **D**—Concatenate means to glue two strings together. No additional spaces or new lines are added between the strings. Therefore, string1 concatenated with string2 becomes "TikTok". The quotation marks indicate that it is a string rather than a variable name.

18. **D**—The index positions for the string "Hannah" are shown in the table below. If we take the substring of *name* starting at position 4 and go to the end, we have the string "nah".

H	a	n	n	a	h
1	2	3	4	5	6

19. **B**—OR means either or both conditions can be true for the condition to be true. Since A is true, then the entire condition is true.

20. **A**—High-level programming languages are more like natural language than low-level ones. The commands in the language are more general and therefore more abstract than low-level languages, which are closer to machine language.

21. **D**—The use of parameters allows a procedure to be called multiple times and apply the same code to different values. Descriptive names for procedures help identify their general function. Therefore, all of these are reasons why procedures are abstract.

22. **D**—Hypotheses can be evaluated without the constraints of the realworld and without adversely impacting the real world.

23. **B**—The API provides the details for how to use the program modules it is associated with.

24. **A**—Models can be used to test events through simulations on a smaller scale to help determine the impact of the same event in real life.

25. **B**—The temperature on Friday morning at 7:00 a.m. will still be 68 degrees from the third "IF" statement, which set it to 68 degrees at 5:00 p.m. the night before. It won't change

until one of the other "IF" conditions evaluate to true.

26. **A**—The list, parkingLot, starts out empty. If elements are not placed into the list, then the DISPLAY statement at the end will show an empty list. Either APPEND or INSERT can be used to add elements to a list. However, we do not have the "name" of the person assigned to a parking place, so answer A, to APPEND the number of the available parking slots to the list, is the best answer.

27. **C**—The variable name is initialized to be an empty text field. This is the variable that is tested in the REPEAT UNTIL condition. An infinite loop will occur unless a way is provided to update the "name" field. The INPUT() command allows the user to enter student names and the value "done" into the "name" variable. This will provide a value to be tested in the condition that will eventually be set to "done" and stop the loop.

28. **B**—The condition to keep hitting the snooze button tests to see if count is greater than or equal to 4. After count equals 4, the flowchart processing continues to the message that it's time to wake up without increasing "count." Therefore, count equals 4 and B is the correct answer.

29. **B**—The keyword NOT flips the value it references to its opposite. Therefore, if age is greater than 42, the opposite of that is age less than or equal to 42. Many students forget to include or remove the equals sign, =, when they apply the NOT operator. The two expressions do not match, and the correct answer is B.

30. **B**—Our list starts with one element, "grapes." The APPEND operation adds the element to the end of the list. The INSERT operation places the element at the index position provided and moves elements to the right, increasing the size of the list. The REMOVE operation deletes the element at the given index position and adjusts the remaining elements down a position. Lists for this course all begin with index position 1. Therefore, the correct answer is B.

31. **C**—The user keys in 3004 as the year to check. The procedure LeapYear(3004) is called with this value. The MOD function returns the remainder after dividing the two numbers. If the remainder is 0, then the year is a leap year. The ELSE IF statement that uses MOD 4 = 0 is true, so the year is a leap year and the correct message is printed. The correct answer is C.

32. **A**—Block 1 correctly sets the alarm time for every day of the week. Block 2 sets the correct alarm time for Monday to Friday. The weekend days do not have an alarm time set, which might be our preferred results, but not the question asked. The correct answer is A.

33. **B**—The first IF statement compares wt1 to the other two values. Since 9 is not greater than or equal to either value, the code moves on to compare wt2, which is 10. This condition is an OR, so only one comparison needs to be true. While 10 is not greater than 11, it is greater than 9. Therefore, the value of 10 for wt2 is returned. The correct answer is B.

34. **C**—A linear search is used to check each item in the list to see if it equals 42.

35. **A**—Procedures are abstractions because they can be used multiple times in programs with different values passed in through parameters without needing to know how they work.

36. **B**—The robot moves forward as long as it can move. If it cannot move, then it rotates left. These steps continue until it reaches the end block pointing right.

❯ Rapid Review

Algorithms are a set of steps to complete a task. Algorithms can be written in natural language, which is our speaking language; pseudocode, which is a combination of natural language and a programming language; diagrammed with a flowchart; and coded in both block (drag and drop) and text-based programming languages.

Programs can be developed for almost any purpose, including for fun and for professional purposes. Programs implement algorithms and use a variety of techniques, such as variables, procedures, and lists, in their processing.

Features to make algorithms more readable and clearer include adding comments, adding blank lines, and using well-named variables and procedures. Variables are a holding place for data. Assignment statements change a variable's value. Lists, like a grocery list, can store many values in one variable name. Individual elements in lists are referenced using their index position. **This exam starts the index position at 1.** Programming languages have built-in functions for common processing needs for lists, such as APPEND, INSERT, REMOVE, and LENGTH. These are on the Exam Reference Sheet (see Appendix), and you will have a copy of it during the exam.

The data types used in programs are integers (whole numbers), real numbers (with decimals), Booleans (true or false), and strings (text). String functions include concatenation, or gluing two strings together, and substring, which is taking a section of a string.

Data abstraction allows us to store data using variables and lists. We can use the name we assign, which makes programs easier to code and understand.

The arithmetic operators used in programming are the same as in math: addition, subtraction, multiplication, and division. MOD provides only the remainder after dividing.

All algorithms can be written using a combination of sequential, selection, and iterative statements. Sequential means each step is executed, in order, one right after the other.

Selection statements filter out some lines of code using an IF (condition) statement. The condition uses the relational operators, $<, \leq, >, \geq, =, \neq$, to make a comparison. The condition will always evaluate to either true or false. These are Boolean values. The logical operators AND, OR, and NOT are used to make more complex conditions.

When the condition is false, the code associated with the IF statement is skipped. An ELSE statement can be added to execute different code when the IF statement's condition is false. Multiple ELSE IF (condition) statements can be added after the IF to construct a nested IF statement. The conditions will be evaluated until the first one is true. All others will then be skipped. ELSE is always last in the structure.

Iterative statements repeat code. The REPEAT n TIMES loop executes a block of code a specified number of times. The REPEAT UNTIL (condition) repeats the code until the condition is true. It checks the condition at the start of each pass. Just like with IF statements, the condition will only evaluate to true or false, a Boolean value. The FOR EACH loop will repeat the code for each element in a list or string.

Binary searches use a "divide and conquer" technique and can only be used with sorted datasets. Lower or higher feedback is provided to determine the next midpoint. Linear searches check every element to either find the item in question or determine that it is not in the dataset. Linear searches can be used with sorted or unsorted datasets.

Procedures are blocks of code that can be used repeatedly in programs. They can have parameters that provide a way for different values to be passed to them, and procedures can return values processed back to the calling program. Using parameters makes a procedure more general, and therefore more abstract, by enabling it to be used with different values each time it is called to run.

Procedures, once working, can be used by anyone, without them having to understand the code or know how it works. They can trust that it works as expected. This provides procedural abstraction, as all the details of how the procedure works are unknown or abstracted away (the "black box" effect). This helps with program complexity and readability. It also simplifies coding by having only one place to make corrections or updates. Application Programming Interfaces (APIs) connect a program to external software, and *import* statements pull in libraries of working code to an application, saving time in the development process. These are also examples of procedural abstraction, as you don't see the source code and can trust that it works as described.

Algorithms can be combined to create a new algorithm. An example is an algorithm to play a video along with the algorithms to provide features to speed it up, slow it down, mute the sound, or display the captions. Be familiar with common algorithms, such as finding the maximum or minimum number, finding the total and average of a group of numbers, and determining if one integer is divisible by another (MOD).

The commands to use to navigate a robot through a maze are MOVE_FORWARD(), ROTATE_RIGHT(), ROTATE_LEFT(), AND CAN_MOVE(direction).

Algorithms can be evaluated for their readability, clarity, and efficiency. There can be more than one correct algorithm to solve a problem, and different solutions can be more efficient with different size datasets. Remember that efficiency includes memory and processing time. There can be trade-offs among different solutions, since more efficient solutions may be more complex and less clear.

Some problems cannot be solved in a reasonable amount of time or with a reasonable amount of resources. As the dataset gets larger, the amount of time and/or memory required becomes too large and is beyond our current capabilities to process. Heuristic approaches can often find solutions that are good enough for the need at hand. Undecidable problems are those that no algorithm can solve for all instances of the problem. There may be solutions for some cases but not all of them.

Simulations enable people to test hypotheses by changing the values of variables with different tests while holding others constant, running multiple tests, and doing so quickly and in a safe environment.

CHAPTER 10

Big Idea 4: Computing Systems and Networks

IN THIS CHAPTER

Summary: This chapter covers how networks are configured so we can use their capabilities to work, play, share, and collaborate with anyone connected to our network. Anytime two devices are connected, a network has been created, and the Internet is a network of networks.

Key Ideas

✪ Redundancy is built into the Internet so that it can still work if parts of it are not operational.

✪ The Internet uses rules, or protocols, such as TCP/IP to send and receive data.

✪ Data to be streamed across the Internet is separated into packets of equal size.

✪ The Internet is scalable, meaning new capacity can quickly be added to meet the demand.

✪ The World Wide Web is a system that uses the Internet to share web pages and data of all types.

✪ Sequential, parallel, and distributed computing systems are different configurations for processing data.

KEY IDEA

Key Terms

Bandwidth
Computing device
Computing network
Computing system
Data stream
Distributed computing
    system
Fault-tolerant
Hypertext Transfer
    Protocol (HTTP)
Hypertext Transfer
    Protocol Secure
    (HTTPS)
Internet Protocol (IP)
    address

Packets
Parallel computing
    system
Protocols
Redundancy
Router
Scalability
Sequential computing
    system
Transmission Control
    Protocol (TCP)
User Datagram Protocol
    (UDP)
World Wide Web (www)

Computing Systems

A computing system is when various types of computing devices, such as desktop or laptop computers, tablets, servers, routers, and/or sensors, plus software, work together for a use such as managing the power grid, traffic signals, a smart home, or a network such as the Internet. Anytime two devices are connected and can send and receive data, a network has been created.

The connections between devices create *paths*. A small network, such as in a home, may have devices directly connected without intermediate steps. Larger networks, such as for schools and businesses, will have several routes between devices. The path consists of all the steps between a sending and receiving device. *Routers* are computing devices along a path that send the information along to the next stop on the path. Each router is only concerned with sending the information to its next stop, not the entire path. The path the router chooses is not known in advance. The routing is determined at the moment it is needed, meaning it is *dynamic*. With the Internet, routers get messages about congestion on a segment and will send the data around that location, keeping everything moving along.

How the Internet Works

The Internet is a network of networks. The word Internet came from "interconnection of computer networks." The Internet is very hardware-driven with wires, cables, and devices such as routers and servers. While some connections are wireless, there are still access points and cables that create the wireless network. The level of collaboration we have today is largely due to the Internet. People from across the globe can work together, create together, and edit together because of these connections.

Packets and Data Streams

Data streams are information transmitted via the Internet. The processing of Internet traffic is done at the sending and receiving locations. At the sending location, the information to be sent, such as a web page, is broken into smaller *packets* of the same size (except possibly the last one, which could be smaller). Header information is attached that includes the destination address and where to place the packet in the final reconstruction of the data stream. The packets are sent on their way to the destination location via different routes. The intermediate routers along the path move the packets to the next destination on the path. The packets arrive at different times and out of order! Once all packets have arrived at the destination, they are reassembled in order. This is called an end-to-end architecture, because the processing is done at each end. In the middle, the packets are only moved along to the next location on the path.

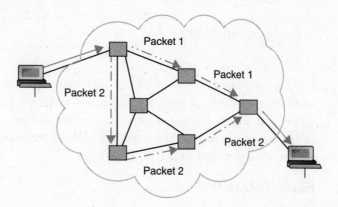

Protocols

Every device on a network is called a "host." When a device connects to the Internet, it is given an "address" similar to the idea of a mailing address given to homes and businesses. These devices can be anywhere in the world. The addresses enable devices to find and communicate with each other. The address is called an Internet Protocol (IP) address. It's how the Internet knows where to route information.

Protocols are a set of rules. These are needed so different equipment made by different companies can communicate with each other. Whether a connection is wired or wireless, before the packets of information can travel across networks, a common protocol, or a set of rules for transmitting and receiving these packets of data, must be used.

The protocols are created by a committee of representatives from different industries who agree on the set of rules for everyone to follow. This committee is the Internet Engineering Task Force (IETF), which is part of the Internet Society. The Internet does not belong to any one country or individual, but its use needs to be agreed on and managed. These standards are continually reviewed and modified as needed to enable new uses for the Internet, and to take advantage of new hardware and other tools to facilitate its structure.

Initially, various businesses were creating their own protocols to use on the Internet. This resulted in incompatibility, and people were unable to send or receive data across the different protocols. The standards now in use are open and available to all to ensure people can communicate across the Internet. This agreement to use an open standard enabled the growth of the Internet.

TIP

NOTE: You do not need to know specific details of the standards for addresses on the exam.

One of the oldest protocols is TCP/IP. TCP creates the packets at the sending location and reassembles them at the receiving one. After receipt of the packets, TCP also sends an acknowledgment back to the sender. If a packet is sent using TCP, but a confirmation message that it made it to its destination is not received, it will be resent. IP moves the packets through the network to their target location. TCP/IP stands for:

Transmission
Control
Protocol
/
Internet
Protocol

UDP is another common protocol and stands for:

User
Datagram
Protocol

UDP is also built on top of IP similar to how TCP works with IP. UDP does not send a confirmation message back to the sender when packets are received. If you use this protocol, you will not know if your entire data stream was received. It is used because it is faster. Some systems do not need the error controls that TCP provides, so UDP provides an alternate protocol to use in those cases.

Fault-Tolerant

We often think of something that is redundant as being unnecessary or not needed. In the case of the Internet, redundancy is a good thing. There is a lot of *redundancy* or duplication built into the Internet on purpose. It is built in by providing multiple paths between devices on the Internet. This means that if one point goes down and is not working, then the traffic will be redirected to a different path to get to its ultimate destination. It is referred to as "fault tolerant" due to these multiple connections and paths. It is also abstract because we don't know where all the connections are or how the paths are determined or redirected. We just know that it works.

Things happen. Equipment fails and cables are accidentally cut among other events that could impact part of the structure of the Internet. This fault tolerance increases the reliability of the Internet. This redundancy was designed into the Internet, making it scalable to meet the demand of more devices and people connecting to it. Of course, it costs more to build in this duplication, but the reliability and convenience of being able to connect to any website make it worth it and outweigh the extra cost.

World Wide Web

The World Wide Web (WWW) is an application that runs on the Internet. Many people use the terms "WWW" and "Internet" interchangeably, but they are two different things. The World Wide Web is a collection of web pages, documents, and files, written in hypertext markup language (HTML). Web browsers read the HMTL code to know how to display the web page with colors, formatting, images, videos, lists, and more.

Hypertext Transfer Protocol (HTTP)

There are standards for how the web browsers and servers on the Web work. HTTP is a protocol used by the World Wide Web. It controls how web page data is requested, sent, and received from the browsers and servers where the web pages are stored.

HTTPS should be used for any secure transaction, such as those involving financial data, medical data, and sites that require a password.

Types of Processing

Sequential Computing Systems

Most of our day-to-day computational work is done on our local devices in a sequential order, with operations executing one after the other in the specified order. This sequential computing model is more than sufficient for what we do. However, it is not efficient enough for certain organizations. Here, efficiency is measured by the time it takes to perform the task. The total time it takes to run a sequential solution is the time it takes to execute all the steps. Sequential systems cannot scale because each step runs after the one ahead of it finishes. You don't get any real gains from multiple processors other than additional speed that could be applied to the parallel model for greater improvement.

Parallel Computing Systems

Some organizations process very complex algorithms. Sequential processing is too slow to handle these algorithms. That's when parallel computing can be used to speed up the processing. The program code is separated into smaller sections and shared across multiple computers. Each one runs its section of sequential steps. The steps are executed simultaneously, in parallel, reducing the overall processing time needed. More computers and processors can be added to scale up and further reduce the amount of time it will take to run the program *to a certain point*.

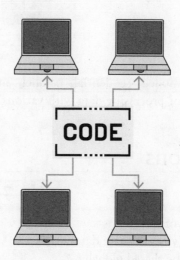

A sequential procedure then combines the results of each processor back to the full output. The longest set of the steps done in parallel **plus** the sequential part to merge the output will determine the total time the parallel computing will take. The *speedup* of a parallel process is determined by dividing the time it took to process the problem sequentially by the time it took to complete it in parallel.

For example, if the sequential time was 600 minutes and the parallel processing time was 120 minutes, the speedup is calculated as: 600/120 = 5.

You can reach a point where adding more computers will not speed up the overall processing, because the sequential steps to combine the outputs cannot be shared. So if you have one computer running and add another to it, the speedup won't halve the time it took the one computer to run the process due to the additional time needed to combine the results.

Distributed Computing Systems

Another model often used with very large sets is a *distributed* computing model. This model can handle the speed and memory requirements for heavy-duty processing needs that a single computer cannot due to resource constraints. In this case, the *data* is spread out among multiple computers. Each computer runs the same program on its section of data at the same time. The results are then passed up to the parent computer to combine as one output. There could be hundreds of thousands of computers involved in a distributed processing model. People sometimes donate time on their computer to help process a section of research data. These devices provide the processing speed and memory needed to handle these incredibly large datasets that a single computer or even several computers could not.

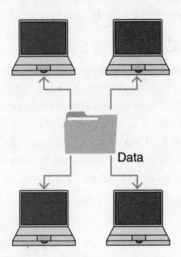

All three models, sequential, parallel, and distributed, have a best use and cost/benefit trade-off for processing data with various levels of speed and efficiency.

❯ Review Questions

Concepts

1. What is a computer network?
   - (A) A way to connect devices to share data
   - (B) Web pages that can be shared globally
   - (C) A dedicated line from one computer to another
   - (D) A set of IP addresses needed to access other computers

2. What are the connected steps between a sending and a receiving location called?
   - (A) A route
   - (B) A heuristic
   - (C) A path
   - (D) A conduit

3. What is bandwidth?
(A) How long it takes 10 megabytes of data to be sent
(B) The amount of data that can be sent in a fixed period of time
(C) The delay in how long it takes between requesting and loading a web page
(D) The amount of data divided by the latency

4. Why is Internet routing usually dynamic?
(A) So that if a path on the route is congested or not working, a new path can be assigned
(B) So that it can speed up or slow down as necessary to avoid data congestion
(C) So that new routes can be tested before being available globally
(D) So that as noise on a route becomes louder, traffic can be limited until it reaches acceptable levels

5. What is the name for the protocol that handles processing at the sending and receiving locations?
(A) Local Area Network Protocol
(B) Point-to-point Protocol
(C) Transmission Control Protocol
(D) Redundancy Protocol

6. What is the number assigned to devices on the Internet?
(A) Internet Protocol address
(B) Domain number
(C) Host number
(D) Router location

7. How do packets know how to get to their destination?
(A) The router knows the path and sends it step-by-step to its final destination.
(B) Each path has an embedded code that directs the packets to the correct location.
(C) The destination location emits pulses that guide the data packets to its location.
(D) The destination IP address is included in each packet.

8. Why is the Internet considered to be fault-tolerant?
(A) It has dedicated lines between devices.
(B) It has duplicate paths to all locations.
(C) It is secured against all threats.
(D) It is open to anyone with a connection.

9. What is the World Wide Web?
(A) A collection of wires and cables to connect devices
(B) Another name for the Internet
(C) A way to search for and share documents and resources
(D) A browser

10. What can be determined by comparing the time it takes different systems to complete the same task?
(A) Efficiency
(B) Reliability
(C) Speedup
(D) Validity

11. A parallel computing system uses multiple computers to run
(A) sections of the data at the same time.
(B) the same data to measure the fastest ISP.
(C) sections of the program at staggered times to avoid overlap.
(D) sections of the program at the same time.

12. Which computing system can process larger datasets when multiple devices are combined because of the additional memory and storage provided?
(A) Distributed
(B) Incremental
(C) Dispersed
(D) Sequential

Application of Concepts

13. Which of the following is true about packets?
(A) Packets leave and arrive at their destination at the same time.
(B) Packets travel along different paths to their destination.
(C) Each router decrypts the packets to confirm their destination.
(D) If a packet does not arrive at the destination, the entire message is resent.

14. Given the network in the diagram, what is an available path for A and B if the link between A and B is down?

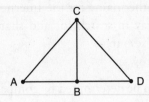

(A) A C B
(B) A C D
(C) C D B A
(D) A C D A

15. What could be added to the diagram to provide redundancy?
    (A) Duplicate routers at each node
    (B) An additional path between A and D
    (C) More cables connecting all locations
    (D) A signal booster to maintain the speed between sending and receiving locations

16. Which of the following is false about HTTPS?
    (A) HTTPS uses Certificate Authorities (CAs) to verify a site's identity.
    (B) HTTPS encrypts data before it is separated into packets.
    (C) HTTPS ensures the secure sharing of data.
    (D) HTTPS trades faster performance for more security.

17. Why is there a limit to adding additional devices to a parallel system?
    (A) The processor speed is limited and additional devices cannot create additional speedup.
    (B) There are only so many configurations to connect devices in parallel.
    (C) Space and connections to power in a building limit the number of devices.
    (D) The amount of time the sequential part takes to run cannot be shortened by adding devices.

› Answers and Explanations

1. **A**—Computer networks connect devices.

2. **C**—A path is the series of steps or nodes between a sending and a receiving location.

3. **B**—Bandwidth is the amount of data that can be sent in a fixed period of time.

4. **A**—Internet routing is usually dynamic so the path can be determined and changed based on the status of the network paths when sending data.

5. **C**—TCP (Transmission Control Protocol) handles processing at the sending and receiving locations. It breaks the data stream into packets, adds header information, and sends them on the way to the requesting location using IP. Once received, TCP sends an acknowledgment and puts the packets back in order.

6. **A**—The Internet Protocol (IP) address is the number assigned to devices on the Internet.

7. **D**—The IP address for the destination is included in the packet header.

8. **B**—The Internet is considered to be fault-tolerant because if one path is down, it has another route it can take.

9. **C**—The World Wide Web is a way to search for and share documents.

10. **A**—Efficiency is determined by comparing the time it takes different systems to complete the same task. More efficient systems may be more complex.

11. **D**—A parallel computing system uses multiple computers to run different sections of the program code at the same time.

12. **A**—Distributed computing systems can solve larger problems than a single computer because of additional memory and storage provided by using multiple devices to run a program on sections of the data.

13. B—Packets travel along different paths to their final destination. They do not arrive at the same time, nor does the router decrypt messages. Only the packets that are missing are resent, not the entire stream.

14. A—If the link between A and B is down, then an available path is A C B.

15. B—A path between A and D would provide another path, increasing available options if a path or paths are down.

16. D—HTTPS provides a secure environment but does not slow down the performance of Internet-based exchanges.

17. D—A parallel system's speed is limited by the time it takes to do all the sequential steps. Adding more devices may speed up the parallel sections, but the overall time is still limited by the time it takes to perform the sequential steps.

› Rapid Review

The Internet is a network of networks that enables people across the globe to be connected. Its structure provides multiple paths to hosts, so if one path is down, information can travel back and forth over a different route. This redundancy makes the Internet "fault tolerant," which makes it more reliable. This structure also enables the Internet to scale up as more devices join and more routes and connection points are needed. Regional or local Internet Service Providers (ISPs) provide Internet connections to homes and businesses.

There are rules, called protocols, for connecting and communicating on the Internet, so the correct information and devices can be found. Each time a device connects to the Internet, it is assigned an Internet Protocol (IP) address.

At the sending location, information is broken into packets, sent along different paths to its destination, and then reconfigured at the destination using the Transmission Control Protocol (TCP). IP is the standard used for transmitting information along the paths. So together, TCP/IP represent the standards used for sending information to the correct locations across all the Internet pathways. User Datagram Protocol (UDP) is another protocol that works with IP to route packets, but it does not send an acknowledgment that the data was received like TCP does. Bandwidth is the amount of data that can be sent or received in a set period of time.

The World Wide Web is an application that uses the Internet to host web pages. These use HTML to format the web pages to host all types of files, including text, images, and videos, in an engaging format. Hypertext Transfer Protocol (HTTP) handles all the details for web pages, and Hypertext Transfer Protocol Secure (HTTPS) should be used for secure data and sites.

With a sequential computing system, processes are executed one at a time. When one finishes, the next one begins. Parallel and distributed computing systems use multiple computers in different ways with the goal of speeding up processing time. Parallel computing deconstructs the program into smaller sections and executes some of them at the same time, thereby speeding up processing. Distributed computing uses multiple computers to run the same program but only on a section of the data to be processed. The results are then aggregated to create one output.

CHAPTER 11

Big Idea 5: Impact of Computing

IN THIS CHAPTER

Summary: Computing has impacted all aspects of our lives, from communication to shopping to research. It has provided ways to share and innovate. These innovations are sometimes used in unexpected ways, causing unanticipated results. Sometimes these are beneficial, such as the World Wide Web expanding from sharing scientific papers to what it is today. Other times these unforeseen results can have privacy, security, legal, and ethical concerns.

The "digital divide" deals with who does not have access to the Internet and the equity and access issues that result. The recognition and impact of bias in computing innovations is another issue that can be difficult to identify but very important to do. Access to information via the Internet has allowed the "crowd" to become involved in many new ways, including "citizen science" and funding new businesses or emergency relief anywhere.

With all of these opportunities on the Internet, our personally identifiable information (PII) is potentially stored or willingly shared, leaving us vulnerable to issues such as identity theft. We are also exposed to malware of various types that attempts to steal our PII or infect and damage our devices. Authentication and encryption help shield us from these attempts.

Key Ideas

- ❂ New technologies can have both beneficial and unintended harmful effects, including the presence of bias.
- ❂ Citizen scientists are able to participate in identification and problem solving.
- ❂ The digital divide keeps some people from participating in global and local issues and events.
- ❂ Licensing of people's work and providing attribution are essential.
- ❂ We need to be aware of and protect information about ourselves online.
- ❂ Public key encryption and multifactor authentication are used to protect sensitive information.
- ❂ Malware is software designed to damage your files or capture your sensitive data, such as passwords or confidential information.

Key Terms

Asymmetric ciphers
Authentication
Bias
Certificate Authority (CA)
Citizen science
Computer virus
Creative Commons
   Licensing
Crowdfunding
Crowdsourcing
Cybersecurity
Data mining
Decryption
Digital divide
Encryption
Intellectual property

Keylogging
Malware
Multifactor authentication
Open access
Open source
PII (Personally Identifiable
   Information)
Phishing
Plagiarism
Public key encryption
Rogue access point
Symmetric key
   encryption
Targeted marketing
Virus

New Ways to Communicate and Interact

Thanks to the Internet and the ease of collaboration and sharing, programs and apps (software applications) can be quickly and easily shared with people worldwide. These can sometimes have a huge impact, positive or negative, on people, and sometimes have additional results not originally foreseen by the software developers. Along with these, advances in programming languages have also spread software development to many other disciplines, such as science and art, resulting in innovation in those fields.

People are wonderfully creative, and there are many computing innovations that have since become widely accepted and a part of our everyday lives. We've changed the way we shop with online e-commerce, and our doctors are available to connect with online before we visit their office. We can get where we need to be without getting lost or stuck in traffic. Our food is ready for delivery, sit-down service, or pick-up from restaurants. The list goes on. These apps and websites are just the tools we need to solve problems, make something easier, or are just fun to have and use. There are few limits to the continued creation of new computing innovations! Some of the positive outcomes impacting our lives daily include:

- The World Wide Web, which was originally designed for scientists to share their research. Now we have much of the world's information within our reach.
- Targeted advertising, which can be helpful for businesses and consumers when looking for a specific item.
- Social media, which has been used to stream events across the globe, sometimes helps to change history. Social media sites and blogs have changed the way many people share information. News of events is shared in "real time," meaning as events are happening, by people who are attending the event. Videos and stories go "viral," meaning they quickly get many views and are shared for even more views. These features allow us to have a better understanding of other parts of the world as well as to be entertained. However, remember that certain governments block some or all content from the Internet for their citizens.

NOTE: Questions about specific social media sites will not be on the AP exam.

- Machine learning and data mining help find patterns and identify insights in data, leading to new innovations.

However, with the benefits of having these, there are also potential downsides when computing innovations are used in unintended ways, including:

- People using social media to bully others by posting anonymously and spreading false information. Others then continue to share the falsehood. People also use social media to spread inaccurate information and scams. These are serious negative impacts of the use of the Internet and social media.
- Homes can be robbed when owners post about being away.
- Discrimination can occur based on information gathered through data mining.

Advances in computing continue to enable innovations in other fields. 3D printers can print artificial limbs, and research is underway for the printing of tissue and organs. 3D printers can also print homes, providing a low-cost option for homeless populations. These were unexpected benefits of 3D printing stemming from its use in different fields.

Medical files, test results, and x-rays can be digitized and sent to specialists in any part of the world for evaluation. Physicians are able to collaborate with experts located anywhere in the world and can be looking at the same test results at the same time. Simulations are increasingly realistic, allowing surgeons and pilots to develop their skills before people are involved.

Online learning is an education model that would not be possible without the tools of communication available via the Internet. Now you can have classmates from anywhere in the world. You can also attend class if you are in a different location from your teacher. Teachers are able to do a combined lesson with a class elsewhere in the world using video conferencing tools. This can expose students to a global perspective that can impact people's understanding of each other, their cultures, and the challenges they face, as well as identify things they have in common.

The list can go on and on. Essentially, every other field has used technology for advances in some aspect of their area of interest. The only limitation is our imagination.

Programmers and businesses try to identify potential negative uses, but it is seldom possible to think of all the ways other people could use an innovation. Of course, some of these, such as targeted advertising, could be positive or negative, depending on your perspective.

The World Wide Web (www), an application running under the Internet, makes it easy to share documents, videos, and all types of computing artifacts as well as create interactive sites where others can provide opinions, advice, and suggestions. This has changed the way businesses and organizations operate. Cloud computing is one example. Businesses have also been able to meet remotely and conduct meetings via technology tools such as video conferencing tools. This saves money on travel expenses and can provide flexibility for employees. It also allows meetings, events, school, and connections to continue during quarantines caused by pandemics!

Access to Information

Cloud Computing

Cloud computing offers new ways for people to communicate, making collaboration easier and more efficient. Storing documents in the "cloud" simply means they are stored on a computer server at a location different than where the owner of the files is located. The documents are accessible via an Internet connection to anyone with verified access to it. This provides several benefits, including the ability for multiple people to update one document at the same time. This eliminates the problem of keeping track of multiple versions of the document—a major headache in the past. People could accidentally overwrite other people's changes or be viewing an out-of-date version.

Another benefit of cloud computing is that people can access the document stored in the cloud from any device, at any time, at any location that has Internet access. This also allows multiple experts to easily evaluate and review documents, leading to better outcomes, whether it's evaluating a medical condition, a business plan, or a group project for a class.

Digital Divide

Technology has had a major impact on the world, enabling innovation through the sharing of resources and computational artifacts. It also allows us to virtually meet with people from anywhere. It is helping us on the path of becoming a true global society.

While the Internet and the World Wide Web have had a global impact on the ease of sharing and collaborating, it is important to remember that not all areas of the world have the same access. Rural and remote areas often have limited, as in slower, or even no access to the Internet. Other areas do not have the infrastructure to support digital access. There are those who cannot afford the fees to connect to the Internet and the web or buy the devices to do so. Many businesses exist to provide this access, but they may not consider it profitable enough to provide the access in some areas, impacting groups and individuals in cities, suburbs, and rural communities.

While the Internet and the World Wide Web are not "owned" by anyone, each government determines which citizens may have access and which websites they may view. The elimination of "net neutrality" has the potential to create an additional divide where those with the funding have faster and better access to the Internet and the web.

The impact of the digital divide includes access to information, knowledge, markets, and different cultures. Perhaps most importantly, the digital divide impacts the ability for all to have a voice and a chance to hear and be heard in their community and across the globe.

Bias in Computing Innovations

Bias, which is intentional or unintentional prejudice for or against certain groups of people, shows up in computing innovations too. Humans write the algorithms, and our biases can make their way into the algorithms and the data used by innovations without us realizing it.

It is a programmer's responsibility to work to remove bias in algorithms. This is difficult when people are not aware of their own bias. In addition to being at the algorithm level, bias can also be introduced at all levels of the software development process.

Artificial intelligence programs are used more and more in ways such as screening applications of job candidates, determining if a person merits credit to purchase a house, and locating what areas have more crime. When these applications have bias built in, it can be difficult to detect it and then even more so to remove it. The reasoning behind decision-making is where bias gets introduced. The decisions are usually based on profitability potential and aren't considering fairness. For example, one business used historical hiring information with its applicant screening software. Because more men had been hired previously, the algorithm continued that trend and eliminated far more female candidates. Determining which attributes to consider can introduce bias into your algorithm and result in skewed results, however unintentionally. The introduction of bias is not easily identified early in the process or may not be seen until further into the process when results are received and analyzed. Although it can be difficult, it is important to identify where in the process the bias was introduced and resolve it for a fairer future outcome.

Crowdsourcing

Crowdsourcing allows people to share information and ask the "crowd"—anyone who accesses the site—for feedback, to help solve problems, find employment, or for funding. Another use of crowdsourcing is when scientists share data and ask nonscientists, or "citizen scientists," to look for and report on patterns or other interesting features of the data or to "donate" computer time during periods of time their machine is inactive. This helps to "scale up" processing capability at little to no cost to the organization seeking the resources. This helps researchers collect data at multiple locations and expand the time period for collecting data. When the research team has too few members to collect all the data they need or does not have an adequate budget to visit all the locations that could provide data, citizen scientists can bridge the gaps. The research teams can likely produce better insights because of the availability of additional data.

Examples of "citizen" science include monitoring monarch butterfly and bird migrations, recording plastics that wash up on beaches worldwide, and classifying galaxies! People are also willing to write documentation, identify photos, and provide all types of assistance. These collaborative efforts help people and society as a whole with discoveries and advances in many fields. As stated earlier, people with different backgrounds look at solving problems in different ways, often because they don't know something "shouldn't be possible." For example, back in 2011, gamers played an online puzzle called Foldit that researchers set up for help folding proteins. Researchers had been working on it for over a decade and the group in the gaming world solved it in three weeks. The gaming community didn't work with preconceived ideas of how proteins should or should not work. Instead, they tried everything! This led to advances in medical research and treatments.

Crowdfunding helps inventors, individuals, and businesses fund their ventures with a little bit of money from many sources. The Internet has made it possible now to see easily what new innovations or events people are trying to raise money for from anywhere in the world.

Legal and Ethical Concerns

Anything a person creates, including any computational artifacts created with a computer, is the intellectual property of that person. The Internet makes it easy for people to share their creations with the world. Unfortunately, it also makes it easy for others to take their work and use it without permission or payment. This is plagiarism and has resulted in people getting a grade of zero on an assignment, failing a class, losing a job, or facing legal issues along with the embarrassment that goes with it. Material created by someone else that you use in any way should always be cited. Fortunately, there are ways to deal with the permissions needed to protect and share your intellectual property.

Over the years, there have been many examples of illegal downloads and sharing of music, games, and videos. Peer-to-peer networks exist that are used to illegally share files of all types. "Mashups" where people combine content created by others is a copyright concern, especially if they earn money from doing so. Many of these have resulted in lawsuits challenging whether someone's intellectual property is changed enough that someone does not have to compensate them for using it.

As mentioned earlier in this chapter, algorithms with bias in them can have both legal and ethical issues. Devices that continually monitor and collect data, such as a voice-activated device we install or video cameras used for facial recognition posted in our communities, can have legal and/or ethical issues. Even when people have approved access to information, choosing to use that access in legal and ethical ways matters. Often digital innovations become accepted with widespread use before legal implications can be determined. There always seems to be something in the news where someone shared, used, or sold information for unethical purposes. These instances cause the legal system to then create laws regarding such use. Often the damage is already done before that can happen. On the other side of the coin, censorship of digital information by government, businesses, or individuals is also harmful and raises ethical, if not legal, concerns.

Creative Commons

Creative Commons provides a way for creators of software, images, music, videos, and any computational artifact to share their creations with stipulations for sharing and permission from the author clearly indicated. Creative Commons provides six levels of licensing that the owner/creator decides for their work. These levels include no restrictions on use, use with and without attribution, the ability to modify with and without attribution, and whether someone other than the original author can sell it.

Digital data is easy to find, copy, and paste, so ensuring you have written permission from the creator or owner is important. Just as it is easy to find many computer artifacts on the web, it is also very easy for people to search for their artifacts to see if someone is using them without permission. If you use something without permission, be prepared for official consequences, including a fine and orders to remove it, among other potential legal actions.

Open-Source Software

Not only do we have access to data but to software as well. "Open source" software is software that is freely shared, updated, and supported by anyone who wants to do so. The availability of this software for everyone has greatly expanded people's abilities to participate in a variety of tasks that many would not have been able to participate in otherwise. Allowing many to develop the software ensures a better product with ideas and solutions to problems from many perspectives. It also is generally a less error-prone product because of all the people testing the software.

Of course, there are also concerns if someone takes code from these openly available programs and either uses it with additional code they wrote, markets it in some way claiming it as their own, or inserts malware into the open-source code, thereby impacting everyone who then downloads it. The malware would be quickly found and corrected due to the many people constantly working and communicating about the code but still impacts those who downloaded it.

Open Access

The sharing of huge amounts of public data by organizations, such as the U.S. government, provides the opportunity for anyone to search for information or to help solve problems. In addition, the availability of open databases in a variety of fields—including science, entertainment, sports, and business—has benefited people everywhere. People identify issues and opportunities, leading to new facets and products for research, production, and sales.

All three of these, Creative Commons, open source, and open access, have provided wide access to digital information. The world's information is accessible—or at least a great deal of it is. But this also reminds us of the digital divide, as many people do not have a device and Internet access to retrieve and contribute to this worldwide source.

Search Trends and Analytics

Social media sites as well as search engines publish what the most frequent searches and posts are about. Our browsers keep a list of our most frequently visited sites on their home page to help us out. The search engines are able to identify when more people than usual are watching a video or searching for a topic. Companies use this information to predict trends and then use their information about related topics to share with those searching and researching. Similarly, analytics identify trends for marketing purposes and help businesses determine what and where customers are searching for their products and their competitors' products, how long an item sits in a virtual shopping cart, and when people buy.

Data Mining

Data mining is a field of study that analyzes large datasets. Companies may use the results to determine when to offer a discount for specific products. Machine learning is a subset of data mining. Machine learning uses algorithms to analyze data and predict behavior and is used in Artificial Intelligence (AI). Companies then use this information to target ads or products to you based on your prior searches or purchasing behavior. It can also be used for a potential fraud alert if your bank detects unusual activity on your account. The machine has "learned" your usual patterns and issues an alert if something is different. If the software used is able to predict more accurately over time, then it is considered machine learning.

Science and business have both benefited from these new sources of information. Data mining has been able to predict when someone will need a new battery for a pacemaker or drop out of a research study so those leading the project can work more closely with the person to try and prevent it. The medical field is working to identify risk factors for diseases to help those at risk make changes to reduce their chance of contracting the disease. For the business world, retaining employees is important to keep knowledge and the company's investment in training the employee in-house. The use of computers to evaluate job candidates has resulted in a higher retention rate.

Personally Identifiable Information (PII)

Any information that identifies you is considered Personally Identifiable Information (PII). It includes data such as your address, age, or social security number. It also includes data about you, such as your medical or financial information. One category many people don't consider is biometric data. If you use your fingerprint to log into your computer, that is biometric data. Retina scans and facial scans can also be stored online. Websites, apps, and networks also track our location.

As with most things, having your PII online has pros and cons. One positive is that creating an account with a website and filling in personal information that will be saved is useful for future purchases. It saves us time and typos by not having to key in the same information each time. Our PII information is also used by websites to show us certain information or related topics based on our prior visits. Again, this can be helpful or feel invasive or creepy. These sites track how long you were on their site, what you viewed, perhaps placed in a shopping cart, actually purchased, or removed without purchasing. This information is used to entice us with additional ads or an offer of a lower price.

Our devices also track our locations. You've probably received a text or e-mail asking about your experience at a store, restaurant, or other venue and asking you to post on social media. (Sometimes I get them when I only walked by a business and never went in!)

All of this data about us is in many different places. A little may be on one website, and some different information may be on another. Since many companies sell the data about us, either notifying us in the very fine print or not at all, this opens the door to all this information being available. As we've discussed throughout the course, software exists to sift through data looking for patterns and similarities. Our information can end up being pieced together.

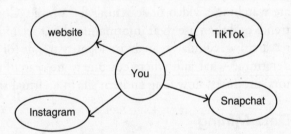

Further, as listed earlier in this chapter, the government, some research sites, and nonprofit organizations provide open access to large databases about many topics. This is great for research and information that would not be available otherwise. Our personal information should not be identifiable and should be only available aggregated with thousands or millions of other records. This means summarizing, removing some aspects, and masking the data findings at such a high level that no individual or group should be identified. However, done incorrectly, individual information can and has been identifiable. It is surprising how one small identifiable piece of data, such as a zip code, can be used with other legally available public sources of data on the web to identify a person. All too often, this invasion of privacy is either posted or shared in ways unknown to those impacted.

Always remember that once data is on the web, it is difficult if not impossible to delete. As soon as you press Send on an e-mail or social media post, it is out of your control and can be forwarded or altered with your name attached to it. Students have been denied or had college admission and scholarships rescinded because of their social media posts. Adults have lost jobs due to their social media posts. People will make assumptions about you based on your posts. You will change as a person over the years, but since data is permanent, be cautious now.

We should always watch and check over our PII because it is our identity, and once stolen, it can impact finances or career and involves a long process to clear up. People can also use it for criminal activities.

Privacy

Digital footprints and fingerprints are the trail of little pieces of data we leave behind as a sign of our presence as we go through our daily lives. Some of the ways our data is collected occurs via:

- GPS coordinates embedded in photographs and apps showing our location
- Financial transactions such as viewing, comparing, and making purchases
- Websites visited
- Cell phones pinging off towers
- Key card access to locations

Many people willingly provide personal information to sites to gain access or privileges, whether it's through sports teams, shopping, or restaurants. Their data is stored and may be sold with or without their knowledge or permission. While the perks of being a frequent customer can be nice, if your information is compromised or used against you, such as your house being robbed because you posted you were out to dinner, the benefit is clearly not worth it.

Sometimes the information is used at a personal level, such as businesses sending special offers to people who visit their stores a certain number of times. Targeted advertising can be useful when you are searching for something, like that perfect gift. However, the downside is that you may only be shown items the algorithm thinks you would like and you may never see other items. This limits your access to other products and information and impacts those potential businesses. These raise privacy and potential security concerns if identifying information about us is still available in the local datasets.

There are ways to search in anonymous mode to prevent this tracking. Many web browsers now have "incognito" or "private" modes so that web searches and file downloads are not recorded in the web history. Some web browsers attest that they do not track and retain your search data. There are also ways to be more anonymous to avoid tracking by websites, such as blocking cookies, installing add-ons to prevent them from tracking your device, and using proxy servers, among other techniques. These are constantly evolving as other software is developed to get around them.

It is a constant challenge, because sometimes by accident, and sometimes on purpose, all the data that has been collected about us is released to those who should not have it or to the world at large. When this involves medical information; financial information, such as credit card numbers; and personal information including social security numbers—it puts our safety, personal and digital, at risk. Once it is online, it is essentially impossible to remove data. Tools such as the Internet archive "The Wayback Machine" can show social media posts that have been deleted. It's never really gone. Backups and screenshots by unknown people mean it can resurface at any time.

Any technology used to harm people is highly unethical and potentially illegal. Internet troll factories attempt to spread misinformation and interfere with many facets of our lives, including tampering with elections and adding racial elements to news and nonrelated events. Organizations or external sources scrape websites for our personal data and sell it to others or release it without our knowledge. Always be cautious and aware that with all the good the Internet provides, others will attempt to manipulate us using the same tools we use in our everyday lives.

Protecting Our Data

Many aspects of our lives are much easier today because of the easy access to all sorts of sites and information that the Internet provides. This can range from shopping, entertainment, and sports sites to price comparisons. We can research health symptoms and medical treatment and find vetted sources for research. We can also find online classes taught by instructors anywhere in the world, as well as illegal sites and transactions as we pick up viruses and other malware along the way.

The Internet has created a way for easy access to worldwide audiences. Providers of goods and services can directly access their customers, eliminating the importance of all types of "middlemen" from brick-and-mortar stores to publishers and music distributors to radio-dispatched taxis. This has changed the way we shop, get our entertainment, schedule a ride, and even obtain financing for projects. But this also raises security, privacy, and ethical concerns related to many aspects and uses of the Internet. Cybersecurity has a global impact because now anyone from anywhere can attempt to gain unauthorized entry to someone else's computer, data, servers, or network.

Security

The security of our data deals with the ability to prevent unauthorized individuals from gaining access to it and preventing those who can view our data from changing it. Strong passwords help block those trying to gain unauthorized access. That is one reason many sites have increased their password requirements to contain components such as:

- A capital letter
- A number
- A special character
- A specified minimum length
- Cannot be the same or almost the same as a previous password
- Cannot be the same as the user ID

Multifactor authentication is another layer that is increasingly used. For example, if someone tries to reset your password, they cannot do it without the second layer of authentication. Sometimes this involves answering questions based on information only you would know, confirming via another account or your cell phone that you are attempting this action, or using a feature of inherence, such as your fingerprint scan.

We trust the companies that maintain our personal information, including social security number and financial information like credit card numbers, to keep it secure. As the news often reports, many companies have had their security defenses breached and customer data stolen. The data often is sold to those planning to use unsuspecting users' identities to open accounts and make purchases. Always check your accounts often!

Cybersecurity

Cybersecurity protects our electronic devices and networks from attacks and unauthorized use. These attacks can come in many forms and can have a major impact on those affected. Many of them come into a network or device through e-mail. An unsuspecting person clicks on a link that downloads a computer virus or other form of malware (the term "malware" comes from "malicious software"). Different types of attacks cause different problems. Data may be damaged or the device may be used to further spread the malware.

Phishing attacks create e-mail and/or websites that look a legitimate hoping to induce a person to click on the malicious link. These sites often prompt a user for their password, credit card number, or other sensitive data under the guise of a valid transaction. The password or other personal information is then used and/or sold for illegal use. This is called social engineering when people are tricked into providing information such as passwords or clicking a link that appears legitimate. We are the weakest link in the steps designed to protect our devices and information.

Computer viruses are like human viruses. They attach themselves to, or are part of, an infected file. There are many types that can damage, delete, or steal your files and use your system to spread to other devices. Viruses spread by being embedded in or attaching to a legitimate program to infect your system. They can then begin to run their code on your computing device. Do not click on files in an e-mail from people you do not know, or even from someone you know, if you are not expecting an attachment. Someone else's system may have been compromised and is propagating the virus by sending out infected messages to everyone in the address book on the infected device. That is a common way viruses are spread. Many websites offering free downloads of games or movies often contain malware. Nothing is really free—there is always a cost of some sort.

Keylogging software is a form of malware that captures every keystroke and transmits it to whomever planted it. They then run software to sift through the keylogger file attempting to identify passwords or other personal information you've entered.

Access points are used to create wireless networks. Public networks such as those at restaurants, stores, and hotels don't require a password to join the network. People can run software on the same open network to intercept your signals and sift through the data looking for passwords. Rogue access points are when someone sets up an access point that is not managed by that organization on their secure network. Anyone on that network could then have their signal intercepted, data captured, or potentially modified. Additionally, someone external to your organization could access your secure network through the rogue access point.

The solution for computer malware is to use antivirus software, firewalls, and caution when downloading or opening files from an unknown or unexpected source. As much as developers try to avoid this, computing systems have errors and design flaws. These vulnerabilities are exploited by those wishing to compromise a system for some type of gain or just to see if they can. Keep current with installing updates for your antivirus software and your operating system. These updates correct errors that are or could be exploited, so they are very important.

Cryptography

Cryptography is the writing of secret codes. It has been used for thousands of years and is the reason we are able to have secured online shopping and keep our data in "cloud" accounts secured with our passwords today. Encryption is converting a message to a coded format. Deciphering the encrypted message is called decryption. Security also relates to encrypting data before it is transmitted to ensure it remains secure if it is intercepted during transmission. The location you sent the data to would decrypt the data for it to then be used as needed.

Ciphers are coded messages, and all ciphers have two parts:

- Key: allows the creation of secret messages
- Algorithm: the set of steps used to transpose the message to be unreadable to anyone but the person who holds the key

Julius Caesar is credited with the Caesar cipher, one of the first ciphers, which is a secret code system. It shifted letters over three spaces and took 800 years to be broken. It is a "symmetric cipher," which means that the same key is used to encrypt and decrypt the message.

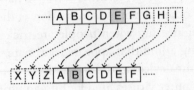

Public Key Encryption

Today's algorithms use asymmetric keys, meaning two keys will be needed, one to encrypt and the other to decrypt the message. Public key encryption uses open standards, meaning the algorithms used are published and available to everyone and are discussed by experts and interested parties and known by all. The key is what keeps information secret until the person it is intended for decrypts it. In this case, the public key is used to encrypt data and is published to anyone. Messages are then decrypted using a private key. The sender does not need the private key to encrypt the message; only the recipient of the message needs it. This is considered a one-way function. That means the function is easy in one direction and difficult in the other. This algorithm creates such large numbers for the key that a brute-force attack, which is checking each possible solution, cannot break the code. In other words, a solution exists, but our current-day computers do not have adequate resources, memory, or time to solve it.

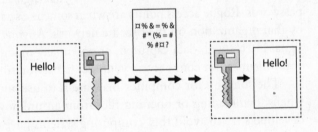

 NOTE: The cryptography algorithms are based on mathematical functions, and these are not covered on the AP exam.

Securing the Internet

The Internet is based on a "trust" model. This means that digital certificates can be purchased from Certificate Authorities (CAs), which identify trusted sites. They issue certificates that businesses, organizations, and individuals load to their websites. The certificates verify to web browsers that the encryption keys belong to the business, thereby enabling online purchases and the sending and receiving of secure documents.

 NOTE: The details of how CAs work is not on the AP exam.

Always check your personal permissions on your social media accounts, permissions you grant websites for information they can collect about you, and what they can do with it. More visibility is being provided about this, but it will probably never be truly transparent. Regularly check your settings because a site may do an update that changes your settings or the intent you had with your settings. Do what you can to protect the privacy of your information.

› Review Questions

Concepts

1. When access to the Internet is unequal based on geographic or socioeconomic reasons, it's referred to as the
   (A) Internet divide.
   (B) wealthy divide.
   (C) distance divide.
   (D) digital divide.

2. What is an example of sharing images and allowing individuals to scan them for certain features?
   (A) Heuristics
   (B) Moore's law
   (C) Citizen science
   (D) Contaminated research

3. What is the name for programming code that is available to anyone to use or modify?
   (A) Licensed software
   (B) Open-source software
   (C) Compiled software
   (D) Open access software

4. What has Creative Commons provided?
   (A) Free use of other people's work
   (B) Ways to share other people's creations without their knowledge
   (C) Licensing options by the owners of artifacts
   (D) Cooperative copyright arbitration

5. The ability to retrieve previously published data and research rather than each organization paying for or collecting their own data to analyze is an example of?
   (A) Creative Commons licensing
   (B) Free access rights
   (C) Open access
   (D) Open source

6. People trading personal information for perks from companies is an example of which of the following?
   (A) The use of proxy servers
   (B) Privacy concerns
   (C) Legal issues
   (D) Authentication exposure

7. What is the term for showing someone information based on their prior searches and purchases?
   (A) Targeted advertising
   (B) Open-source marketing
   (C) Open access marketing
   (D) Aggregation of data

8. Granting access after clearing at least two steps of authentication, such as a password and code sent to your cell phone, is called
   (A) compound authentication.
   (B) complex authentication.
   (C) frequency analysis authentication.
   (D) multifactor authentication.

9. What is one way that does NOT prevent password-cracking programs from easily identifying your password?
   (A) Using a mixture of upper and lowercase letters
   (B) Using special characters as part of your password
   (C) Making it easy to remember so you do not have to write it down
   (D) Using former pet names that hackers could never know

10. Using social engineering to trick users into providing their personal information is called
    (A) keylogging.
    (B) phishing.
    (C) pharming.
    (D) spearing.

Application of Concepts

11. Schools that provide each student with a computing device for school and home use but that do not ensure all students have equally reliable and fast Internet access are contributing to the
    (A) digital divide.
    (B) equity influence issue.
    (C) Internet gap.
    (D) preference issues.

12. Many forms that collect personal information do not include responses for all ethnicities. This is an example of
   - (A) bias.
   - (B) partiality.
   - (C) subjectivity.
   - (D) predisposition.

13. Using an app to notify many people about child abductions, such as an Amber alert, is an example of
   - (A) compliance.
   - (B) consensus building.
   - (C) crowdsourcing.
   - (D) open sourcing.

14. A business's website tracks items that are viewed by visitors to its site. Which question cannot be answered by tracking this data?
   - (A) Which items will sell during each season in different parts of the world
   - (B) The trending colors that could be popular in the next year
   - (C) The income range of prospective customers
   - (D) How many of each item to produce

15. Which of the following is an example of plagiarism?

   1. Writing about an idea you read about
   2. Making minor changes to wording in a paragraph
   3. Retyping text rather than copying and pasting it into a document

   - (A) 1 and 2
   - (B) 1 and 3
   - (C) 2 and 3
   - (D) All of the above

16. What is a symmetric key used for?
   - (A) Sending and receiving information from the web
   - (B) Encrypting data
   - (C) Decrypting data
   - (D) Encrypting and decrypting data

17. Cryptography today uses which of the following?
   - (A) Published algorithms available to all
   - (B) Algorithms known by only a few members of the IETF governing organization
   - (C) The Caesar cipher
   - (D) Undecidable algorithms

18. Computer viruses can replicate after infecting a computer. How are they transmitted?
   - (A) By attaching to a valid program or file
   - (B) By visiting a website that is infected
   - (C) By clicking on a link that takes you to a counterfeit website designed to look like a legitimate one
   - (D) By being on the same network as an infected device

› Answers and Explanations

1. **D**—The digital divide refers to unequal access to the Internet based on geographic or socioeconomic reasons.

2. **C**—Sharing images and allowing individuals to scan them for certain features is an example of citizen science.

3. **B**—Open-source software is available to anyone to use or modify.

4. **C**—Creative Commons allows owners to designate licensing options for their digital creations.

5. **C**—Open access provides access to scholarly articles, data, and research without any restrictions.

6. **B**—People trading personal information for perks from companies is an example of a privacy concern.

7. **A**—Targeted advertising is showing someone information based on their prior searches and purchases.

8. **D**—Multifactor authentication requires the user to clear at least two levels of protection before gaining access.

9. **D**—Using former pet names will not prevent your password from being compromised. Posts on social media and name programs can work in combination to identify your password.

10. **B**—Phishing attacks use techniques such as sending e-mail with a link to a website that looks exactly like a legitimate organization but is bogus. Users provide their password, which is then captured and used on the real website to impersonate you.

11. **A**—The digital divide is when different levels of access to the Internet impact certain groups.

12. **A**—This is an example of bias in the data collection process that leads to inaccurate data for decision-making.

13. **C**—Using information from many people is an example of crowdsourcing.

14. **C**—The data tracked can provide reasonable information about everything except a potential customer's income level.

15. **D**—All of the examples are instances of plagiarism. Ideas must be cited as well as text that is only minimally changed and content you copy either by retyping or pasting into a document.

16. **D**—A symmetric key is used for both encrypting and decrypting data.

17. **A**—Cryptography today uses published algorithms available to all. The key used for decryption is private.

18. **A**—Viruses are transmitted through embedding them in a document or program. Once the document or program is on a new computer, the virus can start running and replicating.

› Rapid Review

Advances in technology have enabled the development of new and innovative creations and solutions in many fields. These advances have changed the way people interact with each other, in both positive and negative ways.

There are many ways to communicate, including e-mail, texting, and social media sites. These sites have also been instrumental in sharing information with a much wider audience and faster than could have been previously reached through nontechnology-related methods. One issue to watch for and test for is bias being included in data collected for a specified purpose. We must remain aware of the digital divide that separates those with access to the Internet from those who without—whether it's due to being in a more remote location or lack of funds to pay for Internet service or devices. In addition, some governments monitor and block certain users and sites on the Internet, usually those critical of the country's leadership.

Technological advances have also enabled easy and real-time collaboration to create documents. Having datasets online and accessible to the public helps share information and provides everyone with the ability to search, or "mine," it for trends and patterns. This could lead to the identification of new issues and opportunities and advances in a variety of fields, including medicine, entertainment, sports, and business.

The use of "citizen scientists" to aid in research and storing or processing digital data is an example of crowdsourcing. Citizen scientists are useful to research teams that have limited time, funding, or members to collect the wide variety or volume of data needed for better analysis and problem-solving.

Plagiarism is easy to commit using the Internet by copying and pasting information without citing the owner of the information. However, it is equally easy to test for plagiarism. Always cite your sources for work and ideas that are not your own. The development of the Creative Commons licensing levels helps people share their creations and allow their reuse for specific uses with a wider audience. The tracking of their use and enforcement can be difficult and leads to issues about intellectual property and copyright. Illegal sharing of digital files is one of the downsides of new technologies and is usually done through peer-to-peer networks. Open-source software and open access to research and other data are legitimate ways to access other people's work.

The unauthorized use or sharing of our personal data is also a major concern that impacts all of us. Combining data to remove the ability to identify an individual's personal data will remain a concern since it is dependent on the abilities of the person or team doing the aggregating to fully understand and implement a complete masking process. Similarly, the tracking of people through their apps, photos, and browsing history is a privacy and security concern. Tied in with this, advertisers use targeted ads based on places we go and sites we visit. People often willingly provide this PII to receive benefits such as discount coupons.

Cybersecurity has become a critical field since the Internet was not designed to be a secure system. While antivirus software and firewalls can prevent many types of malware, hackers often trick people into clicking on unsafe sites or documents using phishing techniques. Hackers also use keyloggers to attempt to gain unauthorized access and create malware to spread viruses and worms. Multifactor authentication uses a variety of ways, including strong passwords, codes sent to a secure device or account, or use of a unique feature such as a fingerprint, to verify that you are the person trying to access your account. Cryptography is a field that deals with ensuring that data is secured via encryption methods before being transmitted across the Internet.

The current technique is public key encryption, which uses an asymmetric system, meaning one key is used to encrypt data and another is used to decrypt it. The key is divided into a public and a private part. The public keys are openly published and available to anyone. The algorithm uses the public key to encrypt, and the receiver decrypts with their private part of the key. This makes it impossible to decrypt because it takes too much memory or time to process. As advances in computer processing power are made, this method may become possible to break, but for now, our data and financial transactions on the Internet are secure.

The Internet is based on a "trust" model, which means that Certificates of Authority (CAs) are issued that ensure the public keys shared by sites we want to do secure processing with are legitimate. If we are buying a product online, our web browsers can trust that the company site is the correct one based on their CA, and we can proceed with our credit card or other transaction.

STEP 5

Build Your Test-Taking Confidence

AP Computer Science Principles Practice Exam 1
AP Computer Science Principles Practice Exam 2

AP Computer Science Principles
Practice Exam 1

Multiple-Choice Questions
ANSWER SHEET

1. (A) (B) (C) (D)
2. (A) (B) (C) (D)
3. (A) (B) (C) (D)
4. (A) (B) (C) (D)
5. (A) (B) (C) (D)
6. (A) (B) (C) (D)
7. (A) (B) (C) (D)
8. (A) (B) (C) (D)
9. (A) (B) (C) (D)
10. (A) (B) (C) (D)
11. (A) (B) (C) (D)
12. (A) (B) (C) (D)
13. (A) (B) (C) (D)
14. (A) (B) (C) (D)
15. (A) (B) (C) (D)
16. (A) (B) (C) (D)
17. (A) (B) (C) (D)
18. (A) (B) (C) (D)
19. (A) (B) (C) (D)
20. (A) (B) (C) (D)
21. (A) (B) (C) (D)
22. (A) (B) (C) (D)
23. (A) (B) (C) (D)
24. (A) (B) (C) (D)
25. (A) (B) (C) (D)

26. (A) (B) (C) (D)
27. (A) (B) (C) (D)
28. (A) (B) (C) (D)
29. (A) (B) (C) (D)
30. (A) (B) (C) (D)
31. (A) (B) (C) (D)
32. (A) (B) (C) (D)
33. (A) (B) (C) (D)
34. (A) (B) (C) (D)
35. (A) (B) (C) (D)
36. (A) (B) (C) (D)
37. (A) (B) (C) (D)
38. (A) (B) (C) (D)
39. (A) (B) (C) (D)
40. (A) (B) (C) (D)
41. (A) (B) (C) (D)
42. (A) (B) (C) (D)
43. (A) (B) (C) (D)
44. (A) (B) (C) (D)
45. (A) (B) (C) (D)
46. (A) (B) (C) (D)
47. (A) (B) (C) (D)
48. (A) (B) (C) (D)
49. (A) (B) (C) (D)
50. (A) (B) (C) (D)

51. (A) (B) (C) (D)
52. (A) (B) (C) (D)
53. (A) (B) (C) (D)
54. (A) (B) (C) (D)
55. (A) (B) (C) (D)
56. (A) (B) (C) (D)
57. (A) (B) (C) (D)
58. (A) (B) (C) (D)
59. (A) (B) (C) (D)
60. (A) (B) (C) (D)
61. (A) (B) (C) (D)
62. (A) (B) (C) (D)
63. (A) (B) (C) (D)
64. (A) (B) (C) (D)
65. (A) (B) (C) (D)
66. (A) (B) (C) (D)
67. (A) (B) (C) (D)
68. (A) (B) (C) (D)
69. (A) (B) (C) (D)
70. (A) (B) (C) (D)

AP Computer Science Principles
Practice Exam 1

Multiple-Choice Questions

Time: 2 hours
Number of questions: 70
The multiple-choice questions represent 70% of your total score.

Directions: Choose the one best answer for each question. The last eight questions of the test have two correct answers; for these, you will be instructed to choose two answer choices.

Tear out the answer sheet on the previous page and grid in your answers using a pencil. Consider how much time you have left before spending too much time on any one problem.

AP Computer Science Principles Exam Reference Sheet

On the AP Computer Science Principles exam, you will be given a reference sheet to use while you're taking the multiple-choice test. A copy of this six-page reference sheet is included in the Appendix of this book (reprinted by permission from the College Board).

To make taking this practice test like taking the actual exam, you should tear out the reference sheet so you can easily refer to it while taking the test. Save these reference pages since you'll need to use them when you take AP Computer Science Principles Practice Exam 2.

If you lose the pages, the reference sheet is also available near the end of the PDF publication "AP Computer Science Principles Student Handouts" on the College Board website. Here is the URL:

https://apcentral.collegeboard.org/pdf/ap-csp-student-task-directions
    .pdf?course=ap-computer-science-principles

GO ON TO THE NEXT PAGE

1. You won the lottery and elected to receive a lump sum! The largest number the bank's computer can store is $2^{31} - 1$, or 2,147,483,647. After depositing your lottery winnings of $2,500,000,000, what will the result be?

   (A) Your winnings were more than the largest number the bank's computers could hold, so an overflow error will occur.
   (B) Since decimal numbers are stored imprecisely in computers, a rounding error will occur.
   (C) The amount will be represented in machine code format, so converting it to decimal will show the balance in a more readable format.
   (D) The amount will cause a runtime error.

2. You stop by and purchase your favorite snack after school one day. You notice the cash register shows the change you are owed as $0.04999999 rather than $0.05. How is this possible?

   (A) The cash register DISPLAY procedure has an error.
   (B) A rounding error occurred.
   (C) It's displaying the change owed in a different currency.
   (D) The amount is represented as a string field rather than a number.

3. You are assigned a parking space in a large parking lot by an automated machine. You recognize that the parking space number is displayed in binary, but the parking spots are labeled in decimal numbers. Convert the parking space number 10011011 to decimal to know where to park and avoid getting towed.

   (A) 154
   (B) 155
   (C) 157
   (D) 9F

4. When designing a web page, you see a color you want to use listed in binary as: 01010000, 11001000, 01111000. Which color is it, given the decimal equivalents (red, green, blue)?

   (A) (32, 76, 414)
   (B) (50, 118, 78)
   (C) (80, 200, 120)
   (D) (128, 310, 170)

5. Your bank asks for your phone number to associate it with your account. What is this an example of?

   (A) A privacy concern
   (B) Multifactor authentication
   (C) A phishing attempt
   (D) Asymmetric authentication

6. You have to change a program written a year ago by someone else. A sample section of code is below. How could the original program author have helped anyone making changes at a later date?

```
PROCEDURE a(x, y, z)
{
    IF x < y
    {
        x ← z
    }
}
```

   (A) Provided the original program requirements
   (B) Added a video describing the program design and functionality
   (C) Used procedure and variable names that described their purpose and content
   (D) Provided written documentation of the application development process

GO ON TO THE NEXT PAGE

Questions 7–8 are based on the code below. Assume all lists and variables have been properly initialized.

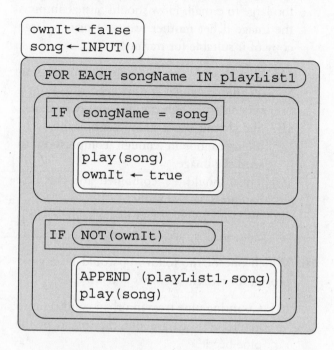

```
ownIt ← false
song ← INPUT()

FOR EACH songName IN playList1

    IF (songName = song)

        play(song)
        ownIt ← true

    IF (NOT(ownIt))

        APPEND (playList1,song)
        play(song)
```

7. What does the code do?

   (A) Plays a song from the playlist.
   (B) If a song requested by the user is in the playlist, plays it; otherwise adds it to the end of the playlist and then plays it.
   (C) Moves a song from its current position in the playlist to the end of it, then plays the next one in the list.
   (D) Identifies songs the user wants to hear but does not own. Provides a way to purchase the song and appends it to their playlist.

8. In the code, if "play" is a procedure, what does "song" represent in the line: play(song)?

   (A) It is the name of the procedure for documentation purposes.
   (B) It is an input value where the user requests the song to be played.
   (C) It is a value being passed to the procedure via an argument.
   (D) It is an expression that must be evaluated to be used in the procedure.

9. Which statement is NOT true?

   (A) Lower level languages are easier to debug because the language is closest to what the computer executes.
   (B) Higher level languages are easier to debug because the language is closer to natural language.
   (C) Lower level languages provide less abstraction.
   (D) Higher level languages are easier for people to code in because they are more abstract.

10. If a simulation of the solar eclipse is set up to test the effectiveness of glasses to safely view the sun, which scenario is most likely if the first test shows the glasses are inadequate?

    (A) The team can modify the degree of darkness and retest quickly to determine the threshold of effectiveness.
    (B) The team should stop the test and notify the company that makes the glasses.
    (C) The team should rerun the test multiple times to ensure the results are valid.
    (D) The team should rewrite the code for the simulation, and then retest.

11. A simulation of conditions for a new sensor to be used with self-driving cars is being designed. The pseudocode for the test is below.

```
When car starts, turn sensor on and
set incident_counter to 0

When detect object 3 feet or closer,
redirect steering wheel away from object

Add one to incident_counter
```

    Which condition is not a useful simulation test for the sensor?

    (A) Multiple obstacles at the same time.
    (B) Zero incidents.
    (C) Set up objects at 3 feet, less than 3 feet, and greater than 3 feet to determine the action taken.
    (D) If the car causes an accident by swerving.

GO ON TO THE NEXT PAGE

12. Which of the following will evaluate to "true"?

   i. (true AND true) OR (true AND false)
   ii. NOT(true OR false)
   iii. NOT(false) AND NOT(true AND false)

   (A) i and ii
   (B) i and iii
   (C) ii and iii
   (D) i, ii, and iii

13. What outcome will the Boolean conditions in the diagram produce at steps 1, 2, and 3?

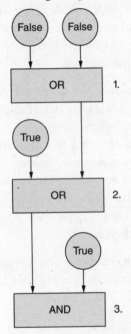

   (A) 1—True, 2—True, 3—True
   (B) 1—False, 2—False, 3—True
   (C) 1—False, 2—True, 3—True
   (D) 1—True, 2—False, 3—False

14. A camera watching an eagle's nest starts recording when a motion detector starts. Which of the following is metadata?

   (A) The latitude and longitude of the nest
   (B) The date and time the motion is detected
   (C) The number of eagles using the nest
   (D) The number of frames per second the camera records

15. Susie's mother wants a copy of a photo from a family vacation that Susie took. The picture is too large to e-mail. How should Susie compress the image if her mother wants to print a large copy of it suitable for framing?

   (A) She should use a lossless compression technique, which will be needed to print a version with high enough quality to frame.
   (B) She should use a lossy compression technique to obtain enough compression to send the image.
   (C) They should be combined for the best compression technique.
   (D) Any compression technique will be sufficient in this case.

16. Which one of the following would be a good project for citizen scientists and why?

   (A) Counting pine trees in urban conditions to get accurate data about the spread of the pine beetle
   (B) Identifying new stars using personal telescopes to keep costs lower for the tracking organization
   (C) Reading different-genre books and evaluating them so book publishers know which types of book manuscripts to accept and market
   (D) Counting fish in a lake to know if the fish are safe to consume

17. What describes the process of searching datasets for incomplete data records to process?

   (A) Classifying
   (B) Cleaning
   (C) Clustering
   (D) Filtering

GO ON TO THE NEXT PAGE

18. A teacher wants to determine student opinions of computer science before and after taking a course. She gives students a survey on the first and last days of class. The survey includes questions about students' impressions of computer science, if the teacher communicated effectively, if the teacher was positive about the course material, and if students gave their best effort in the course. What questions can be determined from the survey data?

   i. If students who moved from a negative to positive impression of computer science after taking the course also thought the teacher communicated effectively

   ii. Which students plan to major in computer science after taking the course

   iii. If the students who did not change their existing view of computer science after taking the course gave their best effort in the course

(A) i
(B) i and iii
(C) ii and iii
(D) i, ii, and iii

19. Given the table of data about car accidents below, which outcome is supported by the data?

(A) Drivers ages 16–25 have the fewest accidents.
(B) More accidents occur on the weekdays.
(C) Drivers age 26–50 have fewer accidents than the other two age groups.
(D) Adult drivers have more accidents on weekdays during rush hour.

20. Why do businesses and scientists attempt to analyze large datasets?

(A) To gain insights smaller subsets of data may not provide
(B) To confirm findings from smaller datasets
(C) To identify potential problems in the metadata
(D) To obtain economies of scale with hardware needed to store the data

21. How do the World Wide Web and the Internet work together?

(A) They perform the same functionality.
(B) The web uses HTTP to share web pages using the Internet.
(C) The Internet uses the web to connect devices to share data.
(D) The Internet is an application that runs using the web.

22. If a fire occurs at a major Internet hub, what is the result?

(A) Internet traffic will be routed to its destination a different way because of the redundancy built into the Internet.
(B) The part of the globe that is served by that Internet hub will be down because of the end-to-end architecture of the Internet.
(C) Different IP addresses will be assigned to devices that were impacted by the unavailability of the Internet hub.
(D) People can use dedicated phone lines as a backup with no change in service.

Most common type of accident	Number of accidents by 16–25-yr.-old drivers	Number of accidents by 26–50-yr.-old drivers	Number of accidents by 51–100-yr.-old drivers	Total number of accidents	Accident occurred on weekday	Accident occurred on weekend
Rear-end collision	311	211	250	772	257	515
Ran light at intersection	215	121	152	488	191	297
Ran stop sign	182	87	92	361	177	184

GO ON TO THE NEXT PAGE

23. The time it took to complete a task sequentially was 25 seconds. The time it took to complete the same task using a parallel computing model was 10 seconds. What is the speedup?

(A) 2.5
(B) 0.4
(C) 15
(D) −15

24. If a company is trying to determine whether to upgrade its bandwidth based on the following graph, what should they measure?

(A) Amount of data uploaded because it includes strategic company backup data
(B) Amount of data downloaded because it has the largest impact on the bandwidth
(C) Frequency of the peak times
(D) Number of devices used on the network

25. Why is the trust model of the Internet important?

(A) It ensures the private security key has not been compromised.
(B) It establishes a dedicated line between two destinations to ensure security.
(C) It enables the secure transfer of data, such as a credit card transaction, which allows online purchasing.
(D) It ensures the privacy of customers making online transactions.

26. You notice a file being uploaded every night to a site you are not familiar with. Opening the file, it looks like a file of your work from the day. This could be an example of a

(A) computer virus.
(B) keylogger file.
(C) network worm.
(D) phishing attack.

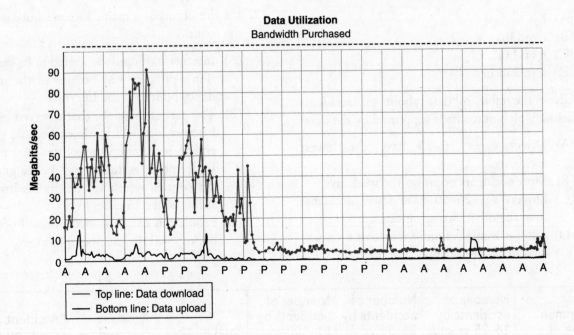

Data Utilization
Bandwidth Purchased

27. You are part of a team that created facial recognition software. However, you just learned an innocent person was taken into custody using only facial recognition software. What can the team do to remove any bias in the future?

    (A) Create better training materials for interpreting the results
    (B) Use photos of a more diverse population to train the algorithm for recognition
    (C) Contact lawmakers to support regulation of the use of facial recognition software
    (D) Add new members to the team to increase the diversity to better identify and avoid bias

28. You make a compressed version of an old classic song to send to a friend. You notice that the sound quality is not as sharp as the original. What is the likely cause?

    (A) The file was compressed with a lossy algorithm.
    (B) The file was compressed with a lossless algorithm.
    (C) The file was corrupted during the copying process.
    (D) The file was copied from a digital version rather than the original analog version.

29. Which of the following is true about packets?

    (A) The receiving device acknowledges the first and last packets to indicate receipt of the data stream.
    (B) Packets travel in order to their destination.
    (C) Packets follow the shortest path to their destination.
    (D) Packets are reassembled at their final destination.

30. How do TCP and IP interact?

    (A) IP forwards the data to the ISP to identify which TCP to use.
    (B) TCP hands off control to HTTP, which passes it to IP.
    (C) TCP creates packets from the data to be sent and transfers control to IP for routing. TCP then reassembles the packets at the destination.
    (D) IP uses UDP in conjunction with TCP to securely send data.

31. An e-mail goes out from your organization's payroll department to all employees stating that everyone needs to confirm or update their banking information to ensure paychecks are deposited on time. It turns out that this was not an e-mail from the payroll department. It is most likely a

    (A) computer virus.
    (B) keylogger attack.
    (C) phishing attack.
    (D) malware insertion point.

32. You need to share a confidential file with another organization. You know the file needs to be encrypted to prevent unauthorized access to its contents. What is the best method of encryption to use?

    (A) Certificate Authorities (CAs) to validate the security of the organization where you are sending the data
    (B) Multifactor authentication to ensure multiple steps of security
    (C) Public key encryption so you do not have to share the encryption key
    (D) Symmetric key encryption so you each have the encryption and decryption keys

33. What is a benefit of the government posting databases for public use?

    (A) It is a way to identify the need for new policies and regulations.
    (B) Consumers can learn more about how their individual data is being collected, stored, and used.
    (C) Companies can opt out to prevent competitors from learning about their business.
    (D) All businesses can access the data at no cost, aiding organizations that would otherwise not have the resources to obtain the data on their own.

GO ON TO THE NEXT PAGE

34. Which algorithm will display the smallest number in a list of positive numbers? Assume *max* is a variable holding the largest number in the list.

(A)
```
smallest ← -1
FOR EACH num IN list
{
        IF (smallest < num)
        {
                smallest ← num
        }
}
DISPLAY (smallest)
```
(B)
```
smallest ← list[1]
FOR Each num IN list
{
        IF (smallest > num)
        {
                smallest ← num
        }
}
DISPLAY (smallest)
```
(C)
```
smallest ← -1
FOR EACH num IN list
{
        IF (smallest > num)
        {
                num ← smallest
        }
}
DISPLAY (smallest)
```
(D)
```
smallest ← max
FOR EACH num IN list
{
        IF (smallest < num)
        {
                smallest ← num
        }
}
DISPLAY (smallest)
```

35. Which of these is a Boolean expression?

(A) `X ← 57`
(B) `Y ← temp * 120 / 100`
(C) `(temp > 32)`
(D) `72 + 12 - (12 * 6) → z`

36. What can be determined from the following program flow?
```
Intro()
Rules()
Play()
Score()
DISPLAY (HighScore())
```

(A) A game is played by calling different procedures.
(B) An error will occur due to invalid procedure names.
(C) Parameters are missing from the procedures, resulting in a runtime error.
(D) A compile time error occurs due to Score() and HighScore().

37. Which statement's format is incorrect?

(A)
```
IF (NOT (x > y))
{
        DISPLAY(message)
}
```
(B) `x ← x + y`
(C) `list[i] ← list[j]`
(D)
```
ELSE
    DISPLAY(new message)
```

38. Which algorithm should be used to find a phone number on a contact list?

I.
Sort the contact list by name
Search for the phone number using a binary search
Display the correct phone number
II.
Sort the contact list by area code
Search for the phone number using a linear search
Display the correct phone number

(A) I.
(B) II.
(C) I and II are equally effective.
(D) A combination of both I and II should be used.

GO ON TO THE NEXT PAGE

39. Why does a computer playing chess use a heuristic algorithm?

(A) It ensures that the computer only wins a certain number of times, making it a more enjoyable experience for people.

(B) It ensures that humans only win a certain percentage based on statistics.

(C) It takes too long to analyze all possible moves, so the computer takes the next best move.

(D) It checks each possible combination of moves for the best move.

40. You are determining the attributes for an AI (Artificial Intelligence) algorithm for a bank to use for approving customers for loans. You select age, income, employment status, and active-loan status as attributes to consider. The bank finds that very few new loans are being offered to college-educated individuals due to existing college loans. This is an example of bias in

(A) analyzing the data.

(B) collecting the data.

(C) preparing the data.

(D) reporting the data.

41. If a list named snacks contains the values:

```
snacks ← ["chocolate", "peanuts",
"granola", "chips", "grapes"]
```

A variable *place* is assigned the value:

```
place ← LENGTH(snacks)
```

What will the value snacks[place] contain?

(A) 5, the number of items in the list.

(B) 6, the number of letters in the word "grapes."

(C) grapes, which is the value in the 5th position of the list.

(D) Error, a list cannot be accessed in this way.

42. Will both of the following two blocks produce correct results? Assume all variables have been properly initialized.

Block 1
```
IF (temp ≥ 80)
{
    hotDay ← hotDay + 1
}
ELSE IF (temp ≥ 60)
{
    perfectDay ← perfectDay + 1
}
ELSE
{
    coldDay ← coldDay + 1
{
```

Block 2
```
IF (temp ≤ 80)
{
    perfectDay ← perfectDay + 1
}
ELSE IF (temp ≤ 60)
{
    coldDay ← coldDay + 1
}
ELSE
{
    hotDay ← hotDay + 1
}
```

(A) Only Block 1 is correct.

(B) Only Block 2 is correct.

(C) Both blocks are correct.

(D) Neither block is correct.

GO ON TO THE NEXT PAGE

43. Determining that an algorithm has a polynomial efficiency means it runs in

(A) an acceptable amount of time even for large datasets.

(B) less time for worst-case scenarios than average scenarios.

(C) an exponential amount of time possibly even for small datasets, making it unable to run for large datasets.

(D) a fractional amount of time for fractional values.

44. Which set of code will calculate the letter grade correctly for a 10-point scale? Assume *average* is a variable holding the student average.

(A)
```
IF (average > 59)
{
    grade ← "D"
}
ELSE
{
    IF (grade > 69)
    {
        grade ← "C"
    }
    ELSE
    {
        IF (grade > 79)
        {
            grade ← "B"
        }
        ELSE
        {
            IF (grade > 89)
            {
                grade ← "A"
            }
            ELSE
            {
                grade ← "F"
            }
        }
    }
}
```

(B)
```
IF (average < 59)
{
    grade ← "D"
}
ELSE
{
    IF (grade < 69)
    {
        grade ← "C"
    }
    ELSE
    {
        IF (grade < 79)
        {
            grade ← "B"
        }
        ELSE
        {
            IF (grade < 89)
            {
                grade ← "A"
            }
            ELSE
            {
                grade ← "F"
            }
        }
    }
}
```

(C)
```
IF (average > 90)
{
    grade ← "A"
}
ELSE
{
    IF (grade > 80)
    {
        grade ← "B"
    }
    ELSE
    {
        IF (grade < 70)
        {
            grade ← "C"
        }
        ELSE
        {
            IF (grade < 60)
            {
                grade ← "D"
            }
            ELSE
            {
                grade ← "F"
            }
        }
    }
}
```

GO ON TO THE NEXT PAGE

(D)
```
IF (average > 89)
{
    grade ← "A"
}
ELSE
{
  IF (grade > 79)
  {
      grade ← "B"
  }
  ELSE
  {
    IF (grade < 69)
    {
        grade ← "C"
    }
    ELSE
    {
      IF (grade < 59)
      {
          grade ← "D"
      }
      ELSE
      {
          grade ← "F"
      }
    }
  }
}
```

45. The code below is a robot algorithm. Which diagram matches the code?

```
MOVE_FORWARD()
MOVE_FORWARD()
ROTATE_LEFT()
MOVE_FORWARD()
MOVE_FORWARD()
ROTATE_RIGHT()
MOVE_FORWARD()
ROTATE_LEFT()
```

(A)

(B)

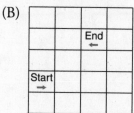

(C)

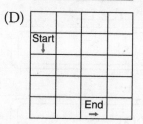

(D)

46. What benefit does an API provide?

(A) It allows programmers to share their code via the API for others to test.

(B) It connects software components providing prewritten and tested code available for use.

(C) It provides algorithms for difficult code to be reviewed.

(D) It provides documentation programmers can use for their programs rather than creating their own.

47. What is the value of *x* after the code below runs?

```
PROCEDURE calcTemp (temp)
{
    newTemp ← (5/9 * (temp - 32))
    RETURN (newTemp)
}
x ← calcTemp(50)
```

(A) −10

(B) 10

(C) 4

(D) −4

48. What is the value of *y* after the following statements?

```
x ← 10
x ← x + 4
y ← x MOD 3
```

(A) 0

(B) 2

(C) 3

(D) 4

49. What is displayed after the following code runs?

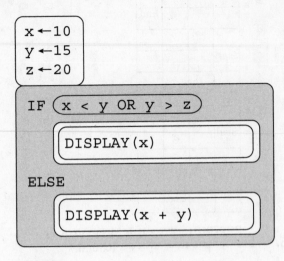

```
x ← 10
y ← 15
z ← 20

IF (x < y OR y > z)
    DISPLAY(x)
ELSE
    DISPLAY(x + y)
```

(A) 10
(B) 15
(C) 20
(D) 25

50. Which of the following two algorithms produces the sum of the elements in the list? Assume the list is initialized and is not empty.

Block 1
```
x   ← 1
sum ← 0
REPEAT (LENGTH(list)) TIMES
{
    sum ← sum + x
    x ← x + 1
}
DISPLAY("The total is: ", sum)
```

Block 2
```
x   ← LENGTH(list)
sum ← 0
REPEAT x TIMES
{
    sum ← sum + list[x]
    x ← x - 1
}
DISPLAY("The total is: ", sum)
```

(A) Block 1
(B) Block 2
(C) Blocks 1 and 2
(D) Neither Block 1 nor 2

GO ON TO THE NEXT PAGE

51. What will the following code produce?

```
x ← 5
y ← x
x ← y + 5

REPEAT UNTIL (x > y)
{
    DISPLAY ("Hello World!")
}
```

A. "Hello World!" will be printed multiple times.
B. The code inside the REPEAT UNTIL loop never executes.
C. The REPEAT UNTIL loop never ends, creating an infinite loop.
D. The program will have a runtime error.

52. What will the code display?

```
snacks ← ["popcorn", "candy", "grapes", "apples"]
FOR EACH snack IN snacks
{
    IF NOT(snack = "banana")
    {
        APPEND(snacks, "banana")
    }
    DISPLAY (snack)
}
```

(A) popcorn, candy, grapes, apples, banana
(B) popcorn, candy, grapes, apples, banana, banana
(C) popcorn, candy, grapes, apples, banana, banana, banana
(D) popcorn, candy, grapes, apples, banana, banana, banana, banana

53. What is the value of snacks after the following code is run?

```
snacks ← ["donut", "french fries", "candy", "popcorn", "candy", "grapes", "apples", "banana"]
j ← 1
REPEAT UNTIL (j = 5)
{
    snacks[j] ← [j + 4]
    j ← j + 1
}
```

(A) 5, 6, 7, 8, candy, grapes, apples, banana
(B) popcorn, candy, grapes, apples, popcorn, candy, grapes, apples
(C) popcorn, popcorn, popcorn, popcorn, candy, grapes, apples, banana
(D) popcorn, popcorn, popcorn, popcorn, popcorn, popcorn, popcorn, popcorn

54. If a procedure accepts two strings as parameters and returns a combined string, what is the procedure doing?

```
The procedure call:
mysteryProcedure("Good luck", " on the AP exam!")

will return: "Good luck on the AP exam!"
```

(A) Appending
(B) Attaching
(C) Bonding
(D) Concatenating

55. What is an iterative software development process designed to do?

(A) Produce better software with a proven process
(B) Shorten the time of developing software by beginning to code while the requirements are being determined
(C) Eliminate the testing step by using only APIs
(D) Develop it right the first time through the iterative process

56. Suppose your program needs to process all values less than a specified value, but your actual test results do not match the expected test results. What is NOT a debugging technique you can use to identify the problem?

(A) Hand-tracing the code

(B) Adding DISPLAY statements to see values in variables at different points in your program

(C) Using a visualizer to view the code as it is executing

(D) Rerunning the code to verify the results

57. Which set of code will move the robot from start to stop and end facing the correct direction? The robot may not move into gray blocks.

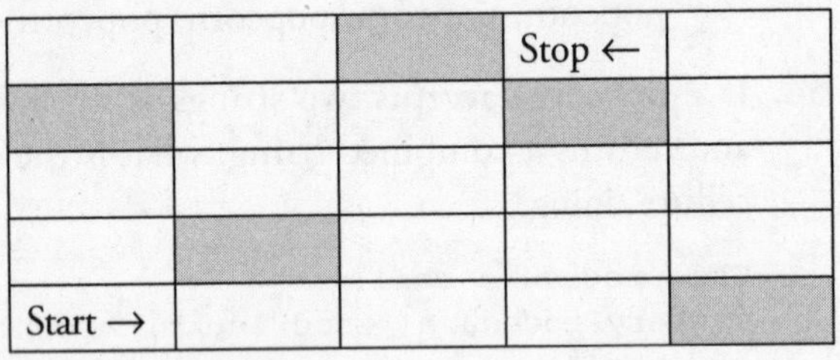

			Stop ←	
Start →				

(A)
```
MOVE_FORWARD(3)
ROTATE_LEFT()
MOVE_FORWARD()
ROTATE_RIGHT()
MOVE_FORWARD()
ROTATE_LEFT()
MOVE_FORWARD(3)
ROTATE_LEFT()
MOVE_FORWARD()
```

(B)
```
MOVE_FORWARD(4)
ROTATE_LEFT()
MOVE_FORWARD(4)
ROTATE_LEFT()
MOVE_FORWARD()
```

(C)
```
MOVE_FORWARD()
ROTATE_LEFT()
MOVE_FORWARD(4)
ROTATE_RIGHT()
MOVE_FORWARD(2)
```

(D)
```
MOVE_FORWARD(3)
ROTATE_RIGHT()
MOVE_FORWARD()
ROTATE_LEFT()
MOVE_FORWARD()
ROTATE_RIGHT()
MOVE_FORWARD(3)
ROTATE_RIGHT()
MOVE_FORWARD()
```

GO ON TO THE NEXT PAGE

Questions 58–62 are related to this passage and chart.

There is an app to help farmers know when fruit is ready to harvest. You are planning to use this and modify it to create a new app to help grocery shoppers know how ripe fruit in the grocery store is. You also plan to let consumers enter any food allergies into the app.

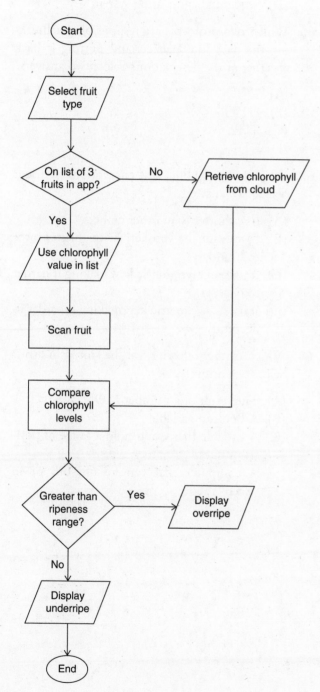

58. What input data is most likely to be needed for the app to work?

(A) Chlorophyll levels of fruit
(B) Image of fruit ripeness levels based on color
(C) Date of harvesting and average number of days to get to store shelf
(D) Scheduled delivery dates of fruit at local grocery stores

59. Which of the following is the most likely potential impact on the economy due to widespread use of the app?

(A) People are less likely to eat overripe fruit, losing the health benefits and incurring higher medical costs.
(B) More food will go to waste if people do not purchase it based on the app results.
(C) As information spreads about which grocery chain has the freshest fruit, other chains will suffer as people move their shopping to the stores with fresher fruit. People could lose their jobs as a result.
(D) Medical costs will go down as people are eating more fruit.

60. Which of the following is the most likely potential benefit of the app?

(A) Less likelihood of people squeezing fruit in the store to test its ripeness and potentially bruising it
(B) Fewer germs left on fruit in the stores from people handling it
(C) Fruit lasting longer in homes and more likely to be eaten, increasing people's general healthiness
(D) Less money wasted with fruit that quickly goes bad

GO ON TO THE NEXT PAGE

61. What is the most likely storage concern of the app?

    (A) If fruit comparison data is stored in the cloud, you must have a strong enough signal to connect to the Internet for the app to work.
    (B) There are so many different types of fruit, the app cannot store them all.
    (C) Maintaining a record of the stores with the freshest fruits will take a lot of storage space, slowing down the app.
    (D) Having to store data in the cloud and retrieving fruit ripeness values stored in the cloud will make the app too slow for most consumers.

62. What process does the app need to perform?

    (A) Measure the size of the piece of fruit
    (B) Record grocery store name and date
    (C) Identify the fruit for correct comparisons
    (D) Compare chlorophyll levels in the piece of fruit to a value representing chlorophyll levels in an average ripe piece of that fruit

63. Cloud-based data storage is best when what conditions are true of those working with the data? Select two answers.

    (A) They are in a secured location.
    (B) They are in separate locations.
    (C) They are dealing with sensitive data.
    (D) They have limited storage at their location.

64. Computers have enabled new innovations in a variety of industries. In the entertainment business, it has become much easier to purchase and share new music. What concern has been raised as a result? Select two answers.

    (A) People are modifying other people's content and claiming the Creative Commons licensing allows it.
    (B) People are being discovered for their music because others are posting it to music-sharing sites.
    (C) People are sharing content without the author/owner's permission.
    (D) Artists are adding their music to streaming services with Creative Commons licensing, bypassing record companies.

65. An organization collects massive amounts of data, more than they can currently process. What options should they consider using to be able to process their data to gain insights? Select two answers.

    (A) Centralized computing system
    (B) Distributed computing system
    (C) Parallel computing system
    (D) Sequential computing system

66. Which two protocols are responsible for breaking the data into packets and putting it back together at the destination? Select two answers.

    (A) TCP
    (B) HTTP
    (C) FTP
    (D) UDP

67. Why should public key encryption be used? Select two answers.

    (A) It is shorter than other ciphers.
    (B) It cannot be broken with brute force techniques.
    (C) It uses an asymmetric key, making it harder to decrypt.
    (D) It uses a symmetric key, making it harder to decrypt.

68. Which of the following can be stored in a bit? Select two answers.

    (A) The result of a number MOD 2
    (B) A Boolean variable
    (C) A variable that could hold a range of positive values
    (D) A computer that can be on, off, or in "sleep" mode

GO ON TO THE NEXT PAGE

69. A company is trying to separate information it has into data and metadata. Which of the following would be considered metadata about documents? Select two answers.

(A) Author of document
(B) File size
(C) Internal page number
(D) Table of Contents

70. What is important to remember when converting a music file from analog data to digital data? Select two answers.

(A) Analog data is a set of continuous values.
(B) Copies of analog data files are more precise.
(C) A higher sampling rate will result in a more accurate digital version.
(D) The samples are compressed to create a smaller digital file.

STOP. End of Exam.

› Answers and Explanations

If further review is needed, the Big Idea where information can be found about the question is included at the end of each answer's explanation.

1. **A**—The huge lottery winnings added to your previous balance were more than the largest integer the bank account could accommodate, so an overflow error occurred. Big Idea 2: Data

2. **B**—Real numbers (e.g., numbers with fractions) are stored imprecisely in the computer's memory and can cause rounding errors. This is why they should not be used for monetary transactions. The clerk owes you a nickel. Big Idea 2: Data

3. **B**—Take the binary number and create a table of the powers of 2, starting with 2^0 in the rightmost position. For every column there is a 1 in the binary number, add the corresponding value of 2^x. Big Idea 2: Data

2^7	2^6	2^5	2^4	2^3	2^2	2^1	2^0
128	64	32	16	8	4	2	1
1	0	0	1	1	0	1	1

$128 + 16 + 8 + 2 + 1 = 155_{10}$

4. **C**—You need to convert the number for each color from binary to decimal:

01010000 for red, 11001000 for green, 01111000 for blue.

Red

2^7	2^6	2^5	2^4	2^3	2^2	2^1	2^0
128	64	32	16	8	4	2	1
0	1	0	1	0	0	0	0

$64 + 16 = 80_{10}$

Green

2^7	2^6	2^5	2^4	2^3	2^2	2^1	2^0
128	64	32	16	8	4	2	1
1	1	0	0	1	0	0	0

$128 + 64 + 8 = 200_{10}$

Blue

2^7	2^6	2^5	2^4	2^3	2^2	2^1	2^0
128	64	32	16	8	4	2	1
0	1	1	1	1	0	0	0

$64 + 32 + 16 + 8 = 120_{10}$

The result is (80, 200, 120), which is option C. Big Idea 2: Data

5. **B**—Multifactor authentication uses two methods to verify someone is who they say they are. Often a pass code or token is sent via text to the phone number or e-mail linked with the account. The code must be typed in by the customer to gain access to the account. Big Idea 5: Impact of Computing

6. **C**—Using well-named procedures and variable names makes code more readable and understandable. The original program requirements would not be useful, as it may not have been updated as the program was modified. Similarly, a video may help to explain the original programmer's thought process, but it may be out-of-date and not very useful for understanding the code they wrote. Documenting the development process will not be useful to someone changing the code. Big Idea 3: Algorithms and Programming

7. **B**—If the song the user typed is in the playlist, it will be played and a Boolean variable marked as true for ownership of the song. Otherwise, after checking all songs in the playlist, if it is not already there, the song will be added to the playlist and then played. Big Idea 3: Algorithms and Programming

8. **C**—When calling the procedure, play, the value is passed to it using an argument. The value in the argument is then loaded into the parameter. It is a parameter when used internally in the procedure. Big Idea 3: Algorithms and Programming

9. **A**—Lower-level languages are written in code closer to machine language. These are more difficult to debug for most people because the code is less like our natural speaking language. Big Idea 3: Algorithms and Programming

10. **A**—A benefit of models and simulations is the ability to modify a variable and retest quickly. Running the test with the same values does not help the analysis. Running one test and then stopping is not an effective use of a simulation. Unless an error was identified, which it was not in this scenario, then rewriting the code will not determine if the glasses are effective to safely protect people's eyes. Big Idea 3: Algorithms and Programming

11. **D**—If the car causes an accident in the simulation, that is not a test of the sensor itself. Ensuring the sensor can read multiple objects and that it does not give a false reading when there are no objects plus ensuring the boundary conditions around the 3 foot limit are all good conditions to test. Big Idea 3: Algorithms and Programming

12. **B**—The only time an AND condition is true is when both conditions are true. An OR condition is true when either or both conditions are true. Evaluating the conditions provided, only i and iii are true. Big Idea 3: Algorithms and Programming

13. **C**—The only time an AND condition is true is when A and B are both true. An OR condition is true when either or both conditions are true. Evaluating the conditions in the diagram will produce the results in answer C. Big Idea 3: Algorithms and Programming

14. **D**—Everything is data about the nest and the eagles using the nest except the number of frames the camera can record, which is data about the data, or metadata. Big Idea 2: Data

15. **A**—Only the lossless compression technique will allow the original uncompressed photo to be restored. Big Idea 2: Data

16. **A**—A project that is good for citizen scientists would be one where specialized equipment, such as a telescope or fish finder, would not be required and that can be based on facts versus personal opinion. Counting trees would be the best use in this example. Big Idea 5: Impact of Computing

17. **B**—Cleaning involves finding and either correcting or eliminating incomplete records. It also involves standardizing the data for the analysis to be performed. It could include filtering out some complete and correct data that is not needed for the planned analysis. Big Idea 2: Data

18. **B**—The survey results will show if students changed their mind in either direction or maintained their viewpoint about computer science if they felt the teacher communicated effectively and if they felt they gave their best effort. It will not show if students plan to major in computer science. Big Idea 2: Data

19. **C**—The data in the table shows that drivers in the 26–50 age bracket have the least number of accidents. The data cannot tell us when the drivers had an accident. Big Idea 2: Data

20. **A**—Smaller datasets may not have enough data to identify patterns or true trends. If a trend is noticed in a smaller dataset, processing larger datasets may not be necessary. The analysis of a large dataset will not identify metadata issues, nor determine when hardware purchases should be made. Big Idea 2: Data

21. **B**—The World Wide Web is an application that uses HTTP to share documents, videos, images, and other files among devices connected to the Internet. Big Idea 4: Computing Systems and Networks

22. **A**—The redundancy designed into the Internet means data can be sent via different paths to reach its destination. Big Idea 4: Computing Systems and Networks

23. **A**—The speedup for a parallel model is the sequential time/parallel time. In this case, it is 25 / 10 = 2.5. Big Idea 4: Computing Systems and Networks

24. **B**—Bandwidth measures the amount of data that can be transmitted in a specified amount of time. Therefore, knowing how much data needs to be downloaded on a regular basis is a key measurement, as people generally download far more than they upload. Big Idea 4: Computing Systems and Networks

25. **C**—Certificate authorities, or CAs, issue digital certificates to customers that confirm ownership of their encrypted keys with secure Internet communications. This enables us to have online shopping, among other secure online transactions. Big Idea 5: Impact of Computing

26. **B**—This is a keylogger file. Your typing keystrokes are recorded and then uploaded to a server where the keylogger is programmed to report. The data is then analyzed, searching for credit card numbers, passwords, or other personal and confidential information. Big Idea 5: Impact of Computing

27. **B**—The facial recognition software needs more examples from a wider population of faces as input to better "learn" to recognize and compare facial features. Big Idea 5: Impact of Computing

28. **A**—The file was compressed using a lossy algorithm. The lossy algorithm cannot restore the file to its original size. You get more compression resulting in a smaller file, but some of the data is lost and a full file restoration is not possible. Big Idea 2: Data

29. **D**—Packets are created at the sending end of the transmission and reassembled at the final destination. Big Idea 4: Computing Systems and Networks

30. **C**—TCP creates packets and passes control of them to IP, which routes them to their final destination. TCP then reassembles the packets to display. Big Idea 4: Computing Systems and Networks

31. **C**—Phishing attacks attempt to get users to type in personal information such as passwords or account information on websites that look just like the real organization's website. Big Idea 5: Impact of Computing

32. **C**—Public key encryption models are the most secure. No key needs to be shared to encrypt or decrypt the file. The public key is used to encrypt, and the receiver's private key is used to decrypt. Big Idea 5: Impact of Computing

33. **D**—One of many benefits is that all organizations can access the data, making it easier for new businesses to have and analyze data the established ones may have. Big Idea 5: Impact of Computing

34. **B**—This is the only option that will capture the smallest number in a list. Big Idea 3: Algorithms and Programming

35. **C**—Booleans can only be true or false, and C is the only option that is a comparison that can evaluate to true or false. Answers A and B assign values to variables and option D would produce an error. Big Idea 3: Algorithms and Programming

36. **A**—The flow of procedures called indicates a game is being played due to the descriptive names they were assigned. The procedure names and parameters are all correct. Big Idea 3: Algorithms and Programming

37. **D**—You cannot have an ELSE statement without an IF statement. Big Idea 3: Algorithms and Programming

38. B—The first algorithm sorts by name but then uses a binary search using phone number. This may not return correct results. Therefore, option II using a linear search on a contact list sorted by area code will return the correct results and is more effective. Big Idea 3: Algorithms and Programming

39. C—A heuristic is finding a good approximate solution when the actual solution would take too long or too many resources. A computer checking all possible chess moves drastically slows the processing down, so a heuristic solution will improve the speed and the overall game experience for the player. Big Idea 3: Algorithms and Programming

40. C—This bias occurred in preparing the data by selecting active-loan status as an attribute to consider. Big Idea 5: Impact of Computing

41. C—Since place is 5, the length of the snacks list, snacks[place], refers to the element at the 5th position of the list, which is "grapes." List elements can be accessed using a constant, such as list[2], or a variable as in this example, list[place]. Big Idea 3: Algorithms and Programming

42. A—Block 1 produces correct results based on the temperature. Block 2 counts all temperatures ≤ 80 to be a perfectDay, rather than separating them by temperature. The condition in the IF statement is set up in the wrong order. Big Idea 3: Algorithms and Programming

43. A—Algorithms with polynomial (cubed, squared, linear) efficiency will run small and large datasets in a reasonable amount of time. Big Idea 3: Algorithms and Programming

44. D—A causes any grade higher than 59 to be assigned the letter grade D. B uses greater than rather than less than in the condition to evaluate. C will be off by one. D is correct. Big Idea 3: Algorithms and Programming

45. D—Only option D ends up in the correct block facing in the correct direction. Remember that ROTATE commands do not move the robot forward a block. They only change the direction in the current block the robot is in. Big Idea 3: Algorithms and Programming

46. B—An API (Application Programming Interface) connects software modules, making working programs such as Google Maps available for use in other programs. Big Idea 3: Algorithms and Programming

47. B—The procedure calcTemp is called with 50 as the argument. 50 is then stored in the parameter temp. Follow the order of operations in the formula to determine the answer the code will return. Big Idea 3: Algorithms and Programming

48. B—MOD calculations provide the remainder when the two numbers are divided. x is assigned the value 10 in the first line of code. In the second line, 4 is added to the current value of x, which is 10, and the new value of 14 is stored back in x. Then the line x MOD 3 takes the current value of x, divides by 3, and returns ONLY the remainder. 14 divided by 3 is 4 with a remainder of 2. The answer to 14 MOD 3 is 2. Big Idea 3: Algorithms and Programming

49. A—An OR condition only needs one of the conditions to be true for the overall condition to be true. Since 10 is less than 15, the value of x will be displayed. Big Idea 3: Algorithms and Programming

50. B—Block 1 calculates the total of the list indices. Block 2 calculates the sum of the elements of the list. Watch for questions like these on the exam. Big Idea 3: Algorithms and Programming

51. B—Code inside the loop will never run because 10 > 5 before the loop runs the first time. Big Idea 3: Algorithms and Programming

52. D—Each time the value in the list is not "banana," the word "banana" is appended to the end of the list. Big Idea 3: Algorithms and Programming

53. A—The value at snacks[j] is replaced by number [j + 4], which is 1 + 4 or 5, then 2 + 4 or 6, then 3 + 4 or 7, then 4 + 4 or 8 as j iterates through the values 1–4. Big Idea 3: Algorithms and Programming

54. D—The procedure concatenates or glues the strings together. Big Idea 3: Algorithms and Programming

55. A—None of the other options will produce better code or even code that works. The iterative development process improves the code in each iteration based on testing and feedback. This process helps ensure working code is produced that meets the requirements. Big Idea 1: Creative Development

56. D—Rerunning the code as it is does not aid in the debugging process. The other three options will provide information to help isolate where the error occurs. Watch for questions that include NOT. Big Idea 1: Creative Development

57. A—This option is correct. The arrow is in the correct square and facing in the correct direction. The ROTATE commands only change the direction in the current block. They do NOT move the robot forward. Big Idea 3: Algorithms and Programming

58. A—As shown in the flowchart, the app uses the chlorophyll levels from the plant to determine ripeness. This level is needed as input. The image of ripe fruit will not be useful for comparing chlorophyll levels. The date of harvesting and days to get to the store shelf would be difficult to track for each fruit shipment, and it's unlikely the app could access such data. The delivery dates at local stores are nice to know from a personal level but does not provide data this app needs to function.

59. B—More food could go to waste if people using the app do not purchase available fruit because they might not eat it in time. It's also possible that once people get it home, they may throw away fruit that is still good to eat. People are already not going to eat fruit that has gone bad, so option A is not significant. Based on deliveries, the grocery store with the freshest fruit is likely to change daily, so this is a minimal impact, if any. There are many medical conditions that eating fruit will not help, so it is not likely there will be a huge impact from option D.

60. C—People will hopefully stop handling the fruit and inadvertently bruising it and leaving germs, but that's not likely since habits are hard to change. Less money may be wasted, but the most likely benefit is C. People can purchase fruit that is not quite ripe and eat it over several days as it ripens.

61. B—There are many types of fruit, and smart devices have a limited amount of space for storing data. You can see in the chart that the app only stores 3 fruit values that the user can chose. The remaining fruit comparison data is retrieved from the cloud as needed. Users will need Internet access if they want to compare a fruit other that the 3 stored locally on the device, but that is not a storage issue. The flowchart does not show the app recording stores with the freshest fruit, so that is not a concern for the app. Option D is possible, but B is the most likely storage issue.

62. D—The app will need to take the chlorophyll level measurement as input, and the processing will involve comparing the measured level to the average chlorophyll level for a ripe piece of fruit. A is the measurement of the size, not the amount of chlorophyll. The grocery store name and date is not relevant to the app's processing. The user will select the fruit as an input value that is used in the process, but that is not the process.

63. **B, D**—Cloud-based storage can be accessed from any location with an Internet connection and is a good solution for storage when local storage options are limited. Sensitive data should not be stored in the cloud. Big Idea 2: Data

64. **A, C**—Some people ignore the Creative Commons licensing guidelines and either take other people's intellectual property and modify it without permission or share it on other sites or with friends without the owner's permission. Big Idea 5: Impact of Computing

65. **B, C**—Both parallel and distributed computing systems can speed up the processing of the data the company collects by spreading out the processing among multiple devices and then combining the results. Big Idea 4: Computing Systems and Networks

66. **A, D**—TCP and UDP make the packets and put them back together. UDP does not send an acknowledgment while TCP does. Big Idea 4: Computing Systems and Networks

67. **B, C**—Public key encryption creates such long keys that brute force techniques are ineffective. The keys are asymmetric, meaning different keys are used to encrypt and decrypt the data. Big Idea 5: Impact of Computing

68. **A, B**—A bit can only hold two possible values, 0 and 1. Therefore, any data it holds can only be represented by these two values. Any number MOD 2 will produce 0 or 1, and Boolean values are either true or false. Big Idea 2: Data

69. **A, B**—The author of a document and the file size for the document are both pieces of metadata. They are about the document, rather than part of the document itself. Page numbers and the Table of Contents are content within the document, not metadata. Big Idea 2: Data

70. **A, C**—Analog data is a series of values that are connected in a smooth data line. The sampling rate determines how closely the digital version matches the analog version. A higher sampling rate will create more instances of data from the analog version to include in the digital version, thereby creating a version that is a closer match to the original analog one. Big Idea 2: Data

Analyzing Your Performance on Practice Exam 1

The exercise below will help you quickly and easily identify the chapters in Step 4 that you most need to review for the AP Computer Science Principles multiple-choice exam. Revise your study plan so that you prioritize the chapters with which you had the most difficulty.

Look at your answer sheet and mark all the questions you missed. Then shade in or mark an X in the boxes below that correspond to the question numbers that you missed. Review the concepts where you missed the most questions. Keep in mind the number of questions to expect from each section, spending more time on those that will appear the most. See Chapter 1 on "What You Need to Know About the AP Computer Science Principles Assessment" for those percentages.

Big Idea 1: Creative Development

55	56	58	62

Big Idea 2: Data

1	2	3	4	14	15	17	18
19	20	28	63	68	69	70	

Big Idea 3: Algorithms and Programming

6	7	8	9	10	11	12	13	34	35
36	37	38	39	41	42	43	44	45	46
47	48	49	50	51	52	53	54	57	

Big Idea 4: Computing Systems and Networks

21	22	23	24	29	30
59	60	61	65	66	

Big Idea 5: Impact of Computing

5	16	25	26	27	31	32
33	40	59	60	61	64	67

AP Computer Science Principles
Practice Exam 2

Multiple-Choice Questions
ANSWER SHEET

1 (A) (B) (C) (D)	26 (A) (B) (C) (D)	51 (A) (B) (C) (D)
2 (A) (B) (C) (D)	27 (A) (B) (C) (D)	52 (A) (B) (C) (D)
3 (A) (B) (C) (D)	28 (A) (B) (C) (D)	53 (A) (B) (C) (D)
4 (A) (B) (C) (D)	29 (A) (B) (C) (D)	54 (A) (B) (C) (D)
5 (A) (B) (C) (D)	30 (A) (B) (C) (D)	55 (A) (B) (C) (D)
6 (A) (B) (C) (D)	31 (A) (B) (C) (D)	56 (A) (B) (C) (D)
7 (A) (B) (C) (D)	32 (A) (B) (C) (D)	57 (A) (B) (C) (D)
8 (A) (B) (C) (D)	33 (A) (B) (C) (D)	58 (A) (B) (C) (D)
9 (A) (B) (C) (D)	34 (A) (B) (C) (D)	59 (A) (B) (C) (D)
10 (A) (B) (C) (D)	35 (A) (B) (C) (D)	60 (A) (B) (C) (D)
11 (A) (B) (C) (D)	36 (A) (B) (C) (D)	61 (A) (B) (C) (D)
12 (A) (B) (C) (D)	37 (A) (B) (C) (D)	62 (A) (B) (C) (D)
13 (A) (B) (C) (D)	38 (A) (B) (C) (D)	63 (A) (B) (C) (D)
14 (A) (B) (C) (D)	39 (A) (B) (C) (D)	64 (A) (B) (C) (D)
15 (A) (B) (C) (D)	40 (A) (B) (C) (D)	65 (A) (B) (C) (D)
16 (A) (B) (C) (D)	41 (A) (B) (C) (D)	66 (A) (B) (C) (D)
17 (A) (B) (C) (D)	42 (A) (B) (C) (D)	67 (A) (B) (C) (D)
18 (A) (B) (C) (D)	43 (A) (B) (C) (D)	68 (A) (B) (C) (D)
19 (A) (B) (C) (D)	44 (A) (B) (C) (D)	69 (A) (B) (C) (D)
20 (A) (B) (C) (D)	45 (A) (B) (C) (D)	70 (A) (B) (C) (D)
21 (A) (B) (C) (D)	46 (A) (B) (C) (D)	
22 (A) (B) (C) (D)	47 (A) (B) (C) (D)	
23 (A) (B) (C) (D)	48 (A) (B) (C) (D)	
24 (A) (B) (C) (D)	49 (A) (B) (C) (D)	
25 (A) (B) (C) (D)	50 (A) (B) (C) (D)	

AP Computer Science Principles
Practice Exam 2

Multiple-Choice Questions

Time: 2 hours
Number of questions: 70
The multiple-choice questions represent 70% of your total score.

Directions: Choose the one best answer for each question. The last eight questions of the test have two correct answers; for these, you will be instructed to choose two answer choices.

Tear out the answer sheet on the previous page and grid in your answers using a pencil. Consider how much time you have left before spending too much time on any one problem.

AP Computer Science Principles Exam Reference Sheet

On the AP Computer Science Principles exam, you will be given a reference sheet to use while you're taking the multiple-choice test. A copy of this six-page reference sheet is included in the Appendix of this book (reprinted by permission from the College Board).

To make taking this practice test like taking the actual exam, you should tear out the reference sheet so you can easily refer to it while taking the test. Save these reference pages since you'll need to use them when you take AP Computer Science Principles Practice Exam 1.

If you tore out the pages earlier and have lost them, the reference sheet is also available near the end of the PDF publication "AP Computer Science Principles Student Handouts" on the College Board website. Here is the URL:

https://apcentral.collegeboard.org/pdf/ap-csp-student-task-directions
   .pdf?course=ap-computer-science-principles

GO ON TO THE NEXT PAGE

1. When running a program that counts the number of records in a large dataset, you receive an error on your computer screen, in binary format: 11110001.

   Convert the error message from binary to decimal to be able to look it up.

   (A) 239—Invalid operation. Corrupt data caused the error.
   (B) 240—Decimal numbers are stored imprecisely in computers. A rounding error occurred.
   (C) 241—Overflow error. The object exceeded its maximum size. The dataset is too large to run on your computer.
   (D) 404—Error message not found.

2. You read in the news about an employee who took advantage of decimal numbers used with currency exchanges to steal money. What is the most likely way the employee accomplished this?

   (A) The employee redirected the overflow amount when it occurred and deposited it in his account.
   (B) The employee took advantage of rounding and deposited the fractional amounts.
   (C) The amount is represented in binary and when the right-most bit was a 1, he replaced it with a 0 and deposited the difference.
   (D) The employee converted to euros and then back to U.S. dollars. The difference in the exchange rate was deposited into his account.

3. Saving your information from an online form to be able to autofill fields in future forms captures some of your Personally Identifiable Information (PII). This could be an example of

   (A) an ethical matter.
   (B) a legal problem.
   (C) a privacy concern.
   (D) a security issue.

4. What order should the following procedures be used in creating an app to reserve a study room in the library?

   - checkAvail()—checks the availability of the time requested since multiple people can use the app at the same time
   - recordResv()—records the room reservation
   - requestTime()—asks for a reservation time for the study room
   - timesAvail()—displays the times the room is available
   - updateTimes()—updates the times available to be displayed

   (A) requestTime(), recordResv(), timesAvail(), checkAvail(), updateTimes()
   (B) requestTime(), timesAvail(), recordResv(), updateTimes()
   (C) timesAvail(), requestTime(), checkAvail(), recordResv(), updateTimes()
   (D) requestTime(), recordResv(), updateTimes()

Questions 5 and 6 are based on the code below. Assume the variables and list already have values.

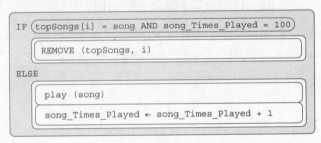

```
IF (topSongs[i] = song AND song_Times_Played = 100)
    REMOVE (topSongs, i)
ELSE
    play (song)
    song_Times_Played ← song_Times_Played + 1
```

5. What is the code doing?

   (A) Playing a song from the topSongs list
   (B) If a song is in topSongs, playing it, then removing it
   (C) Removing a song from topSongs if it has been played 100 times; otherwise playing the song and increasing the number of times played
   (D) This code will not run as written.

6. In the above code, after a song has been deleted from the list once, it keeps being removed after the user adds it back to the list. What is the best way to fix this error?

   (A) Change the program to allow songs to be played 1,000 times before being deleted.
   (B) Send the user a message to confirm they want to delete the song, stating it can never be added back to the list.
   (C) Write a new procedure to add a song back to the list if it had been on the list previously.
   (D) Set song_Times_Played back to 0 after removing a song.

7. Which of the following will evaluate to false?

   ```
     i. false AND (true OR NOT(false)
    ii. true AND (NOT(true AND false))
   iii. NOT (false OR (true OR false))
   ```

   (A) i and ii
   (B) ii and iii
   (C) i and iii
   (D) i, ii, and iii

8. Which of the following will evaluate to true?

   ```
     i. (true OR false) AND NOT(true OR
        NOT(false))
    ii. NOT (true AND
        (NOT(true OR false)))
   iii. (NOT(true) OR (true AND false))
   ```

   (A) i
   (B) ii
   (C) i and iii
   (D) ii and iii

9. A group that is watching sea turtle nests records data about their nests. Which of the following is metadata?

   (A) Daily temperature of the nest
   (B) Date the eggs were laid
   (C) Nest tag
   (D) Number of data fields tracked

10. The video the nest watchers took of the baby sea turtles making their way to the water is too large to send. How can the volunteers compress the video to get it to the scientists in full resolution?

    (A) Lossless compression will allow the scientists to see the video in full resolution.
    (B) Lossy compression will make the file small enough to send.
    (C) They should be combined for the best compression.
    (D) Any compression technique will be sufficient.

11. When analyzing a list of potential employees for promotion that an algorithm produced, the team noticed that there were no members of a particular group included. With further research, it was determined that part of the criteria that the algorithm used included prior employees in that position, which had few from that particular group. What is this is an example of?

    (A) Bias
    (B) Citizen science
    (C) Single criteria elimination
    (D) Targeted data

12. Which of the following techniques would be best to use to further analyze patterns that emerged during data mining?

    i. Classifying data to categorize it into distinct groups
    ii. Cleaning data to determine which data to include in the processing
    iii. Clustering data to separate data with similarities into subclasses
    iv. Filtering to set conditions so only records meeting the criteria are included

    (A) i, ii, iii
    (B) i, iii, iv
    (C) i, ii, iv
    (D) i, ii, iii, iv

13. The data you are analyzing shows a surprising correlation between parking tickets and pizza orders. What should you do with this information?

    (A) Document the trend to share with management.
    (B) Perform additional data collection from new sources to verify the correlation.
    (C) Determine if the pizza order caused the parking ticket.
    (D) Determine if the parking ticket caused the pizza order.

14. A good business practice is to send a copy of data off-site in the event of a catastrophic event such as a fire at the organization's primary server location. How can organizations keep their data secure while transmitting and storing in an off-site location?

    (A) They should encrypt their data using public key encryption.
    (B) They should use a symmetric key encryption algorithm to protect their data.
    (C) They should only send nonsensitive data off-site.
    (D) They should make physical copies of their data and ship it to the off-site location weekly.

15. In putting together a team, the project manager wants to have members with different backgrounds, even if they are in nonrelated fields. What is the best reason for this idea?

    (A) Different experiences will help develop leaders on the team.
    (B) There will be support for the project from all areas that have team members involved.
    (C) The team members will ensure the project excels in their area of expertise.
    (D) Different perspectives will help develop a better product.

16. What should an organization with extra computers and large amounts of data that they are unable to process consider?

    (A) Utilizing a distributed computing model
    (B) Adding extra servers to their location to be available when needed
    (C) Limiting the amount of data collected to balance the available processor speed
    (D) Maintaining a sequential computing model

17. Which of the following will help organizations gain insights about their business?

    (A) Collecting and analyzing large amounts of data to identify patterns and trends they can use to their advantage
    (B) Separating large amounts of data into smaller datasets and analyzing those for faster results
    (C) Developing decryption data techniques to be able to drill down and analyze data the government posts online
    (D) Creating copies of company data to let each division do their own analysis without impacting others

18. How does data streaming on the Internet work?

    (A) Data is sent along the shortest path to reduce buffering.
    (B) Packets are created at the sender's end and reassembled at the receiver's end.
    (C) It uses HTML to share documents among users when requested through their web browsers.
    (D) It creates redundancy, so when part of the Internet is down, information can keep flowing.

GO ON TO THE NEXT PAGE

19. How do Internet packets travel to their destination?

    (A) Router to router based on the travelling salesman algorithm

    (B) Along the same path to stay in order

    (C) Timed to arrive at the destination in their correct order

    (D) Along a variety of different paths

20. What action does the Internet Protocol (IP) perform?

    (A) It ensures packets can be transmitted across different equipment used with the Internet.

    (B) It enforces the Internet's rules for website names.

    (C) It classifies the data into clusters used for Internet traffic analysis.

    (D) It measures the latency on the Internet to determine the fastest path to send the data.

21. You are writing code to count duplicates in an existing list. What code could replace <missing code> for the algorithm to work correctly? Assume all variables have been correctly initialized.

```
<listNums is a list of integers>
PROCEDURE countDups(listNums)
{
   index = 2
   numDuplicates = 0
   FOR EACH number in listNums
   {
      REPEAT UNTIL (index ≥
        LENGTH(listNums))
      {
         IF (<missing code>)
         {
         numDuplicates ←
           numDuplicates + 1
         }
         index ← index + 1
      }
   }
RETURN numDuplicates
}
```

    (A) listNums[index] > listNums[index − 1]

    (B) listNums[index] < number

    (C) listNums[index] = number

    (D) listNums[index] = listNums[index + 1]

22. What is bandwidth?

    (A) The amount of data that can be transmitted in a specified amount of time

    (B) The speed at which that data can be downloaded

    (C) The size of the cable that connects homes and businesses to the Internet

    (D) The amount of delay between requesting data and receiving it

23. How can consumers ensure that a website is not a phishing scam before making an Internet purchase?

    (A) Go to the website directly rather than clicking a link from an e-mail.

    (B) Call the company directly.

    (C) Use antivirus software and keep it up-to-date.

    (D) Use a firewall to block malware.

24. With regard to multifactor authentication methods, a security token texted to your cell phone is an example of which category?

    (A) Knowledge

    (B) Possession

    (C) Inherence

    (D) All of the above

25. Which of the following ensures you have a strong password?

    (A) You can remember it without writing it down

    (B) A string that includes special characters and uppercase and lowercase letters

    (C) It is at least 8 characters long

    (D) All of the above

26. Why is the Internet designed to be fault-tolerant?

    (A) So the system doesn't crash when people make typos in their web requests

    (B) So the Internet can keep running even when it has malware

    (C) So it can keep running when sections of it are not working

    (D) So as companies expand to new locations, IP conflicts can be resolved

GO ON TO THE NEXT PAGE

27. When analog data is converted to digital data,

    (A) the data match exactly.
    (B) the digital data is an approximation of the analog data.
    (C) the analog data approximates the digital data.
    (D) the digital data has more values than the analog data.

28. While crowdsourcing is often used to fund projects, what is another use in practice today?

    (A) Diagnosing medical conditions by asking if others have similar symptoms
    (B) Asking those who register with a company to evaluate new products
    (C) Lowering costs by using the crowd's computers during periods of activity
    (D) Matching people needing work with job openings

29. If data analysis identifies new patterns, what should a company do with the information?

    (A) Further analyze the data pattern identified to make strategic decisions.
    (B) Change the prices on their products to match the findings for increased sales.
    (C) Get their products to market faster to increase their profit.
    (D) Use it to place targeted ads with people who are repeat customers.

30. What value will the following code display? Assume all values are correctly initialized.

    num is a variable holding an integer value.

    ```
    DISPLAY (num MOD 10)
    ```

    (A) The value in the *ones* position
    (B) The value in the *tens* position
    (C) The current value in the variable *num*
    (D) The quotient of *num* divided by 10

31. Which code segment will correctly add a name to a team roster?

    Assume all variables and lists are appropriately initialized.

    Block 1
    ```
    x ← 1
    REPEAT UNTIL (x <= 0)
    {
        APPEND (roster, name)
        x ← x + 1
    }
    ```

    Block 2
    ```
    FOR EACH name IN roster
    {
        APPEND (roster, name)
        DISPLAY(name)
    }
    ```

    (A) Block 1
    (B) Block 2
    (C) Both Block 1 and Block 2
    (D) Neither Block 1 or Block 2

32. Which algorithm will determine if a number is even?

    (A)
    ```
    num ← INPUT( )
    IF (num MOD 2 = 0)
    {
        DISPLAY (num, " is even")
    }
    ```

    (B) Assume list is initialized with integers.
    ```
    FOR Each num IN list
    {
        IF (num / 2 = 0)
        {
            DISPLAY (num, " is even")
        }
    }
    ```

    (C)
    ```
    num ← INPUT( )
    IF ((num / 2) * num = num)
    {
        DISPLAY (num, " is even")
    }
    ```

    (D)
    ```
    num ← INPUT( )
    IF (NOT (num MOD 2 = 0))
    {
        DISPLAY( num, " is even")
    }
    ```

GO ON TO THE NEXT PAGE

33. Why is a binary search the most effective way to search a sorted dataset?

(A) The item searched for bubbles to the beginning of the dataset after one pass.
(B) It uses machine learning with each pass of the data to learn where the data is located in the file.
(C) It eliminates half the dataset with each iteration of the search.
(D) It merges sections of data to only have to search one section with each iteration.

Questions 34–38 are related to this passage and chart.

To help people who are expecting a package to be delivered while they are away from home, a new "open it yourself" app is being developed. The purpose is to give certain people and/or organizations a special code to key in to open and close your door.

Here is a chart with basic information:

Input	Processes	Output	API needed	Average delivery time with app	Average delivery time without app
request for garage door access code	generate random code	text message of unique code	garage door company to send open signal	2	1
	send code	text confirmation message to home owner	text message app		
	code expires after 90 seconds				

34. What input is needed for the application?

(A) An address
(B) Product description and dimensions
(C) Time of day
(D) A code requested by the delivery person

35. What is a security concern related to the data?

(A) Neighbors or people walking or driving past the house could see the delivery.
(B) Your data is accessible by companies in the cloud.
(C) The code is not encrypted.
(D) If there is a power outage, the garage door will stay up.

36. What output is provided?

(A) Signal to open door
(B) Alert text message to delivery company
(C) Unique code to delivery person
(D) All of the above

37. What is a most likely benefit?

(A) Packages are not left out so they are not vulnerable to "porch pirates."
(B) Weather will not ruin packages.
(C) More online sales result for everyone because safe delivery is ensured.
(D) A regular delivery person for a route ensures the process is done correctly.

38. What is an impact to society?

(A) More delivery drivers will be employed because these deliveries take longer.
(B) The economy will get a boost with more purchases due to safer deliveries.
(C) Most businesses will use or offer this service.
(D) Less theft will occur as businesses will have proof that a delivery was made, lowering overall costs for everyone.

GO ON TO THE NEXT PAGE

39. If a programmer tested the following code with the values indicated, would the program correctly calculate the average of the test scores?

Assume all variables and lists have been appropriately initialized.

```
FOR EACH score IN testScores
{
    IF score > 0
    {
        total ← total + score
    }
    count ← count + 1
}
DISPLAY ("The average score on
    the test was: ", total / count)
Test1 [100, 90, 80, 80, 85, 50, 0,
    85, 90]
Test2 [192, 85, 74, 100, 96, 88]
```

(A) Yes, the code works as it should for both test cases.
(B) No, the code does not average the test scores correctly for either test.
(C) No, the code only works for the Test1 scores.
(D) No, the code only works for the Test2 scores.

40. When should a heuristic algorithm be used?

(A) When a problem is unable to process in reasonable time but a "close enough" solution is acceptable
(B) When the data is not sorted and cannot be placed in the order needed
(C) When a problem is undecidable because not enough information is known
(D) When searching is needed but efficiency is a requirement

41. How many times do FOR EACH loops run with lists?

(A) Once
(B) Until the index for the list is 0
(C) For the LENGTH of the list
(D) Until the user types STOP

42. Which code below can replace the missing code to select data that is less than the targetValue and even? Assume all variables have been properly initialized.

```
IF  < missing code >
{
    DISPLAY ("Found it!")
}
```

(A) (num MOD 2 = 0) OR (targetValue < num)
(B) (targetValue > num) AND (targetValue MOD 2 = 0)
(C) (num MOD 2 = 0) AND (targetValue > num)
(D) (targetValue > num) OR (NOT(num MOD 2 > 0))

43. Which type(s) of statement is needed to find all records in a list that are positive?

(A) Sequential and iterative
(B) Selection and sequential
(C) Selection
(D) Iterative and selection

44. Grace and Ada write algorithms and test them with increasingly large datasets. Algorithm 1 is still running while Algorithm 2 completed before midnight. What can you determine about the algorithms?

(A) 1 has an exponential efficiency and 2 has a polynomial efficiency.
(B) 1 has a polynomial efficiency and 2 has an exponential efficiency.
(C) 1 is unsolvable and 2 is decidable.
(D) 1 is decidable and 2 is unsolvable.

45. Each of the following can make an algorithm more readable except:

(A) Well-named variables and procedures
(B) Consistent formatting within the code
(C) Procedures that have one purpose
(D) Minimizing the use of loops so the program flow will be clearer

46. For a block of code under an ELSE statement to run, the selection criteria result must be which of the following?

(A) Repetitive
(B) Compound
(C) True
(D) False

GO ON TO THE NEXT PAGE

47. Which set of pseudocode will correctly cause an alarm clock to chime at the correct time?

(A) Compare alarm time to current time
If the times are not equal, check a.m./p.m. indicator
If a.m./p.m. is equal, turn on alarm

(B) Compare alarm time to current time
If the times are equal, check a.m./p.m. indicator
If a.m./p.m. is equal, turn on alarm

(C) Compare alarm a.m./p.m. indicator to time a.m./p.m.
If not equal, compare alarm time to current time
If the times are equal, turn on alarm

(D) Compare alarm a.m./p.m. indicator to time a.m./p.m.
If not equal, compare alarm time to current time
If the times are not equal, turn on alarm

48. Which diagram matches the code below?

```
MOVE_FORWARD(2)
ROTATE_LEFT(3)
MOVE_FORWARD(3)
ROTATE_RIGHT(1)
MOVE_FORWARD(1)
ROTATE_LEFT(3)
MOVE_FORWARD(1)
ROTATE_RIGHT(3)
```

A.   B.

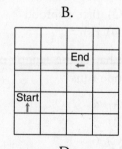

C.   D.

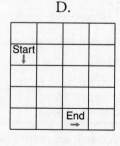

49. You need to swap the first and last values in a list. Which option produces the correct process?

(A) ```
list[1] ← list[LENGTH]
list[LENGTH] ← list[1]
```

(B) ```
tempValue ← list[LENGTH]
list[1] ← tempValue
list[LENGTH] ← list[1]
```

(C) ```
tempValue ← list[LENGTH]
list[LENGTH] ← list[1]
list[1] ← tempValue
```

(D) ```
tempValue ← list[LENGTH]
list[1] ← tempValue
list[LENGTH] ← list[tempValue]
```

50. What is the value of carChk after the code below runs?

```
PROCEDURE carMaint (miles)
{
   checkUp ← false
   IF (miles ≥ 4999)
   {
        checkUp ← true
   }
   RETURN (checkUp)
}

carChk ← carMaint(4999)
```

(A) False
(B) True
(C) 5000
(D) 4999

51. Which of the following places the numbers in ascending order?

  i.   01011110
  ii. 01011101
  iii. 92

(A) i, ii, iii
(B) i, iii, ii
(C) ii, iii, i
(D) iii, ii, i

GO ON TO THE NEXT PAGE

52. Will the code run as expected to dispense items purchased in a vending machine?

```
DISPLAY("Please insert money and make
  a selection")

REPEAT UNTIL (amtPaid ≥ cost)
{
    amtPaid ← INPUT( )
    DISPLAY("Please enter $ ", cost -
      amtPaid, "to make your purchase")
    amtPaid ← amtPaid + INPUT( )
}

IF (amtPaid > cost)
{
    DISPLAY ("Your change
      is $ ", (cost - amtPaid))
    Dispense(item)
    Dispense(change)
}
ELSE
{
    Dispense(item)
}
DISPLAY("Enjoy your selection!")
```

(A) Yes, the code works as expected.
(B) The REPEAT UNTIL loop is an infinite loop.
(C) The calculation of the amount of change to return is incorrect.
(D) The > sign should be < in the IF statement.

53. What is displayed after the following code runs?

```
rate ← 10
hours ← 40
totalPay ← 0
overtimePay ← 0

IF ( hours > 40 )

    DISPLAY("You earned overtime pay.")

ELSE

    DISPLAY("Regular Pay = $", hours * rate)
```

(A) You earned overtime pay.
(B) Regular Pay = $40 * 10
(C) 400
(D) Regular Pay = $400

54. How many times does the following loop run?

```
numSold ← true
price ← x
REPEAT numSold TIMES
{
    sales ← numSold * price
    numSold ← numSold - 1
}
```

(A) The REPEAT loop will run 5 times.
(B) The REPEAT loop executes once and exits the loop after numSold's value changes.
(C) The REPEAT loop never ends, creating an infinite loop because numSold's value keeps changing.
(D) The program has an error and will not run.

Questions 55–57 refer to the following code.

```
count ← 1
pets ← ["dog", "dogfood", "cat",
  "catfood", "fish"]
FOR EACH animal IN pets
{
    IF (animal = "fish")
    {
        DISPLAY (animal)
        INSERT(pets, count, "fishfood")
    }
    count ← count + 1
}
```

55. What will the code display?

(A) dog, dogfood, cat, catfood, fish
(B) dog, dogfood, cat, catfood, fish, fishfood
(C) fish, fishfood
(D) fish

56. What is the length of the list "pets" after the code runs?

(A) 4
(B) 5
(C) 6
(D) 7

57. What is value of pets[3] after the following code is run?

```
INSERT (pets, 1, "horse")
INSERT (pets, 2, "carrots")
REMOVE (pets, 3)
```

(A) It is an empty field.
(B) dog
(C) dogfood
(D) cat

GO ON TO THE NEXT PAGE

58. What is this code doing? The list named *numbers* contains integers. Assume all variables are correctly initialized.

```
value1 ← 0
value2 ← 0
FOR EACH num in numbers
{
    value1← value1 + num
    value2 ← value2 + 1
}
value3 ← value1 / value2
```

(A) Calculating how many numbers are in the list

(B) Calculating the sum of all the values in the list

(C) Calculating the average of the values in the list

(D) Calculating the minimum value in the list

59. What should project teams do to produce a better software product?

(A) Break down the problem into manageable units.

(B) Code while requirements are being finalized to have more time for testing.

(C) Spend testing time only on the complicated sections.

(D) Not allow any changes from the user.

60. A soccer league tracks certain stats by team as seen in the table below. Which of the following CANNOT be determined by the data?

(A) If a team wins more often when the number of red cards is less than 1 per game

(B) If a team wins more when they were the home team

(C) If days where the temperature was 80°F were also rainy

(D) Team winning percentage

61. What is this block of code doing?

```
price ← p
numItems ← num
taxRate ← foodTax
amtPaid ← 20.00
inv ← currInv
amtOwe ← (price * numItems) * taxRate
IF (amtPaid ≥ amtOwe)
{
    change ← amtPaid - amtOwe
    inv ← inv - 1
}
ELSE
{
    DISPLAY("Please pay an
    additional $", amtOwe-amtPaid)
}
```

i. Calculates the tax rate for an item

ii. Calculates current inventory numbers

iii. Calculates the change owed the customer or if the customer needs to pay more for their purchase

(A) i and ii

(B) i and iii

(C) ii and iii

(D) i, ii, and iii

Team #	Wins	Losses	Average number of red cards per game	Game day temperature higher than 80°F	Rain day before a game	Home games won
55	22	12	0	17	10	19
42	11	23	1.5	13	15	4
37	19	15	0.5	14	17	12

GO ON TO THE NEXT PAGE

62. Which set of code will move the robot from start to stop? The robot may not use gray blocks.

				Start ↓
	Stop ↑			

(A)
```
MOVE_FORWARD(2)
ROTATE_RIGHT(1)
MOVE_FORWARD(4)
ROTATE_LEFT(1)
MOVE_FORWARD(2)
ROTATE_RIGHT(1)
MOVE_FORWARD(1)
ROTATE_LEFT(1)
```

(B)
```
MOVE_FORWARD(3)
ROTATE_LEFT(3)
MOVE_FORWARD(2)
ROTATE_LEFT(1)
MOVE_FORWARD(1)
ROTATE_LEFT(3)
MOVE_FORWARD(1)
ROTATE_LEFT(3)
```

(C)
```
MOVE_FORWARD(3)
ROTATE_RIGHT(3)
MOVE_FORWARD(2)
ROTATE_RIGHT(1)
MOVE_FORWARD(1)
ROTATE_RIGHT(3)
MOVE_FORWARD(1)
ROTATE_RIGHT(3)
```

(D)
```
MOVE_FORWARD(1)
MOVE_FORWARD(1)
ROTATE_RIGHT(1)
MOVE_FORWARD(1)
MOVE_FORWARD(1)
MOVE_FORWARD(1)
ROTATE_LEFT(1)
MOVE_FORWARD(1)
MOVE_FORWARD(1)
```

63. Which of the algorithms below will produce the same result? Select two answers.

(A) Processing a list from the beginning to the end and counting the number of elements that begin with the letter "a"

(B) Processing a list from the end to the beginning and counting the number of elements that begin with the letter "a"

(C) Processing the list with a merge search to group the elements that begin with "a" and then counting them

(D) Processing the list with a procedure to see if the element begins with the letter "a" and keeping count with a local variable

64. An alarm company records the number of times each door is opened and closed. The alarm cannot be set if a door is still open. How can the alarm company code this option in its software? Select two answers.

(A) If the door count multiplied by 2 gives an odd number, then the door is open.

(B) If door count MOD 2 = 1, then the door is open.

(C) If the number of times a door is opened does not equal the number of times it is closed, then the door is open.

(D) If the quotient of dividing the door count by two is an even number, then the door is open.

65. A simulation for a new app to allow students to place a lunch order by 11:00 a.m. to speed up the lunch line is being tested. What information will the simulation provide? Select two answers.

(A) If a new line at the pick-up station will cause a slowdown

(B) If students will use the app often enough to make it worth the cost of developing

(C) If the app will decrease the amount of wasted food

(D) If the app can speed up the lunch line

GO ON TO THE NEXT PAGE

66. If two people need to collaborate on a document but are in two different locations, what is the best solution? Select two answers.

 (A) One person should travel to the other person's location for better communication.
 (B) Assign a different person to work on the document that is located in the same place as one of the others.
 (C) Use a cloud-based service for the document so both can edit the current version of the document.
 (D) Hold video conferences for them to speak face-to-face to discuss the document.

67. Why are "citizen scientists" being used on projects? Select two answers.

 (A) They can record local data to be included in global databases.
 (B) They are paid minimum wage.
 (C) They can record data over a longer period of time.
 (D) Retired scientists can maintain involvement in their area of expertise.

68. Which items can be represented by two *binary* digits? Select two answers.

 (A) Pizza with 10 slices
 (B) Number of eyes humans have
 (C) Number of letters in the word "dog"
 (D) Number of donuts in a dozen

69. Which expressions are equivalent to: number ≤ 42 AND (grade ≥ 9)? Select two answers.

 (A) NOT (number > 42) AND (grade = 9 OR grade > 9)
 (B) (number < 43) AND (grade > 8)
 (C) (number < 42) AND (NOT (grade < 9)
 (D) (number > 43) AND (grade > 10)

70. What data structures provide the ability to code once and repeat multiple times in a program? Select two answers.

 (A) Selection statements
 (B) Sequential statements
 (C) Iterative statements
 (D) Procedures

STOP. End of Exam.

> Answers and Explanations

If further review is needed, the Big Idea where information can be found about the question is included at the end of each answer's explanation.

1. **C**—11110001 converts to 241. The error is that the number was larger than the computer could handle, resulting in an overflow error. Big Idea 2: Data

2. **B**—The way floating point numbers are stored can cause rounding errors. The employee sent the fractional part of numbers to the separate account, and it accumulated over time. For example, if the number was $1.988889, then $0.008889 could be sent to the extra account. Big Idea 2: Data

3. **C**—Storing personal information about you can be a privacy issue if the data is not protected. Additionally, the data could be sold without your knowledge. Big Idea 5: Impact of Computing

4. **C**—The program should display available times so people can see if the time they want is available. They can then request a time. The app should check to ensure the time has not already been taken since multiple people can use the app at the same time. Then the reservation can be recorded and the list of available times updated. Big Idea 3: Algorithms and Programming

5. **C**—If the song has already been played 100 times, it will be removed from the list topSongs. Otherwise, it will be played and the number of times it is played will increase by 1. Big Idea 3: Algorithms and Programming

6. **D**—The number of times the song has been played is still set to 100, so even after the user adds it back to the list, the next time it is played, both conditions in the IF statement will be true, and it will be removed again. Resetting it back to 0 after it has been removed from the list is the best way to resolve the problem. Big Idea 3: Algorithms and Programming

7. **C**—The first and third conditions evaluate to be false. The only time an OR condition is false is when both are false, and the NOT operator takes the opposite of the value, so true would become false and false would become true. Big Idea 3: Algorithms and Programming

8. **B**—Only the second condition evaluates to be true. Both values must be true with an AND to be true, and one or both need to be true with an OR for it to be true. Big Idea 3: Algorithms and Programming

9. **D**—Metadata is data about data, and the number of data fields volunteers track is about the data. The other fields are data about the sea turtle nests. Big Idea 2: Data

10. **A**—Only the lossless compression technique will allow the original uncompressed video to be restored for the scientists to review. Big Idea 2: Data

11. **A**—This is an example of unintended bias in the algorithm. By using prior experience in a position as criteria for future hiring, the data would have naturally excluded this group, leading the algorithm to also exclude them from future promotions. Big Idea 5: Impact of Computing

12. **D**—All of the methods can be used with further analysis. Big Idea 2: Data

13. **B**—A correlation identified in the data analysis may not show that a cause and effect relationship actually exists. Further research and data from new sources is needed to confirm if the relationship exists. Big Idea 2: Data

14. **A**—Sending transaction data off-site can present a security concern if the data is not encrypted. Public key encryption has not been broken and is the standard today. Big Idea 5: Impact of Computing

15. **D**—A team with diverse skills and backgrounds can deliver a better product in a collaborative environment. Big Idea 1: Creative Development

16. **A**—A distributed computing model uses multiple devices to run a program. This can greatly speed up the processing time for the data. Big Idea 4: Computing Systems and Networks

17. **A**—Smaller datasets may not have enough data to identify patterns or true trends. Big Idea 2: Data

18. **B**—The Internet has an end-to-end architecture because packets are created by breaking the information into smaller segments at one end (the sender's) and are reassembled at the other end (the receiver's). Big Idea 4: Computing Systems and Networks

19. **D**—Packets travel along many different paths to reach their final destination. They arrive out of order and are then reassembled at the destination. Big Idea 4: Computing Systems and Networks

20. **A**—Protocols are rules that are followed to ensure data can communicate across all equipment. Big Idea 4: Computing Systems and Networks

21. **C**—When the element at the current index position in the inner REPEAT UNTIL loop equals the value in the outer FOR EACH loop, then a duplicate exists and the counter should be incremented. Big Idea 3: Algorithms and Programming

22. **A**—Bandwidth measures the amount of data that can be transmitted in a specific amount of time. Therefore, knowing how much data needs to be downloaded on a regular basis is a key measurement. Big Idea 4: Computing Systems and Networks

23. **A**—Phishing scams can make a website look very realistic. To be sure you are at an authentic website, search to find the link yourself or type it into your browser rather than clicking on a link. Big Idea 5: Impact of Computing

24. **B**—Multifactor authentication usually requires two of three categories: *knowledge*—such as a password, *possession*—something they have, such as a unique security token, or *inherence*—something they are, used with fingerprint login. The security token texted to a cell phone is an example of *possession*. Big Idea 5: Impact of Computing

25. **D**—A good password should be easy to remember, contain uppercase and lowercase letters, contain symbols, and be at least 8 characters long. Big Idea 5: Impact of Computing

26. **C**—Fault tolerance means the Internet will continue to function and reroute packets when parts of it are down. Big Idea 4: Computing Systems and Networks

27. **B**—The digital data approximates the analog data by taking samples of the analog data at a specified rate based on the need. A higher sampling rate will more closely approximate the analog data. Big Idea 2: Data

28. **D**—Crowdsourcing is used in many ways and more are coming into use. Helping people find available jobs is one use. Big Idea 5: Impact of Computing

29. **A**—Companies should take the findings from the data-mining results and make strategic decisions to determine when and how to take advantage of the new information. The other decisions can be made based on current sales and projections and do not need data-mining techniques. Big Idea 2: Data

30. **A**—MOD provides the remainder after dividing. The remainder of a number after dividing by 10 will be the value in the *ones* column. Big Idea 3: Algorithms and Programming

31. **B**—Block 1 is an infinite loop. Block 2 will add the new name correctly. Big Idea 3: Algorithms and Programming

32. **A**—The MOD operator returns the remainder when two numbers are divided. If a number is divided by 2 and the remainder is zero, then it is an even number. Big Idea 3: Algorithms and Programming

33. **C**—The binary search is most efficient as a divide-and-conquer algorithm because half the data can be removed with each iteration of the search. The item can be found or determined that it is not in the dataset in a minimal number of passes. Big Idea 3: Algorithms and Programming

34. **D**—For the application to be able to open the garage door, a code specific to that delivery needs to be provided to the delivery person and entered into the app. The address and time of day are needed to schedule the delivery, but are not needed by the app. The product dimensions are needed for loading the truck efficiently, but the app does not need the information.

35. **B**—Having your data controlled by the app company is a security risk. You have no idea who has access to it and how safely it is maintained. For option A, anyone traveling past your home at the right time would know you had received a delivery. This is not an issue related to the app's use of data. Similarly, with D, if the garage door stayed open for any reason, it is not an issue with the app. Option C could be an issue if the code stayed active, but the table shows that it expires 90 seconds after it is entered.

36. **C**—The app sends output, first to the delivery person with the unique code. Then once the code is typed in, the app outputs an alert text message to the app owner. The app does not send a message to the delivery company, nor does it send the signal for the garage door to open.

37. **A**—The most likely benefit is that packages will remain safe. "Porch pirates" who take packages off people's doorstep will be thwarted! Depending on a location's overhang, the weather may not have ruined them previously, but this is not the most likely benefit. People may order online more often due to safe delivery, but this is not the most likely or measurable benefit. And let's hope the regular delivery person ensures the delivery is correct, following the algorithm, but this is not the best benefit of using the app.

38. **A**—The chart shows the average delivery time without the app and the amount of time it takes to make a delivery if using this app. It takes about twice as long to make the delivery using the app once the driver arrives at the location. Therefore, more delivery drivers will be hired to ensure timely delivery is still possible. While some people may purchase more online since they can get safe deliveries, this is difficult to measure whether it is related to the app or not. Maybe they just got a raise and have more income for purchases. More delivery businesses may offer the service as a result, but that is not a huge impact to society. There may be a lower theft rate, but it is not indicated in the data we have.

39. **D**—The code only includes test scores that are greater than 0. Test1 scores have a 0 that will not be included in the average, but it should. The IF statement should be removed to correctly calculate test averages in all cases. Big Idea 3: Algorithms and Programming

40. **A**—A heuristic is finding the best approximate solution when the actual solution is intractable due to current memory and/or space limitations. Big Idea 3: Algorithms and Programming

41. **C**—FOR EACH loops will run for each element in a list. Big Idea 3: Algorithms and Programming

42. **C**—To test if a number is even, you can use MOD with 2, and a remainder of 0 means it is even. Use less than "<" to determine if a number is less than another. Use AND for both conditions to be true to select the number. Be sure to use the correct variable, "num", to test the conditions. Big Idea 3: Algorithms and Programming

43. **D**—Iterative code will loop until every item in the list is checked, and a selection statement is needed to determine if a number is positive. Big Idea 3: Algorithms and Programming

44. **A**—Tractable algorithms run efficiently for large and small datasets and have a polynomial efficiency, while intractable algorithms cannot run efficiently for large datasets and have exponential efficiency. Big Idea 3: Algorithms and Programming

45. D—Readability is a feature of algorithms that are clear and easy to understand. Every feature except D helps others understand what its intended purpose is. Loops should be used to shorten the code, which makes it more readable. Big Idea 3: Algorithms and Programming

46. D—The selection criteria must be false for the code associated with an ELSE to run. Big Idea 3: Algorithms and Programming

47. B—Option B compares the time first, and if equal, it then checks the a.m./p.m. indicator. Big Idea 3: Algorithms and Programming

48. C—This diagram starts and ends in the correct block facing in the correct direction. Remember that rotating left three times is the same as a right turn, and rotating right three times is the same as a left turn. Big Idea 3: Algorithms and Programming

49. C—The temporary variable is assigned the value at the end of the list. Then the last element can be assigned the value in the first position. Finally, the first position in the list is assigned the value in the temporary variable. Big Idea 3: Algorithms and Programming

50. B—checkUp is set to true if miles ≥ 4999. Since miles is 4999, checkUp will be true. Big Idea 3: Algorithms and Programming

51. D—The binary number $01011101 = 93_{10}$, and the binary number $01011110 = 94_{10}$, so the numbers in ascending order go from iii, ii, i for 92, 93, 94. Big Idea 2: Data

52. C—The amount of change due calculates a negative number. The calculation should be amtPaid – cost rather than cost – amtPaid. Big Idea 3: Algorithms and Programming

53. D—The ELSE condition will run because hours is not greater than 40. Therefore, the program will display answer D. Big Idea 3: Algorithms and Programming

54. D—The criteria for the REPEAT loop is incorrect. It must be a constant or a variable holding an integer value, not a Boolean value. Big Idea 3: Algorithms and Programming

55. D—The only time the animal is displayed is when it is a fish. Big Idea 3: Algorithms and Programming

56. C—The length of the list, pets, is 6 as there are 6 elements in it. Big Idea 3: Algorithms and Programming

57. C—The INSERT command moves current values over a position each time.

The REMOVE command shifts list values to the left.

After these commands, pets[3] = dogfood. Big Idea 3: Algorithms and Programming

58. C—*value1* is storing the sum of all the values in the list. *value2* counts the number of items in the list. *value3* is the sum divided by the number of values, which provides the average value of all the elements in the list. Big Idea 3: Algorithms and Programming

59. A—None of the other options will produce better, or even working, code. Big Idea 1: Creative Development

60. C—The only information that cannot be determined from the table is if it rained on days that were 80°F or warmer. Big Idea 2: Data

61. C—The block of code calculates the current inventory, change owed, if any, and the additional amount to pay, if any. It does not calculate the tax rate. That is provided and used to calculate the total amount due. Big Idea 3: Algorithms and Programming

62. B—The code starts and stops in the correct block facing the correct direction. Remember that rotate blocks do not move forward. They rotate the direction within the current block. Big Idea 3: Algorithms and Programming

63. **A, B**—Processing a list from the beginning to the end or the end to the beginning with the same code in each to find and count the elements that start with an "a" will produce the same results. A merge search does not exist (but a merge sort does). The local variable that counts the words would not be available outside of the procedure. Big Idea 3: Algorithms and Programming

64. **B, C**—If one variable represents the number of door openings and closings, then modulus math, which gives the remainder after division, can determine if a number is even or odd. An odd number would mean a door is open. Option C uses two variables for the same door, one to count the number of times a door opened and the other to record the number of times it closed. If these are not the same, then a door is open and the alarm cannot be set. Big Idea 3: Algorithms and Programming

65. **A, D**—The simulation can show if the lunch line will speed up and if a new bottleneck will be created at the pick-up line. The simulation will not show how often the app will be used or if food will be wasted. Big Idea 3: Algorithms and Programming

66. **C, D**—Cloud-based storage can be accessed from any location with an Internet connection and is a good solution for storage when people are in different locations. Video conferences will help the collaboration effort. Big Idea 1: Creative Development

67. **A, C**—With training, "citizen scientists" can provide a wealth of data over longer periods of time and they could be anywhere in the world, creating more data from a variety of locations. Big Idea 5: Impact of Computing

68. **B, C**—Two binary digits can hold up to the decimal equivalent 3, so only the numbers 0, 1, 2, and 3 can be stored using two binary digits. Big Idea 2: Data

69. **A, B**—Both of these are different ways of stating (number ≤ 42) AND (grade ≥ 9). NOT (number > 42) is the same as (number ≤ 42) as is (number < 43). (grade = 9 OR grade > 9) is a longer way of stating (grade ≥ 9). (grade > 8) also represents (grade ≥ 9). Big Idea 3: Algorithms and Programming

70. **C, D**—Procedures can be coded once and called as many times as the program needs. Iterative statements, also called loops, can repeat a block of code as many times as needed in a program. Big Idea 3: Algorithms and Programming

Analyzing Your Performance on Practice Exam 2

The exercise below will help you quickly and easily identify the chapters in Step 4 that you most need to review for the AP Computer Science Principles multiple-choice exam. Revise your study plan so that you prioritize the chapters with which you had the most difficulty.

Look at your answer sheet and mark all the questions you missed. Then shade in or mark an X in the boxes below that correspond to the question numbers that you missed. For what concepts did you miss the most questions? As you review, keep in mind the number of questions to expect from each section, spending more time on those that will appear the most. See Chapter 1 on "What You Need to Know About the AP Computer Science Principles Assessment" for those percentages.

Big Idea 1: Creative Development

15	34	36	59	66

Big Idea 2: Data

1	2	9	10	12	13	17
26	27	29	51	60	68	

Big Idea 3: Algorithms and Programming

4	5	6	7	8	21	30	31	33	39	40	41	42	43
44	45	46	47	48	49	50	52	53	54	55	56	57	58
61	62	63	64	65	69	70							

Big Idea 4: Computing Systems and Networks

16	18	19	20	22	26

Big Idea 5: Impact of Computing

3	11	14	23	24	25
28	35	37	38	67	

5 Minutes to a 5

180 Activities and Questions in

5 Minutes a Day

INTRODUCTION

The questions in this section are designed to help you review and study, with a little time spent each day. The questions cover each of the Big Ideas from the course, and they are designed to ensure that you understand and can explain the concepts. If you can explain something, you have a good grasp of it. Each question also includes a formatted label to find information about the specific concept in the Conceptual Framework document. This document is available online from the College Board at the link: https://apcentral.collegeboard.org/pdf/ap-computer-science-principles-conceptual-framework-2020-21.pdf. This document is freely available to teachers and students.

The numbering scheme for the label follows an outline format and starts with the Big Idea abbreviation:

Big Idea 1	Creative Development	CRD
Big Idea 2	Data	DAT
Big Idea 3	Algorithms and Programming	AAP
Big Idea 4	Computing Systems and Networks	CSN
Big Idea 5	Impact of Computing	IOC

The first number in the next section represents the Enduring Understanding. There are multiple ones for each Big Idea, numbered sequentially. Next is a letter representing a Learning Objective related to the Enduring Understanding. These also increase in alphabetic order. The last number references the Essential Knowledge statement linked to the Learning Objective, and these also increase sequentially.

As an example, DAT-2.B.3 would be Big Idea 2 about Data, the second Enduring Understanding listed, Learning Objective B, and the third Essential Knowledge statement associated with it. I have my students check off each concept on their copy of the document as they master it. As the exam date gets closer, this helps them focus most of their time on those they need to review.

There are answers and explanations for each question at the end of the question section. Remember, a little bit of time each day will build your knowledge and confidence!

Check off each activity as it is completed.

1. ❑	46. ❑	91. ❑	136. ❑
2. ❑	47. ❑	92. ❑	137. ❑
3. ❑	48. ❑	93. ❑	138. ❑
4. ❑	49. ❑	94. ❑	139. ❑
5. ❑	50. ❑	95. ❑	140. ❑
6. ❑	51. ❑	96. ❑	141. ❑
7. ❑	52. ❑	97. ❑	142. ❑
8. ❑	53. ❑	98. ❑	143. ❑
9. ❑	54. ❑	99. ❑	144. ❑
10. ❑	55. ❑	100. ❑	145. ❑
11. ❑	56. ❑	101. ❑	146. ❑
12. ❑	57. ❑	102. ❑	147. ❑
13. ❑	58. ❑	103. ❑	148. ❑
14. ❑	59. ❑	104. ❑	149. ❑
15. ❑	60. ❑	105. ❑	150. ❑
16. ❑	61. ❑	106. ❑	151. ❑
17. ❑	62. ❑	107. ❑	152. ❑
18. ❑	63. ❑	108. ❑	153. ❑
19. ❑	64. ❑	109. ❑	154. ❑
20. ❑	65. ❑	110. ❑	155. ❑
21. ❑	66. ❑	111. ❑	156. ❑
22. ❑	67. ❑	112. ❑	157. ❑
23. ❑	68. ❑	113. ❑	158. ❑
24. ❑	69. ❑	114. ❑	159. ❑
25. ❑	70. ❑	115. ❑	160. ❑
26. ❑	71. ❑	116. ❑	161. ❑
27. ❑	72. ❑	117. ❑	162. ❑
28. ❑	73. ❑	118. ❑	163. ❑
29. ❑	74. ❑	119. ❑	164. ❑
30. ❑	75. ❑	120. ❑	165. ❑
31. ❑	76. ❑	121. ❑	166. ❑
32. ❑	77. ❑	122. ❑	167. ❑
33. ❑	78. ❑	123. ❑	168. ❑
34. ❑	79. ❑	124. ❑	169. ❑
35. ❑	80. ❑	125. ❑	170. ❑
36. ❑	81. ❑	126. ❑	171. ❑
37. ❑	82. ❑	127. ❑	172. ❑
38. ❑	83. ❑	128. ❑	173. ❑
39. ❑	84. ❑	129. ❑	174. ❑
40. ❑	85. ❑	130. ❑	175. ❑
41. ❑	86. ❑	131. ❑	176. ❑
42. ❑	87. ❑	132. ❑	177. ❑
43. ❑	88. ❑	133. ❑	178. ❑
44. ❑	89. ❑	134. ❑	179. ❑
45. ❑	90. ❑	135. ❑	180. ❑

Name each of the three types of computing innovations, and give an example of each.
CRD-1.A.2

Day 2

How can diverse collaborative teams help reduce or eliminate bias? CRD-1.A.3, CRD-1.A.4

Explain who and how many people should be interviewed for a project and why.
CRD-1.A.5, CRD-1.A.6

Explain ways feedback can be provided to a programming team. CRD-1.B.1

Day 5

What is a benefit for programmers using pair programming to work together to create a program? CRD-1.B.2

Day 6

What is the way users interact with a program called? What is the way a program performs while executing called? CRD-2.B.4

Day 7

Describe three different forms of input to programs. CRD-2.B.3, CRD-2.C.1

Day 8

Describe what an event is in terms of program input, and give two examples.
CRD-2.C.2, CRD-2.C.3

5 Minutes to a 5

Day 9

What impact do events have on program flow? CRD-2.C.5

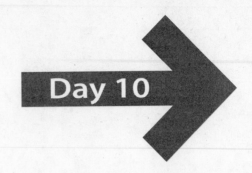

What is output? Describe at a high level how output is produced. CRD-2.D.1, CRD-2.D.2

Day 11

Why were development processes created? What steps are generally used in most development processes? CRD-2.E.1, CRD-2.E.2

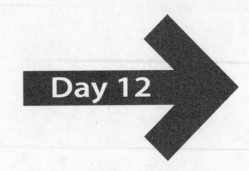

Compare and contrast the iterative development process and the incremental development process. CRD-2.E.3, CRD-2.E.4

Day 13

What is the purpose of the investigative phase of the development process? CRD-2.F.1, CRD-2.F.2

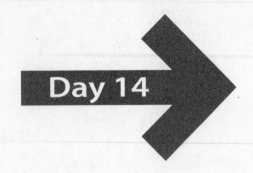

Describe three methods that could be used in the investigative phase to gather information.
CRD-2.F.3

What should be identified and included in the program specification? CRD-2.F.4, CRD-2.F.5

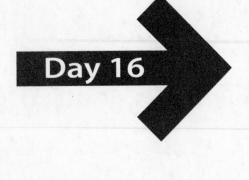

Day 16

What is the purpose of the design phase? Describe three steps a design phase may include. CRD-2.F.6, CRD-2.F.7

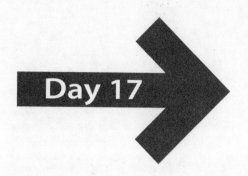

Day 17

Why is the testing strategy identified in the design phase? CRD-2.F.7

Day 18

Why should program documentation about the code and how it was developed be written? CRD-2.G.1, CRD-2.G.4

Day 19

When should a program comment be used? CRD-2.G.2

Day 20

Are program comments the only type of documentation needed? CRD-2.G.5

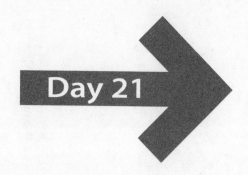

Day 21

Does it matter when documentation is written as long as it is written? CRD-2.G.3

Day 22

Why should code written by others or obtained from a library be acknowledged? CRD-2.H.1, CRD-2.H.2

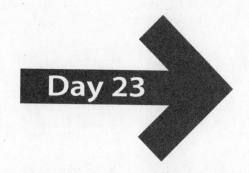

Day 23

Give an example of a logic error. When do logic errors occur, and why can they be difficult to recognize? What is the best way to identify logic errors? CRD-2.I.1

Day 24

What must happen before a program with syntax errors can run? CRD-2.I.2

Day 25

Why can runtime errors be hard to identify? CRD-2.I.3

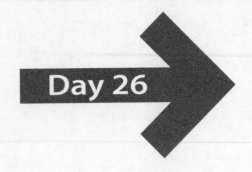

Day 26

Describe three different ways to find and correct errors. CRD-2.I.5

It's time out: work on exam directions ...
who now CRD-2.J.1

Describe the testing process. CRD-2.J.1

If a program only works for certain input, should other values even be tested? Why or why not? CRD-2.J.2

Day 29

Describe how all values are represented at the computer's lowest level. DAT-1.A.2, DAT-1.A.3

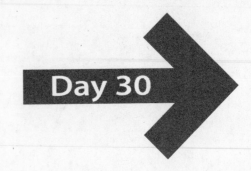

What is the largest decimal number that can be written with a byte, and why is it the largest? DAT-1.A.4

Day 31

State at least three types of values bits can represent. Describe how the computer determines when a binary value represents different types. DAT-1.A.6, DAT-1.A.7

Summarize the key factors used when making something abstract. How are abstractions useful? DAT-1.A.5

Day 33

Draw a picture of analog data and a picture of digital data. Describe how the digital data representation of analog data is an abstraction. DAT-1.A.8, DAT-1.A.9

Day 34

Describe the process to convert analog signals to digital data. DAT-1.A.10

Explain how you can determine when an overflow error has occurred. DAT-1.B.1

Day 36

Describe how real numbers are stored in computer memory, and provide an example. What impact, if any, could this have on a program's results? DAT-1.B.3

Day 37

Explain place value with number systems. DAT-1.C.4, DAT-1.C.5

Illustrate how 222_{10} equals the binary value 1101110_2. DAT-1.C.1, DAT-1.C.2, DAT-1.C.3

Day 39

Describe how data compression algorithms work. What determines the degree of compression that can be obtained by the algorithm? DAT-1.D.2, DAT-1.D.3

Day 40

Explain the significance of having two key types of data compression algorithms and when each should be used. DAT-1.D.4, DAT-1.D.7

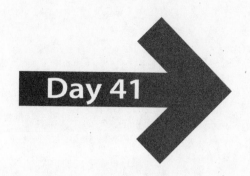

Day 41

What are the limitations of lossless and lossy compression algorithms? DAT-1.D.5, DAT-1.D.6, DAT-1.D.8

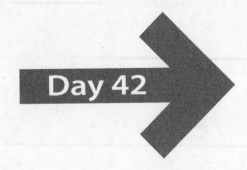
Data is just a series of numbers or characters. Describe how computers help make it meaningful. What do we call meaningful data? DAT-2.A.1, DAT-2.A.2

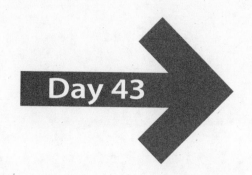

Day 43

If computer processing of data shows a correlation, how can you confirm the relationship exists between the data values? DAT-2.A.3, DAT-2.A.4

What is the definition of metadata? Give an example. DAT-2.B.1

Day 45

How does metadata affect the primary data? For example, if metadata about a video showing a working prototype of a new innovation includes the file size, date, and device type of the camera, what happens to the primary data if the file type of the video is converted to a new file type? DAT-2.B.2

Day 46

What is a benefit of using metadata? DAT-2.B.3, DAT-2.B.5, DAT-2.B.4

Day 47

What are examples of issues with raw data? What, if anything, should be done about these issues? DAT-2.C.2, DAT-2.C.3, DAT-2.C.4

Describe how bias is introduced into a dataset. Can additional data balance out the bias? DAT-2.C.5

Communicating results from analyzed data is important. What common tools can help communicate this effectively? DAT-2.D.2

Day 50

Describe how raw data is processed to start finding possibilities for new insights.
DAT-2.E.2, DAT-2.E.3, DAT-2.E.4

Day 51

There are many ways data can be grouped and filtered in iterative ways. What is the point of this data maneuvering? DAT-2.E.5

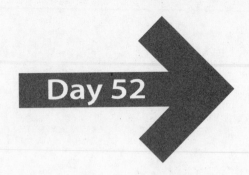

Day 52

Why are descriptive variable names an important feature of programs? AAP-1.A.2

Day 53

Name the four different data types used in most programming languages, and describe the type of data each one holds. AAP-1.A.3

Describe how the assignment statement works, and provide an example. AAP-1.B.2

How can you retrieve a former value in a variable after an assignment statement loads a new value? AAP-1.B.3

Day 56

Diagram how to access an individual value in a list. AAP-1.C.2, AAP-1.C.3

Day 57

Describe how strings are similar to lists. AAP-1.C.4

Day 58

How is a list, as a data abstraction, useful in a program? AAP-1.D.3, AAP-1.D.4, AAP-1.D.6

Day 59

Explain what happens when a list index is larger than the list length. AAP-1.D.8

Day 60

Can an algorithm be an infinite task? AAP-2.A.1

Day 61

Specify at least three ways algorithms can be represented so people will know what to do with them. AAP-2.A.2

Describe three statements used to write algorithms. AAP-2.A.4

What is an expression in programming? Describe how expressions are evaluated in a program. AAP-2.B.3, AAP-2.B.4

When implementing an algorithm in programming code, why are clarity and readability important as long as the code works? AAP-2.B.7

How is the modulus operation similar to regular division, and how is modulus different than regular division? AAP-2.C.1

Day 66

Describe what happens when two strings are concatenated. AAP-2.D.1

Day 67

Describe how to access part of a string, such as finding the last three characters in an e-mail address. AAP-2.D.2

When using relational operators, what data type is the outcome? Why? AAP-2.E.2

Day 69

How are logical operators applied to a programming condition? AAP-2.F.1, AAP-2.F.3, AAP-2.F.4

Day 70

Why use the logical operator NOT in a condition rather than just saying the opposite condition? AAP-2.F.2

Describe how truth tables can be used to help evaluate complex conditions.

Provide an example. AAP-2.F.3, AAP-2.F.4, AAP-2.F.5

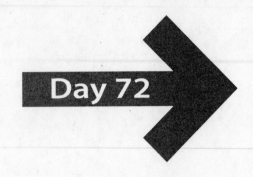

Day 72

How do sequential, selection, and iterative statements work with the flow of a program?
AAP-2.H.1

Day 73

What happens internally to a program when the IF condition is false and an ELSE statement is present? AAP-2.H.3

What happens internally to a program when the IF condition is false and the ELSE IF condition is present? What happens in a program when the IF condition is false and the ELSE IF condition is false? AAP-2.I.1, AAP-2.I.2

Day 75

Diagram what happens to the flow of a program when a loop is encountered.
AAP-2.J.1

What has to change for the REPEAT UNTIL loop to stop? AAP-2.K.2

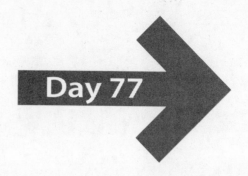
Is a loop that never executes considered a logic error? AAP-2.K.5

Day 78

Do similar algorithms always perform the same? Why or why not? AAP-2.L.2

Describe the meaning of the statements:

    rain = true

    IF (rain)

Is it equivalent to IF (rain = true)?

Support your answer. AAP-2.L.3, AAP-2.L.4

Can algorithms be reused, or are they customized and remain specific to one purpose?
AAP-2.M.1, AAP-2.M.2, AAP-2.M.3

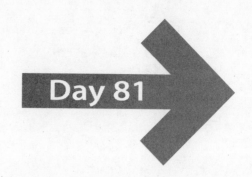

Day 81

Can a variable's value be copied to a list? AAP-2.N.1

Draw what happens in computer memory when the current value of list2 is copied to another list. AAP-2.N.1

Day 83

If you insert a new value and existing values need to shift one position to the right, how should the elements be copied over to avoid accidentally overwriting an element's value? AAP-2.N.1

What is a risk when processing a list in a loop and removing an element? How can it be avoided? AAP-2.N.1

Day 85

How can you use the LENGTH(list) function to reference the last element in a list? Why is this useful? AAP-2.N.1

What does "traverse" a list mean in computer science terms? AAP-2.O.1

What is the programming structure designed to **process each element in a list?** Describe how it works. AAP-2.O.2

What values does *item* take on in the FOR EACH *item* IN listName loop? AAP-2.O.3

Day 89

What is the pseudocode to determine the minimum value in a list? AAP-2.O.4

Day 90

Write the pseudocode to compute the average of a list of numbers. AAP-2.O.4

Day 91

Diagram how a linear search works, and describe the process. AAP-2.O.5

Describe how a binary search works using pseudocode. AAP-2.P.1

Day 93

What is the prerequisite required for a binary search? Explain why it is needed.
AAP-2.P.2

Compare the efficiency of a binary search to the efficiency of a linear search. When is each one most efficient? AAP-2.P.3

Define what a procedure is, and describe how procedures are used in computer science.
AAP-3.A.1

Day 96

Describe how the concepts of "global" and "local" apply to variables in a program.
AAP-3.A.3

Day 97

What, if anything, is the difference between an argument and a parameter?

Which one is local to the procedure? AAP-3.A.3

Diagram how a procedure works with the flow of a program. AAP-3.A.4

What is the minimum and the maximum number of parameters a procedure can have?
AAP-3.A.5

What does the DISPLAY() command do? How is it useful with debugging? AAP-3.A.6

Day 101

How can you interrupt the flow of a procedure? AAP-3.A.7

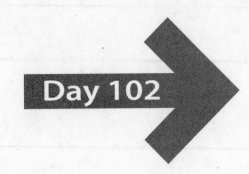

Day 102

If a procedure returns a value, how can the value be used back in the calling procedure?
AAP-3.A.8

Day 103

How can a value the user enters via the INPUT() command be used elsewhere in the program? AAP-3.A.9

Sometimes procedures in a library or Application Programming Interface (API) are called "black box" procedures. How does this phrase relate to procedural abstraction? AAP-3.B.1

Day 105

Describe how the use of procedures helps create an application. AAP-3.B.2, AAP-3.B.3

Do parameters make a procedure more or less general (e.g., more or less abstract)? How? AAP-3.B.5

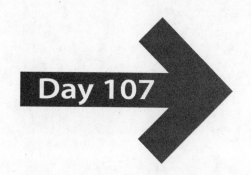

We write instructions in "natural language" code that is very English-like. The computer reads binary. What is the function of compilers and interpreters with program code? DAT-1.A.7

Day 108

Can you modify programs or procedures in a software library? AAP-3.D.1

Day 109

How can you learn what the API or library modules do and how to use them?
AAP-3.D.4, AAP-3.D.5

Describe how the RANDOM procedure works. What does inclusive mean when setting the range for random values? AAP-3.E.1, AAP-3.E.2

Day 111

What should you do if you need to use a randomly generated value later in a program?
AAP-3.E.1

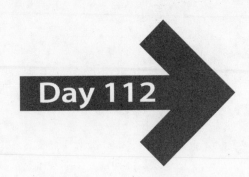
Describe how a simulation is an abstraction. Provide an example. AAP-3.F.1, AAP-3.F.2

Day 113

Why are simulations used? How are simulations constrained? AAP-3.F.3

Day 114

How could bias be introduced into simulations? AAP-3.F.5

Day 115

When are simulations usually created, and how are they used? AAP-3.F.4, AAP-3.F.6, AAP-3.F.7

Day 116

How do simulations use random numbers? AAP-3.F.8

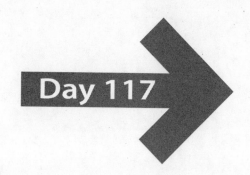

How is the efficiency of an algorithm described? What factors are included? AAP-4.A.3

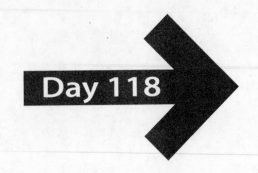

Day 118

Compare how an algorithm's efficiency is determined versus how it is measured.
AAP-4.A.4, AAP-4.A.5

Day 119

If more than one algorithm can be written for the same problem or requirement, will they all have the same efficiency? Why or why not? AAP-4.A.6

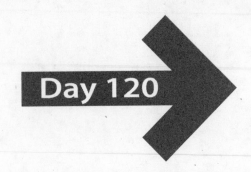
Algorithms that run in an unreasonable amount of time have what type of efficiency? If an algorithm has a "cubed" efficiency, is it considered to run in a reasonable or an unreasonable amount of time? Support your answer. AAP-4.A.7

What is the difference between a decision problem and an optimization problem? Describe what a heuristic solution is and when it is used. AAP-4.A.8, AAP-4.A.9, AAP-4.A.2

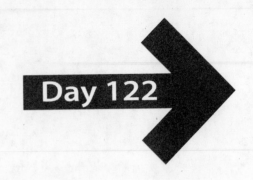

Day 122

Describe when a problem is considered *decidable* versus *undecidable*. AAP-4.B.1, AAP-4.B.2

Day 123

Are there any cases when an undecidable problem may have a solution? AAP-4.B.3

What is an example of a computing system? Explain what makes it a computing system. CSN-1.A.1,CSN-1.A.2

Day 125

As a computing system, a network serves what purpose? CSN-1.A.3, CSN-1.A.4

Diagram a path between two computing devices on a computer network. CSN-1.A.5

Day 127

People often use the terms "router" and "access point" interchangeably, but they have two different functions. Describe the role of each in a network. CSN-1.A.6

Day 128

Explain how bandwidth is measured. What do people usually forget to consider about bandwidth? CSN-1.A.7, CSN-1.A.8

Day 129

Define what the Internet is in three to four sentences, and illustrate how it works. CSN-1.B.1

Explain how a device connects to the Internet. CSN-1.B.2

Day 131

Describe the role protocols perform for the Internet. CSN-1.B.3, CSN-1.B.4

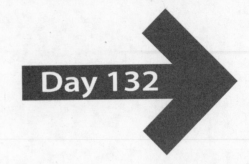
Explain why Internet routing was designed to be dynamic. CSN-1.B.5, CSN-1.B.6, CSN-1.B.7

Describe the packet creation process. What is a benefit of using packets? CSN-1.C.1

What information is included in a packet? CSN-1.C.2

Day 135

What options exist for a packet to arrive at its destination? This is a little tricky.
CSN-1.C.3

What does IP stand for? What is an IP address? When is it assigned? Do you keep the same one all the time? CSN-1.C.4

Day 137

Identify the differences between IP, TCP, and UDP. CSN-1.C.4

Describe how the World Wide Web is organized. CSN-1.D.1

Day 139

Does the World Wide Web use the same protocol as the Internet? If so, which one or ones? If not, what protocol(s) does it use? CSN-1.D.2, CSN-1.D.3

What is the relationship between the World Wide Web and the Internet? CSN-1.D.1, CSN-1.D.3

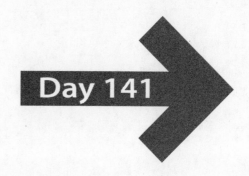

Day 141

What would the Internet be like if it was NOT fault-tolerant? CSN-1.E.1

What is one benefit and one harm of having redundancy built into the Internet? CSN-1.E.2, CSN-1.E.6

Draw a diagram that indicates where redundancy is designed into the Internet. CSN-1.E.3, CSN-1.E.7

Day 144

When is sequential processing usually insufficient? CSN-2.A.1

Describe how parallel computing uses multiple computers. CSN-2.A.2, CSN-2.A.3

How is the efficiency of different computing models determined? CSN-2.A.4

Day 147

Describe how the times to run sequential solutions and parallel solutions are determined.
CSN-2.A.5, CSN-2.A.6

Day 148

Describe how speedup is calculated. Why is it important to know what the speedup is? CSN-2.A.7 CSN-2.B.1, CSN-2.B.2, CSN-2.B.5

Day 149

What types of processing can a distributed system handle? CSN-2.A.3

Day 150

When would a distributed computing system be used? CSN-2.B.4

Day 151

What has been the result of other fields implementing technology in their areas? IOC-1.A.5

Explain how a computing innovation can have an impact beyond its intended purpose.
IOC-1.B

Day 153

Identify and explain the causes of differences in Internet access across communities (e.g., the "digital divide"). IOC-1.C.1, IOC-1.C.5

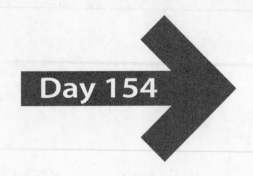

Discuss ways bias makes its way into algorithms. IOC-1.D.1

Explain one way bias can be identified, and identify at least one way to correct bias.
IOC-1.D.1

A lot of data are available publicly in "open access" format. Should an organization use it? Why or why not? IOC-1.E.1, IOC-1.F.5

Day 157

Describe the role of a "citizen scientist." Describe a benefit and a potential harm of using citizen scientists. IOC-1.E.3

Day 158

Describe one positive aspect and one negative aspect of "crowdsourcing." IOC-1.E.6

Define "intellectual property." Describe how using computers has impacted people's intellectual property. IOC-1.F.1

If you created a cool design that you posted on the web for others to view, and you want others to be able to post it on other websites, how would you go about it? IOC-1.F.4

Peer-to-peer networking software was invented to easily share large files. Describe the ethical or legal concerns that exist when peer-to-peer software is used to share digital media such as games, movies, or music. IOC-1.F.11

Day 162

Software exists or can be written to "scrape" data from other websites, such as social media sites. The data can then be processed to look for patterns and other insights. What legal or ethical concerns exist from this form of data collection? IOC-1.F.11

Day 163

Describe three examples of personally identifiable information (PII) we leave behind when we visit websites. IOC-2.A.1

Describe a potential benefit and a potential harm from search engines tracking searches. IOC-2.A.2, IOC-2.A.6

5 Minutes to a 5

Day 165

Identify a potential benefit and a potential problem with your location being tracked by multiple devices, such as cell phones, along with cell towers and networks tracking when and where you connected to them and websites tracking your visits and links clicked. IOC-2.A.3, IOC-2.A.4

Day 166

Describe how someone or an organization can combine publicly available information plus posts on social media and data collected from your digital footprint to identify you. IOC-2.A.7, IOC-2.A.14, IOC-2.A.15

Explain what it means to say that electronic messages and posts are out of your control once they have been sent. IOC-2.A.11, IOC-2.A.13

Provide examples of what others can do with your PII if they obtain it. IOC-2.A.12

Day 169

Why have password requirements become more stringent over the years? What are four factors that make a strong password? IOC-2.B.2

Describe each of the three multifactor categories and how each one is usually used.
IOC-2.B.3, IOC-2.B.4

Describe how symmetric encryption works, and give an example. IOC-2.B.5

Day 172

Describe how public key encryption works. IOC-2.B.5

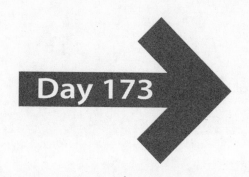

Describe or diagram how a certificate authority (CA) is used. IOC-2.B.6

Day 174

Why should organizations and individuals install new software releases? IOC-2.B.7, IOC-2.B.10

Day 175

What are two common ways malicious software impacts a computing device? IOC-2.B.8, IOC-2.B.9

Day 176

What do permission settings on programs do? Can users do anything with these settings? Have you ever looked at the permission settings for your social media accounts? IOC-2.B.11

Describe how a phishing attack could be set up. IOC-2.C.1

How does a keylogging attack work? How could it be detected? IOC-2.C.2

Day 179

Describe what a rogue access point on a network could do. IOC-2.C.3, IOC-2.C.4

How can a rogue access point be detected? IOC-2.C.3, IOC-2.C.4

Answers

Day 1

The virtual reality headset or a GPS (Global Positioning System) are examples of computing innovations that are physical. They are real objects to hold. Any software program, such as a computer game, is a nonphysical computing innovation. E-commerce and crowdfunding are examples of nonphysical computing concepts that are computing innovations.

Day 2

When a team is diverse, people bring different knowledge and experiences with them. Their differing perspectives help identify potential issues and when or where they could occur to prevent bias from inadvertently being included in the final product.

Day 3

A variety of people who will be future users of the software should be interviewed and observed to fully understand how they would use it. People with different job responsibilities must be included, because each will have differing requirements the software needs to meet. Even people with the same job may be using existing software differently. People are inventive with figuring out workarounds, and these need to be identified and analyzed to understand why they happened too!

Day 4

Feedback to the programming team needs to be constant during the design and coding/testing phases. The use of online tools makes providing feedback easier. People who are not in the same physical location can provide feedback using a shared document, an audio file, or, most effectively, through a video recording showing their screen at the same time that they are discussing features to help others understand their point.

Day 5

There are several benefits to using pair programming. One is the collaboration that will occur as the two people share their ideas and discuss their use. Another benefit is having a second set of eyes to help prevent or find errors in the code. Two heads really are better than one! We know what we meant to type, so it can sometimes be hard for the original programmer to see an error.

Day 6

The way users interact with the program is through the user interface. Time needs to be included in the project plan for designing the user interface and obtaining feedback on how well it works. A software application may be great, but if it is difficult to use or not clear about how to proceed, then it is doomed to fail by those who have to interact with it. The way a program performs and the way users interact with it are included in the description of the program's behavior.

Day 7

Input can come from the user typing something in using the keyboard. This is text-based input. Input can also be an image, audio, or video file. Editing software can use each of these in various ways, as can software that runs social media sites. Input can also be tactile, such as through a touchscreen or a virtual keyboard or from a game controller or sensor transmitting data as input.

Day 8

With event-driven programming, the program continuously waits for an event to occur to trigger certain code to execute. Examples of events include a swipe across the screen or the pressing of a button, virtually or physically, or a command sent through a game controller.

Day 9

Events cause certain segments or modules of code to run when they occur. After the device is turned on and initialized, it waits with nothing happening except checking for events to occur. There is not a sequential flow to the program.

Day 10

Output is data in any form, including, but not limited to, text displayed, a sound or sounds, an image, or an event, such as setting a temperature alarm. Output is based on the input to a program. For example, temperature readings could be compared to a threshold temperature. An alarm could sound as one form of output, and a message could be sent to a variety of devices about the temperature being too high or too low as another type of output.

Day 11

There are many software development processes. Some have come in and out of favor as new ones become available. The point of having one is to follow a structured process to ensure that steps are not forgotten. Most of them include the following steps:

- Investigating and reflecting—ensuring the requirements are identified and understood
- Designing—creating a solution to meet the requirements and obtaining user feedback and approval
- Prototyping—developing a mock-up or sample code without all the features to obtain feedback from users before going further
- Testing—creating the test plan to know expected results for comparison to the actual test results. There are many forms of testing, including unit testing, where the programmer runs the code to get any errors or "bugs" out, integration testing of all the modules used, and acceptance testing by the user.

Day 12

Both the iterative and incremental development processes include testing and feedback throughout the processes. The iterative process tests and obtains feedback and then revises the code through additional iterations of coding, testing, and feedback until the code works and the users accept it. The incremental process keeps breaking the problem into smaller chunks until a section is small enough and has definable requirements to code. Each section is tested, and feedback is provided until it is working and approved. The pieces are then combined into the whole program or application, and their interfaces with other modules are tested. Programming each module in the incremental process will also use an iterative process to test and revise until completed.

Day 13

The investigative phase is where the requirements are identified. It is important that the project team understand the requirements and not just write them down. Additionally, constraints, risks, and concerns should be identified during this step.

Day 14

There are several commonly used methods to gather information. The use of some of these depends on factors such as the time available or the proximity the development team has to the users. Direct observations are always very valuable. Programmers have the chance to immediately ask users questions for clarification about how they are currently doing the process that will be automated or updated.

Surveys are useful, and the programming team can refer back to the data collected as needed. However, the survey must be comprehensive or combined with additional methods to fully identify the requirements. It's easy to make invalid assumptions when writing the survey questions.

Interviews can also provide the opportunity for follow-up questions, but the questions asked may unknowingly miss some of the user requirements if interviewing is the only method used.

Day 15

The program specification should include the requirements, describe how the program or application will work at a high level, and include any required user interactions the software needs to accommodate.

Day 16

The design phase determines how the requirements will be met. Common steps include brainstorming, storyboarding, creating mock-ups of the user interface, and outlining the program modules and their functionality.

Day 17

Since the requirements for the program or programs have been identified, the testing strategy should be documented to ensure each requirement is included and the code is working correctly. Programmers are an optimistic group and often assume code is working correctly when the output appears reasonable. That's why the test plan is needed with expected results to ensure the actual results match.

Day 18

Program documentation is needed and should be kept up-to-date as programs are modified or updated. It helps anyone, including the original programmer, to understand the purpose and flow of a program. If a couple of weeks or months go by, it can be difficult to remember exactly how and why you wrote code a certain way. Anyone picking up the code to modify it will appreciate the documentation versus having to take additional time to figure out how the code works or was intended to work.

Day 19

Comments should be used at the top of a program to include the programmer's name, the date the program was written or modified, and a description of the purpose of the program. Comments should also be included to document procedures and any section of code that is complicated, tricky, or key to the functioning of the program.

Day 20

Program comments are NOT the only type of documentation needed. Program comments are for the programmers about what the code is designed to do and how the code accomplishes it.

Other documentation needed is a user guide for anyone learning to use the system. A "help" document is also needed for the users to explain errors the program was designed to identify and how to avoid them. This documentation can be online or in print form, but it is needed to ensure the programs are easy to learn and use from the user side as well as the programmer side.

Day 21

Program documentation should be written as the program is being developed because people forget details or reasons why something was done a certain way. The documentation will be better prepared and more thorough if it is written as the code is written. When projects are behind, writing documentation is often one of the areas that is cut. If the documentation wasn't already created as the program was written, it definitely gets minimum attention and then is minimally useful.

Day 22

All code not written by the programmer should be cited in the program documentation. This is to give credit where it is due as well as to identify where code came from in the event future errors occur.

Day 23

An example of a logic error is using the wrong variable in a calculation or as output. Another example is using the wrong mathematical operation in an equation, such as addition rather than multiplication.

Logic errors occur when a program is running. A syntax checker will not identify these because they are valid commands. Additionally, the section of code with the error may not run each time. It may only run when a certain condition is true. This makes them difficult to identify.

That is why the test plan is so important. It shows us the expected output values for certain input. If we compare these with the actual output and they are different, we know to start looking for the logic error!

Day 24

Syntax errors must be corrected before a program will run. Syntax errors break the "grammar" rules for the programming language and include things such as missing punctuation, mismatched parentheses, or a typo in a variable name.

Day 25

Runtime errors occur when the program is running, hence the name. Depending on the input, a runtime error may not occur each time the program executes, making it harder to find. An example is when a variable is used as the divisor and sometimes has the value zero. The runtime error would occur when it's zero because you cannot divide by zero, but the program would execute successfully with other values.

Day 26

Test cases with expected results are very effective at identifying errors. Tracing through your code step-by-step by hand is great for finding problems and thoroughly understanding what the code is actually doing versus what was intended to occur.

Many IDE (Integrated Development Environments) include visualizations and debuggers where you can step through the code line-by-line. These automated versions are similar to the hand-tracing method.

Using temporary DISPLAY or print statements to show intermediate values or to ensure a section of code is being executed is very helpful for finding errors.

Day 27

The testing process includes *unit testing*, which corrects syntax errors (the grammar rules for the programming language) and ensures correct output is produced by the code.

Integration testing is the term used when all the modules making up the functionality are tested to ensure that they work together correctly. For example, a program may have one module for shopping, one for ordering, one for shipping, and one for updating inventory. These are tested individually in unit testing, and then integration testing makes sure they interact correctly with calls to modules, passing arguments to procedures, error handling, and output.

Acceptance testing is when clients start using the software with sample data to test the accuracy of the system. After any needed updates are made, the users sign off that the application is ready to be in "production" mode.

There are many other types of testing as well, but you should always do these tests at a minimum, plus more depending on the type of software and its planned use.

Day 28

Yes, programs should always account for invalid input data and either provide a prompt to reenter with valid data or end the program gracefully with a clear error message rather than crashing.

Programs should also carefully test for "boundary" conditions. This means if a condition is true when a value is less than 100, be sure to test with the values 99, 100, and 101 to ensure the code does not run one too few or one too many times. This is a common error for both new and experienced programmers.

Day 29

At the lowest level, all values are represented by a series of 0s and 1s, or binary digits. These binary digits, called *bits* for short, represent electrical current or no electrical current running through a hardware circuit. They represent numbers, characters, sounds, and colors, among other types.

Day 30

The largest decimal (base 10) number that can be converted to binary and written using a byte (8 bits) is 255. Starting in the ones column on the far right, each power of two increases by one, which doubles the value from the column to its immediate right.

2^7	2^6	2^5	2^4	2^3	2^2	2^1	2^0
128	64	32	16	8	4	2	1

If you add all the values together, you will get 255, the largest number that can be represented in 8 bits. $128 + 64 + 32 + 16 + 8 + 4 + 2 + 1 = 255$

Another way to look at it is 2^8 is 256. This is in the ninth bit, so the largest number that 8 bits can hold is one less than the next column, or 255 in this case.

Day 31

Bits can represent a variety of data, including numbers, colors, sounds, characters, and machine instructions. The software in use knows how to interpret the bits for its program instructions. For example, image-editing software interprets the bits as colors for the pixels in the image. The software for a podcast knows the bits represent sounds. Software performing a math equation interprets the bits as numbers.

Day 32

Creating an abstraction involves removing or hiding features that are not important to this abstraction so the focus can be on the one or the few details that are relevant. This reduces the complexity of what the abstraction represents, making it easier to understand and work with. For example, if you saw this image, you would know it is not a real house but an abstraction of one. The details are removed, and it is a general representation.

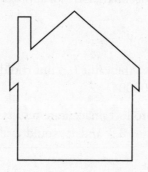

Day 33

The graphs help us to see that the analog and digital data representations are not exactly the same. The digital data are discrete points and approximate the analog data. All the values from the analog data are not represented and have been simplified in the digital version.

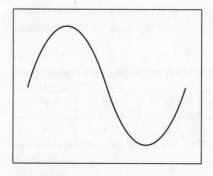 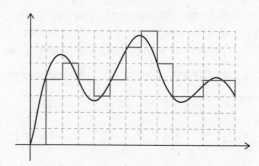

Day 34

When analog data is converted to a digital version, samples of the analog data are taken and represented digitally. When samples are taken more frequently, a closer approximation to the analog data is achieved. With music, when the samples are taken often enough, the human ear cannot distinguish the difference between the analog and digital versions.

Day 35

Programmers should start looking for possible overflow errors when dealing with very large numbers that take many bits to represent. This includes negative numbers because the same number of bits are required to represent the negative version of a number as the same positive number. There is a "sign bit" before the number that indicates if a number is positive or negative. An overflow error occurs when more digits are needed than are available and ends up flipping the sign bit. Therefore, if you are expecting a very large positive number but you end up with a very small negative number, check for an overflow error. Similarly, if you expect a small negative number but end up with a large positive number, check for an overflow error.

Day 36

Real numbers, or those with decimals, have an approximate value in computer memory. For example:

num = 0.1 + 0.1 + 0.1

The variable *num* should have the value 0.3 but could be stored in computer memory as 0.299999998 or 0.3000000004.

This approximation could produce inaccurate results in a program. A program could compare our variable, *num*, to 0.3 and it would evaluate to false when it should be true.

if (0.3 = num)   The result will be false if num is not exactly 0.3.

Day 37

Just like base 10, base 2 starts in the ones column on the far right. It's the value of 2^0, and any number to the power 0 is 1. Since binary only uses 0 and 1, when we need to represent 2, we need to carry over to a new column, the twos, which is 2^1. We run out of positions when we need to represent 4, so the next column is the fours, 2^2. Each column to the left represents the next power of 2, which is its place value. The binary number 101_2 represents 1 four, 0 twos, and 1 one, and in the decimal number system, 101_{10} represents 1 hundred, 0 tens, and 1 one.

Create a diagram to show the place values for a byte to help visualize this concept.

2^7	2^6	2^5	2^4	2^3	2^2	2^1	2^0
128	64	32	16	8	4	2	1

Day 38

We need to convert 222 to binary. Let's set up the table of our binary columns.

2^7	2^6	2^5	2^4	2^3	2^2	2^1	2^0
128	64	32	16	8	4	2	1

1. Find the largest value in the table that can be subtracted from 222 and result in 0 or a positive number. In this case, we can subtract 128, so we put a 1 in the 2^7 column.

$$\begin{array}{r} 222 \\ -128 \\ \hline 94 \end{array}$$

2. Now find the largest value in the table that can be subtracted from 94 with a difference of 0 or a positive number. We can subtract 64, so we put 1 in the 2^6 column.

$$\begin{array}{r} 94 \\ -64 \\ \hline 30 \end{array}$$

3. Repeat the steps to find the largest value to subtract from 30. It is 2^4 or 16, so we need to also put a 1 in that column.

$$\begin{array}{r} 30 \\ -16 \\ \hline 14 \end{array}$$

4. 8 is the largest value that can be subtracted from 14, so a 1 goes in the 2^3 column.

$$\begin{array}{r} 14 \\ -8 \\ \hline 6 \end{array}$$

5. 4 can be subtracted from 6, so 1 goes in the 2^2 column.

$$\begin{array}{r} 6 \\ -4 \\ \hline 2 \end{array}$$

6. 2 can be subtracted from 2, so 1 goes in the 2^1 column.

7. We can't forget the ones column; otherwise the values will be off. A 0 goes in the ones column along with the columns that do not have a 1.

2^7	2^6	2^5	2^4	2^3	2^2	2^1	2^0
128	64	32	16	8	4	2	1
1	1	0	1	1	1	1	0

$222_{10} = 11011110_2$

Day 39

There are different data compression algorithms. They generally look for repeating strings of values in a dataset and replace them with a shortened code to represent them. The new smaller dataset is a compressed version of the original. Datasets that have more repeating values can be compressed more than ones that have less redundancy in their values.

Day 40

Lossless and lossy compression algorithms each have uses they were designed to meet. If you need the full file restored after compression, then a lossless compression algorithm must be used. If you don't need the full file restored and speed is an important consideration, then a lossy compression algorithm will result in a greater degree of compression and therefore transmit faster.

Day 41

Lossless data compression algorithms cannot achieve the same level of compression that lossy algorithms can. Lossless must be used if you want the full file restored, though.

Lossy data compression algorithms can get greater levels of compression, but the original file can never be restored, because bits are discarded during the compression process.

These limitations generally make it easy to pick which technique is needed for compression.

Day 42

Computers can help identify patterns in data that people could not identify. People get tired and bored and miss things. Computers are perfect for work like this. Once patterns are identified, people can analyze them to identify information. This is when data can be used for making decisions and ultimately become knowledge.

Day 43

To determine if a correlation does exist, see if one event actually does cause the other. To fully analyze the possible correlation, data from several different sources may be required to make a conclusion. Additional data from the same source do not provide the same level of assurance as data from a different source to confirm the correlation.

Day 44

Metadata is data about data. Sounds like a circular argument, doesn't it? Metadata helps us find a file or tag data with possible search criteria so we get useful results. The tags we provide to images, videos, and websites are part of the metadata. Examples include the author of anything someone created, the file type, the file size, the date created, the date last modified, and even the device used to create it.

Day 45

Fortunately, changes made to metadata do not impact or change the primary data at all. If the file type is changed, the video still shows the prototype as it did previously.

Day 46

Metadata provide a way to organize and structure the data, which helps in finding it later. In addition to finding data, metadata can also provide additional information about data. For example, if an image is the data, having the metadata of the date the image was created or the longitude and latitude of the location can be helpful.

Day 47

Raw data is data that comes in from any source. It could be incomplete or invalid, or it could be a duplicate, among other issues. Data provided by multiple people have greater opportunities for differences in how the same data is represented. If I write Dr., it could be Drive in an address or Doctor as an abbreviation. The data would need to be cleaned to ensure the correct meaning of Dr. is consistently used or spelled out to avoid confusion.

Day 48

Bias can be included in a dataset or software without people being aware that it is happening. Sometimes it occurs because people select from data that is available to them. That data can already include bias in what or who the data is about. For example, data about employee tenure at a company may include gender. If a great deal of historical data is included, fewer women could be included, especially if the data includes employees in management positions. In this case, pulling in additional years of data from the same company would include the same bias issues. If the study is less about this company and more about working women instead, additional data from other sources could be available and useful or simply provide more bias. Project teams have to be very careful about this, and having a diverse team can help identify or prevent bias in the data used or software written.

Day 49

Humans are very visual, so providing a way to communicate using tables, diagrams, or interactive displays helps get the message across.

Day 50

Programs are used to clean digital data, meaning identifying incomplete data and removing it along with duplicates and making the data uniform. After the data has been cleaned up, other programs can start classifying data into clusters or groups where it belongs for various analyses. Different groups within an organization may want to use the same data but in different ways. Each will provide the filtering and grouping criteria, and programs will be written to process the data in ways that will hopefully lead to new insights that can be used by the organization.

Day 51

The point is to identify patterns that can lead to insights into the data. Programs can sift through the data and process the data multiple times with different criteria to group and filter the data, searching for new patterns. Further analysis can determine if the identified pattern is new and valid information. This provides organizations with opportunities to do things better or in new ways to make their business more valuable.

Day 52

Programmers decide on names for variables. Giving a variable a name that describes the data it holds helps make the program easier to understand.

Day 53

The four different data types used in most programming languages are:

- Numbers, which can be integers (whole numbers) or real numbers (with decimals).
- Strings, which are text fields. Even if a number appears in a string, it is considered text, and mathematical operations cannot be performed on it.
- Booleans, which are values that are either true or false.
- Lists, which are collections of data stored within one variable name.

Day 54

For this course, the ← symbol is used to indicate assignment. The right-hand side of the ← is solved if it is an equation or condition. The result is then stored in or "assigned to" the variable on the left of the ←.

In math, you can write an equation in either format, but in programming, the variable receiving a new value is always on the left.

areaCircle ← 3.14 * (radius * radius)

Day 55

This is a bit of a trick question because you can't retrieve a previous value from a variable that has been overwritten with a new value. If you need the old value later in the program, create another variable to copy the previous value to before assigning the new value.

Day 56

If we have a list named *courses* and it holds a schedule of classes, and we want to reference our favorite class, APCSP, we need to use the index position of it.

DISPLAY(courses[1])   will show APCSP.

DISPLAY(courses[3])   will display Chemistry.

value	APCSP	Algebra	Chemistry	English	Government
index	1	2	3	4	5

Remember that the index position starts at 1 for this course.

Day 57

Strings are a sequence of characters, and lists hold a sequence of values. You can reference each letter of a string or an element of a list using the index.

stringName[index]

listName[index]

Day 58

A list can represent multiple data values in one list name. Therefore, individual variable names for each data value are not needed. This makes programs much easier to create, modify, and understand.

Day 59

When a requested index position is larger than the list length, an index-out-of-range error occurs. This can also happen if you try to reference an index position that is too small. What is happening is that the program is trying to reference a position in the list that does not exist.

Day 60

Algorithms cannot be infinite. By definition, they are finite. Think of space vehicles like Mars Exploration Rover that operate indefinitely until something breaks or they are destroyed. These are very complex systems that are made up of multiple algorithms, each doing a specific task. These tasks may start over or repeat, but each has a starting point and an ending point, even though they may appear to be running infinitely.

Day 61

One way is using our natural language (English, in my case). I can give a list of instructions using words for the algorithm.

Another way is using diagrams, such as a flowchart. Assembly instructions for how to put anything together are algorithms. As we all know, some are good, and others are terrible!

A third way is to use pseudocode, which is a combination of natural language and a programming language. As you get more comfortable with programming languages, you'll find you begin to use the code constructs more often. Be aware that this is not writing the actual code but designing the program before coding it. If you know you'll need a loop, you may choose to add the loop structure using the programming language and use words for the loop contents. Remember that pseudocode cannot run on a computer. It is not a programming language.

Day 62

The three statements used to write algorithms are:

1. Sequential statements. These execute in the order given. When one finishes, the next statement begins.

2. Selection statements start filtering out some of the code based on the condition in an IF statement. Program statements associated with the IF are only executed when the condition is true. Otherwise, they are skipped.

3. Iterative statements, also known as "loops." These repeat code a specified number of times.

Day 63

Expressions are any set of values and operators that need to be evaluated to a single value. An equation using operations, values, or variables is one example. A condition that needs to be evaluated as true or false is another example of an expression. These are evaluated using the order of operations from mathematics.

Day 64

Although working code is important, unless you want to be stuck maintaining a program indefinitely, making your code clear and readable helps anyone else who needs to maintain or use your code to understand what it does and how it accomplishes the functionality. It also helps you. The details may be fuzzy if you're looking at a program you wrote a few days or months ago, but a readable, clear, and well-documented program will go a long way to providing details and clarity!

Day 65

The modulus operation uses division. The similarity is that it does divide. However, it throws away the quotient and only returns the remainder, so that is different than regular division. This course uses MOD for this operation. It has the same precedence as multiplication and division.

Day 66

When two strings are concatenated, their values are glued together. The individual strings are not changed because strings are immutable (unchangeable). Instead, a copy of the new string is created in computer memory and printed or stored in a different variable.

For example:

greet = "Hello"

who = " world"

concatenating these two strings results in: "Hello world"

Day 67

Many programming languages provide common methods for working with strings. To take a segment of a string, use the "substring" function. It needs the beginning location and ending location or length and returns the characters within those values to be printed, displayed, or stored in a variable.

Day 68

Relational operators, $= \neq \geq \leq < >$, are used for comparisons. These are used in both IF (condition) and REPEAT UNTIL (condition) statements. Comparisons check to see if the relationship between the operands on either side of the operator are true or false. Therefore, the data type is Boolean. For example:

$x \leftarrow 99$

$x = 100$ false

$x < 100$ true

$x >= 99$ true

Day 69

Logical operators are used to build more complex conditions by providing a way to combine conditions. Games often need multiple conditions to determine the outcome for the players.

The AND logical operator is only true when both operands are true. The OR logical operator is only false when both operands are false. For example, this Boolean expression has to evaluate comparisons that then become operands for another comparison.

$(x > 42)$ AND $(y = z)$ OR $(a > -5)$ OR $(60 < temp)$

    1   2   3   4

         5   6

            7

The multiple conditions are evaluated one by one because you can only compare one operand on each side of a relational operator at a time.

1. Compare $x > 42$, and mark as true or false.

2. Compare $y = z$, and mark as true or false.

3. Compare $a > -5$, and mark as true or false.

4. Compare $60 < temp$, and mark as true or false.

5. Compare the results of 1 AND 2, and mark as true or false.

6. Compare the results of 3 OR 4, and mark as true or false.

7. Finally, compare the results of 5 OR 6, and mark as true or false.

Day 70

You can accurately say both, such as:

    $x < y$ or $NOT(x >= y)$.

Sometimes, one format is clearer than the other. NOT is part of mathematics, and computer science mirrors the rules of mathematics.

Day 71

Truth tables can be used to evaluate complex conditions by listing all possible combinations to evaluate complex Boolean expressions. It's easy to make a mistake if you try to do it in your head. Using the prior example, let's assign values to the variables and build a truth table to evaluate the complex condition.

    $a \leftarrow -3$

    $temp \leftarrow 67$

    $x \leftarrow 40$

    $y \leftarrow 11$

    $z \leftarrow x - y$

    $(x > 42)$ AND $(y = z)$ OR $(a > -5)$ OR $(60 < temp)$
       1   2   3   4
           5   6
             7

1	2	3	4	5	6	7
40 > 42	11 = (40 – 11)	–3 > –5	60 < 67			
F	11 = 29	T	F			
F	F	T	F	1 AND 2	3 OR 4	
				F AND F	T OR F	
				F	T	5 OR 6
						F OR T
						T

Day 72

Sequential statements execute one right after the other. The flow of the program is in the order of the statements, and hopefully, they are in the correct order. Selection statements interrupt the flow by only executing certain sections of code when a condition is true. When a selection statement is a nested condition, with ELSE IF statements or an ELSE statement, once a true condition is found, other conditions will not even be checked and will be skipped. Iterative statements also interrupt the sequential flow by repeating sections of code before continuing with the next statement after the loop completes.

Day 73

When the IF condition evaluates to false, the code associated with the IF section is skipped. This code is shown in this course between braces { } after the IF (condition) statement.

When an ELSE is present and the IF condition is false, the code in braces { } after the ELSE is executed. This code is skipped when the IF condition is true.

Day 74

When the program code has an IF condition and an ELSE IF condition structure, the IF condition is always evaluated first. If it is false, the condition associated with the ELSE IF will be evaluated. If it is true, the code associated with the ELSE IF is executed. When the IF condition and the ELSE IF are false, neither section of code under the IF or the ELSE IF will be executed.

Day 75

The flow of a loop is:

```
  ┌──→Start of loop (run loop?)
  │    {
  │
  │        code repeated in the loop
  │
  └───}
```

Using the structure above, the loop starts and tests to see if it should run. If so, the code within the braces is executed. Then the program moves back to the top of the loop to determine if it should repeat the loop again. These steps repeat until the program determines that no more iterations of the loop are needed.

Day 76

The REPEAT UNTIL statement has a condition that is checked before each iteration of the loop. The condition has to have the chance to change or the code will have an infinite loop.

Day 77

Although a loop not executing is often an error, there are valid examples for this to occur. For example, a vending machine program needs to ensure a customer enters enough money for the product before dispensing it. A loop could run until the amount deposited is the same or greater than the cost of the product. If the exact change is initially deposited, the loop does not execute.

Many loops are set up with a condition that never changes, such as:

    REPEAT UNTIL (False)

and then break out of the loop when the condition is met.

Day 78

There is always more than one right way to write an algorithm, and algorithms do not all function the same way. A simplified example of this would be a part of an algorithm checking for greater than a specified value and another checking (less than or equal to). These algorithms perform the same condition check.

When implementing algorithms, programmers should always test that the code is not "off by one" and processing one too many or one too few data elements.

Day 79

The statements assign a Boolean value of *true* to the variable *rain*. It then tests the value of *rain* in the condition. It is read as "if rain." In this case, rain is true, so it evaluates as "if true." The code associated with the IF statement would execute.

This statement is equivalent to IF (rain = true) and is a shorthand way to write the same condition.

Day 80

Algorithms can be reused and are all the time! Reusing algorithms helps create new code faster because the algorithms are already defined and correct. This can also reduce the amount of time needed to test and can help identify where errors in the code could be. Sometimes new algorithms are derived by modifying existing ones or combining them in a new way.

Day 81

Yes, a variable's value can be copied to a list, but you must provide the index position where it should go. The variable's value does not append to the end or insert into a location without the program code specifying it.

Day 82

When the current value of list2[j] is copied to another list, the memory references look like:

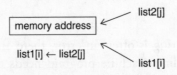

After this line of code is executed, list1[i] contents are updated to the value at the memory location where list2[j] was pointing. In the computer's memory, both variables point to the same location, so if the value is changed in an expression using one of the lists, it will also be changed in the other list.

Day 83

Start from the end of the list, and work your way down to copy elements to their new index position before their current index position is overwritten. The last step is to insert the new value at the specified index location.

listExample = [1, 2, 3, 4, 5]

We want to insert the number 42 at index position 3 with the command:

INSERT(listExample, 3, 42)

First, the numbers at index positions 4 and 5 need to shift one to the right. If we copy the value at index 4 into index 5, then we've lost the value at index 5, and our list would look like: listExample[1, 2, 3, 4, 4]

Instead, we need to start with the last index position (here it is 5) and copy it to its new index position, which is 6. Then move down the list, copying over the value at each index position until we reach our insert location.

listExample[1, 2, 3, 4, 5, 5]

listExample[1, 2, 3, 4, 4, 5]

listExample[1, 2, 3, 3, 4, 5]

As the last step, we insert the new value at index 3, and our list is:

listExample[1, 2, 42, 3, 4, 5]

As you can already see, a loop should be used since we are repeating the steps to copy over values.

Day 84

When processing a list and an element is removed, the other elements move down one. The risk is that the element right after the one that was deleted has now moved into its position. The loop has already processed that position, so this element would be skipped, possibly leading to invalid results. This is a logic error when it occurs.

One way to avoid the problem is to process the list from the beginning, and when an element is removed, reset the index position back by one so it checks that index position again. You can also start from the end of the list and remove elements that way. When elements shift down, you have already checked that element, so nothing is skipped.

Day 85

For this course, the last element in a list will always match the length of the list. Therefore, the last element can be referenced using:

listName[LENGTH(listName)]

This makes the code more flexible because it can be used with any size list without having to modify the code.

Day 86

Traversing a list means to process the elements in the list. All or some of the elements can be processed. This could mean that if a particular value is found in the list, all processing stops. It could also include only processing every even *index* position. Don't confuse this with the case that only elements of the list that are even are processed. In that case, you would still have to traverse the entire list to determine if an element is even or odd, not the index.

Day 87

Loops or iterative statements are the structures of choice to easily process lists. The code can be written to keep repeating until the current index position equals the length of the list using the LENGTH(list) command for a REPEAT UNTIL loop. The FOR EACH loop is structured to process every element of a list without having to specify how many times to repeat.

Day 88

In the FOR EACH loop format on the Exam Reference Sheet, *item* is a variable. It will take on the value of each element in the list. For the first iteration of the FOR EACH loop, *item* takes on the value at index position 1. In the next iteration, *item* takes on the value at index position 2. This continues until the loop finishes processing the list.

Day 89

The pseudocode to find the minimum value in a list is:

1. Set the current minimum value to be the first element in the list.

2. Set up a loop to process all the elements in the list.

3. Compare the current minimum value with the next element.

4. If the element is less than the current minimum value, set the current minimum variable to be the element's value.

5. Repeat steps 3 and 4 until all elements in the list are checked.

Day 90

The pseudocode to calculate the average of a list of numbers is:

1. Initialize a variable to hold the sum of the numbers in the list.

2. Set up a loop to process all the elements in the list.

3. Add the value of the current element to the sum.

4. After all list elements have been processed, divide the sum by the length of the list to calculate the average.

Day 91

In a linear search, each element in a list is checked, starting at the beginning and working through the list to the end. You could also start at the end and work your way down to the first element. The current element is compared with the element you are searching for. If it is found, save the index position of the element to be able to locate it again. Exit the search loop.

numList = [5, 4, 3, 2, 1]

index = 1

searchFor = 2

found = false

numList	5	4	3	2	1
index	1	2	3	4	5

⤷ does the value at index 1 = searchFor? 5 = 2 is false
 ⤷ does the value at index 2 = searchFor? 4 = 2 is false
  ⤷ does the value at index 3 = searchFor? 3 = 2 is false
   ⤷ does the value at index 4 = searchFor? 2 = 2 is true
    ⤷ the last index position is not checked. The value was already found.

loop through the list

   if numList[i] = searchFor

      set found to true

      save the index position of the found element

      break out of loop

Day 92

A binary search works in this way:

1. Check the value of the element at the midpoint of the list. You can take the length of the list and divide it by 2 to find the middle index position.

2. If the value you are searching for is higher than the midpoint value, there is no need to check elements from index position 1 through the midpoint. Those are discarded from the search algorithm.

3. If the value being searched for is lower than the midpoint value, there is no need to check elements from the midpoint index position to the end.

4. Calculate the new midpoint index position for the remaining elements in the search.

5. Repeat until the element is found or determined not to be in the list.

Day 93

A binary search must be performed on sorted data. Otherwise, the search algorithm would not work. There is no way to know if the value is in the half to be discarded during each iteration.

Day 94

A binary search is more efficient than a linear search when searching large datasets because each iteration of the search throws away half of the remaining data. A binary search can find a value or determine that it is not in a list of 100 elements within 7 iterations. It can do the same with a list of 1,000 elements in 10 iterations.

A linear search can be more efficient if the value being searched for is near the beginning of the list. A binary search is more efficient in all other cases. A binary search has a logarithmic efficiency, while a linear search's efficiency is linear. Here is a chart comparing the two.

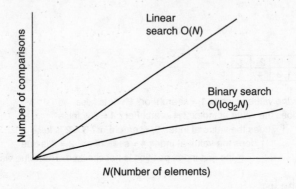

Day 95

Procedures are sections of code that are in a module of their own within a program. They can be built-in procedures that come with a programming language or customized ones. They can be used as many times as needed in a program, which makes code much shorter. This makes it more readable, and it's easier to fix or update because code that does the same thing is not repeated. Therefore, you only have to change it in one place rather than multiple places.

Day 96

Global variables are available to the whole program. Local variables are only "known" and available within the procedure or loop where they are defined. At the end of the procedure or loop, local variables and their values are "garbage collected," and the link to their memory location is removed. If you need the value in a local variable later in a program, use the RETURN statement in the procedure to send the value back to the calling location.

Day 97

Arguments are used to send data to a procedure. The parameters are local to the procedure and are assigned the values of arguments that are sent with the call to the procedure. The number of arguments must match the number and data type of the parameters. If there is more than one parameter, the first value sent as an argument is assigned to the first parameter, the second argument is stored in the second parameter, and so on. That's why it is important to send the arguments in the expected order.

Day 98

When the program calls the procedure, the code in the main program is paused while the code in the procedure is executed. Once it finishes, control is returned to the point where the call to the procedure occurred.

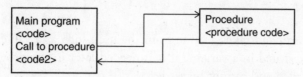

Day 99

A procedure may have zero parameters or an unlimited number. Too many parameters can get confusing, so if you find yourself needing quite a few, see if you can break the procedure down further into multiple procedures. Remember that one procedure can call another.

Remember to include the parentheses after the procedure name when defining a procedure and when calling it. Any parameters or arguments are included within the parentheses.

procedureName( )

Day 100

The DISPLAY( ) command is a built-in procedure for this class. It mirrors the information in the parentheses onto the screen. You can include multiple types of values in the parentheses, separating them by commas. The types can include strings with quotation marks around them, numbers, equations to evaluate, or calls to procedures.

The DISPLAY() command is useful with debugging to indicate when sections of code execute or to show the values of variables midway through the program.

Day 101

When the RETURN statement is used in a procedure, it immediately exits the procedure, and control of the program is reverted to the point where the procedure was called. All the statements in the procedure may not have executed.

If a procedure does not have a RETURN statement, once the procedure finishes executing its code, control is sent back to the point the procedure was called.

Day 102

If a procedure returns a value to the calling program, the value must be stored in a variable or list if it is needed later in the program. Otherwise, it is lost forever in cyberspace.

If you do not plan to use the value later in the program, you can use the call to the procedure in a DISPLAY() statement or as input to a calculation or expression to evaluate. Here are a couple of examples.

catchMe ← procedureName(arg1)

The variable catchMe stores the value returned by the call to procedureName() with the argument, arg1.

DISPLAY("The value is", procedureCalc(arg1, arg2))

During the DISPLAY() statement, the call to procedureCalc is executed with arguments arg1 and arg2. The value returned by procedureCalc is then displayed, finishing the execution of the DISPLAY() statement.

Day 103

The INPUT() command takes a value from the user, such as a value typed on a keyboard. It must be stored in a variable if it is needed later in the program. Otherwise, the value is not saved and cannot be retrieved.

username ← INPUT()

Day 104

These "black box" procedures exemplify procedural abstraction because you know what input is needed and what output to expect, but you do not know the details of how the input is processed to produce the output, only that it works. If the code of the procedure is modified, users of the procedure do not need to know, hence the mysterious, but correct, black box designation.

Day 105

By breaking the program design into smaller modules, these procedures can each provide specific functionality. The main program can be built by calling the procedures to provide the full features needed. These modules can also be imported into other programs and reused, saving time and money and producing readable and correct code because they have already been tested.

For example, if we were building a game, we could call procedures for the main functionality needed. These modules have descriptive names, so it is easy to understand what each does.

initialize()

play()

updateScore()

gameOver()

highScore()

Day 106

Parameters make a procedure more general. The procedure can be called with different values sent to it through the arguments each time it is invoked. By being able to accept various values, the procedure is more flexible and abstract.

Day 107

Compilers and interpreters convert our program code to machine code (binary). Compilers convert the entire program to executable code. The executable code is saved in a new file, so memory is required. The executable module is then executed by the computer, which is faster than how interpreters work.

Interpreters convert the code line-by-line to machine code. Interpreters require less memory since the intermediate code is not saved. This method is faster at checking the source code for errors, but it is slower at running the executable code than compilers. Often the difference is negligible.

Day 108

You cannot modify programs or procedures from a software library. You only get the compiled version of the code, meaning the code has been translated from the natural language-type programming language to one the computer understands at a lower level. This is abstraction in action! You only need to know what the program or procedure does to know if you want to use it. Then you need to provide any expected arguments and handle any expected output.

Day 109

For any given programming language, there are common sites and official documentation that list libraries that are available for use. Always get them from a reliable source! Check for verified and vetted libraries unless you know the person sharing them. The documentation accompanying the library describes how to use the program via the API or application programming interface.

Day 110

The RANDOM() procedure expects two arguments when it is called. These are the starting number and the ending number for the range of numbers that the generated number can be between. Both the starting and ending numbers are also included in the pool of numbers, meaning they are inclusive. The procedure generates a random number in the range and returns the number. Each number is equally likely to be selected each time the RANDOM() procedure executes.

Day 111

To keep the random number for use later in the program, assign it to a variable. Otherwise, the number generated is no longer available. The next time the random function is used, a new value will be produced, which could be the same because the range is the same, but it could also be a different value in the range.

This is a common error with new programmers. You must set up a variable to "capture" the value generated to be able to use it later in the program.

Day 112

Simulations take models of an event or an object and then run the model through a test environment. The test environment is not real, though some simulations try to mimic real-life events. Many of the details are removed so that the focus can be on just the aspect being studied. This fits the definition of abstraction!

I used to work for an airline, so an airplane simulator immediately comes to mind. A real plane is not used for cost and safety considerations! The controls for the aircraft are real, but the results of pilot actions under a variety of conditions are computer generated.

Day 113

Cost, timeliness, and safety are the three main reasons that simulations are used. For example, a building won't be built in an earthquake-prone area with just the hope that its structure is earthquake resistant. A simulation can determine the effectiveness of the planned building structure with different magnitude earthquakes. Simulations are also needed because the real-life events may not happen often enough for testing purposes. Simulations don't have the constraints of the real world. Each test can modify a different variable while holding others constant to see the impacts of various scenarios.

Day 114

Just like with other uses, such as surveys or data collection, bias is usually introduced into simulations because of the choices made of what to include or exclude in the model and tests. Sometimes the reason is convenience because of the ease of including or eliminating certain features. Sometimes the reason is that a correlation appears to exist but has not been confirmed and the variables are included or excluded based on a false conclusion. Sometimes it's just poor judgment.

Day 115

Simulations are ideal when a real-world event or object is too large or small, too fast or slow, too costly, or too dangerous to study in real life. Simulations begin with a hypothesis about how the object being studied will react under a certain set of conditions. The simulation works to match those conditions to either prove or disprove the hypothesis. The hypothesis is then refined or tossed out based on the results. A real benefit of simulations is the ability to continue to modify the values of a variable in a controlled environment to continue to see the impact on the object or event being tested.

Day 116

As we often experience ourselves, real life is unpredictable! Therefore, simulations will use numbers that are randomly generated to inject the arbitrary nature of the real world. The intent is to make the simulations more realistic and introduce or combine factors in ways that people think would not occur, therefore creating a more effective simulation.

Day 117

The amount of resources used determines how efficient an algorithm is. The time it takes to process and the amount of memory used make the determination. Since different algorithms can perform differently with larger or smaller datasets, efficiency is described as a function of the input size.

Day 118

Mathematical reasoning is used to determine the efficiency of an algorithm. The efficiency is measured by counting the number of times one or more statements actually execute.

Day 119

We know that more than one correct algorithm can be written to solve a problem or perform a task. These algorithms can have different efficiencies, especially for complex algorithms or those that process very large datasets. Think about programs you wrote when you first started programming. If you look back at them after learning more and having more experience writing code, you'll probably see better ways you could have structured the code, but it is still correct code!

Day 120

Algorithms that run in an unreasonable amount of time have an exponential or factorial efficiency. An algorithm with a polynomial efficiency, such as cubed, runs in a reasonable amount of time.

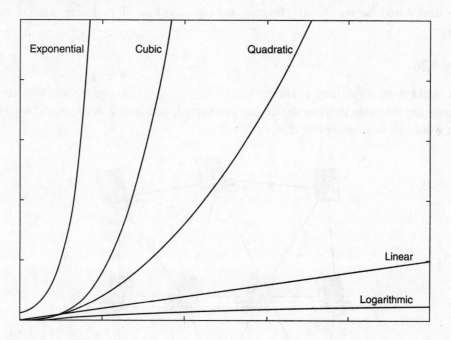

Day 121

A decision problem simply needs a yes/no answer to a question or problem. An optimization problem is looking for the best solution. When an optimization problem is too complex to be solved with our current resources, meaning it takes too much time or needs too much computer memory, a heuristic solution can often be used. Heuristics are solutions that work, but they are not the best solution available. Heuristics can be processed on a computer, so they are a solution, and often a quite good one, but the best solution is beyond our current capabilities.

Day 122

A problem is *decidable* when an algorithm exists that can handle all input and provide correct output. An *undecidable* problem is when an algorithm cannot be written that can produce a yes/no answer that is correct for all input values possible.

Day 123

Yes! An undecidable problem may have some instances where there is a solution, often with smaller-sized datasets. However, there is not an algorithm that solves all instances of it, which then qualifies it as undecidable.

Day 124

The traffic light system in any town is part of a computing system. An air traffic control system is also a computing system. These are considered computing systems because there are multiple computing devices and software working together to maintain these processes.

Day 125

A network connects different devices for the purpose of sending and receiving data. The data could be documents, images, messages, videos, or websites, among many others!

Day 126

You could draw something as simple as: A _____ B, and it would be correct because anytime two or more devices are connected, you have a network. A better version would be something like this:

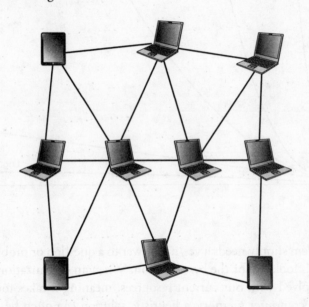

Day 127

An access point sends out radio waves to provide wireless access to a network. Devices can connect to the access point to gain access to the network.

A router manages the devices and communication on it. It also provides access for devices on smaller networks, such as those in homes or small offices, to the Internet. A router can provide wireless access for small networks, but most access points cannot provide routing capabilities.

Day 128

Bandwidth measures the amount of data that can be sent in a fixed amount of time. We are usually speaking about upload and download speeds to and from the Internet, but it can be other networks. People usually forget the "amount of time" part. Bandwidth is measured in bits per second and notated as bps. However, with today's speeds, you are more likely to see Mbps, which is megabits per second, or Gbps, which is gigabits per second.

Day 129

The Internet is a network of networks. It uses protocols, or rules, to manage the connections and communication between devices of any type. It breaks information into packets to send across the network to the recipient, where they are put back together in order. It has redundancy built in to make the Internet fault-tolerant.

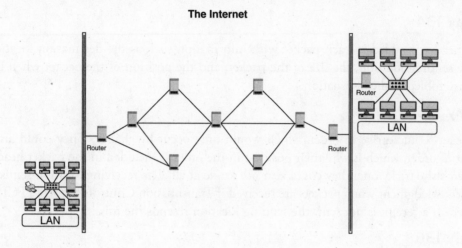

Day 130

The device will need to connect to an Internet Service Provider (ISP), usually through a phone line. Businesses may have fiber-optic cables to provide faster connection speeds. There are many ISPs, though some communities only have one to provide Internet connectivity. The ISP provides the router and cabling to connect to their network, which then usually connects to a larger Regional ISP or Network Service Provider (NSP), which finally provides the connection to the Internet.

Day 131

Protocols are the rules that companies need to follow to produce equipment for connecting to and for the transfer of data across the Internet. These rules were created and are reviewed and modified as needed by the Internet Engineering Task Force (IETF) and are open and available to everyone. These protocols allow anyone to use any equipment that follows the protocols to connect and communicate across the Internet.

Day 132

Dynamic routing on the Internet means the paths packets of information take are not preset. This was designed into the Internet to make it able to handle links that are down by routing data away from those areas.

The Internet was designed to allow new networks to be added to the structure without needing to bring the Internet down to do so. New networks and devices can be added or removed without impacting the rest of the structure.

Dynamic routing takes advantage of scaling, so as more networks and paths are added to the Internet, dynamic routing can start using them without any internal reworking required.

Day 133

Packets are created by dividing the information requested into sections of equal size. The last one might be smaller, depending on the size of the data. A benefit is that the packets don't all have to take the same path, so sections of the network don't become congested.

Day 134

A header is added to each packet with information such as the destination location, the sending location, the size of the packet, and the position of the packet when it is reassembled at the destination.

Day 135

Packets could arrive in order, which would only occur by chance. They could arrive out of order, which is why their position in the order is included in the packet header. Here's the tricky one: they could also not arrive at all. The receiving location sends an acknowledgment when packets are received if Transmission Control Protocol (TCP) is used. If a receipt is not sent, the sending location resends the missing packet.

Day 136

IP stands for Internet Protocol, which is the set of rules for transmitting data across the Internet. Devices are assigned a unique IP address when they connect to the Internet by the ISP. Although you can assign a static IP address to a device, most of us are assigned a dynamic IP address, meaning it changes each time we connect to the Internet. It is used as part of the header when making packets so routers know where to send it and what address it is coming from.

Day 137

TCP and User Datagram Protocol (UDP) are similar protocols that divide the information into packets and reassemble them at the destination location. TCP will send an acknowledgment that the packet reached its destination, but UDP does not. IP is the protocol that finds the destination address and moves the packets through the network to the destination.

Day 138

The World Wide Web is a lot of pages, documents, files, images, and videos, among other types. They are linked so they can be shared. Its original purpose was for scientists to be able to share documents and data with their peers.

Day 139

It does both. The World Wide Web (WWW) uses a different protocol than the Internet. It uses Hypertext Transfer Protocol (HTTP), which handles the requests and delivery of web pages from a web browser using Hypertext Markup Language (HTML), which formats web pages. The WWW uses TCP and IP to send data across the web.

Day 140

Many people use the terms *World Wide Web* and *Internet* interchangeably, but they are not the same thing. The World Wide Web was created to share scientific documents, and it still shares information, though it's much more than just documents! The World Wide Web is a separate application that uses the Internet to send and receive information. HTML formats the information so the information is displayed in a readable way with colors, images, different sizes and types of fonts, and videos, as well as documents.

Day 141

If the Internet did not have the redundancy built in to make it more reliable, people across the globe would not use it as we do today. We would likely not use e-commerce as much because we could not rely on our purchases to be sent. Sharing data in the cloud would be minimal because people could not depend on it being available when needed. Gaming leagues and multiplayer games would be nonexistent because players could not team up with others reliably, or their game could stop midstream. These are only a few examples.

Day 142

A huge benefit is the reliability that redundancy provides. Although some sections of the Internet may fail, it simply redirects that traffic so that the entire Internet does not fail. This duplication does cost more to build, maintain, and power.

Day 143

The redundancy is seen at each node since each one has multiple paths drawn to it.

Day 144

When datasets are large or the processing is complex with many calculations performed on the data, sequential processing can become slow and take too long.

Day 145

Parallel processing breaks a program into smaller segments and uses multiple computers to spread out or distribute the processing. Assigning multiple computers for parts of the program is where the efficiency gains are made. Simulations often use parallel computing models.

Day 146

The efficiency is determined by measuring the time the different models take to complete the same task. The results are compared to determine the efficiency and the computing model's rank as compared with the other models that were included in the measurement.

Day 147

A sequential computing model executes the steps in order, one after the other. A parallel computing model has two parts: a sequential part and the parallel part. The time it takes to process is the sum of the time for the sequential processing plus the longest part of the parallel processing.

Day 148

Speedup is the increase in efficiency between using one computer (sequential) versus multiple (parallel). It is calculated by dividing the sequential processing time by the parallel processing time.

It's important to know this because the efficiency will reach a point where adding more computers will not speed up the processing. This is because the time it takes for the sequential part of the processing cannot be reduced, so adding more computers will not help.

Day 149

A distributed model divides the data to be processed among multiple computers. Distributed models also communicate their actions among all of the devices involved. A traffic system is an example. Some of the features it provides are different devices to handle traffic lights, caution lights, highway entrance light systems, and congestion at locations. Settings are updated as needed, making the processes appear as one system handling it all.

Day 150

A distributed model breaks the data into sections, and multiple computers run the different sections of data. This is a very efficient way to process very large datasets and processing needs. Although parallel computing systems share memory, distributed models do not; rather, they have their own memory and processors. The Internet and cellular service are examples of distributed computing models.

Day 151

There have been advances in many areas due to computing innovations. For example, movies are now wholly created in a digital format. We've all seen the improvements in computer-generated imagery (CGI) in movies to create scenes with aliens, chases, and explosions. The medical field now has robotic surgery and can consult with experts across the globe. There are many other advances in many other fields.

Day 152

Global Positioning System (GPS), originally created for the military, is now available on mobile devices and is built into vehicles and includes additional information such as restaurants, hotels, and gas stations.

The World Wide Web provides a great way to share information with anyone on the planet with an Internet connection. However, along with the helpful, funny, and interesting information on the web are criminal activities, cyberbullying, and stalking.

It's difficult to envision all the ways people will think of to use a new innovation for good or for bad.

Day 153

There are several reasons the digital divide exists in a variety of communities. One major reason is lack of access. The ISP companies have not found it cost-effective to provide the infrastructure to communities that are more isolated. Rural areas of the country have been particularly impacted by this. Often when they do have access, it is much slower than what cities will have available (e.g., dial-up access rather than high-speed access).

Another cause is the cost of the technology devices. Even if they have Internet access in their community, many families cannot afford the devices to use, or the devices may be older and cannot perform some features, such as streaming or connecting to online classes and meetings.

Another way the digital divide occurs is the lack of access to devices for the disabled. Depending on the person's disability, there may not be a device to adequately help the person use the Internet.

Day 154

Bias can enter algorithms in a variety of ways. One is through the data. If the data feeding into the algorithm is biased, for example, by underrepresenting certain groups, the algorithm will work and have skewed results. Some historical data underrepresents women and people of color. Even selecting current data based on zip code can under-report certain groups.

Algorithms can also have bias due to the way they are used. If an algorithm is designed for use in a densely populated area but is also used for rural areas, the results may not be reliable.

There is also the problem of people not fully understanding the implications when they select the data to use or when and where to apply the algorithm.

Day 155

Programming teams and anyone using the results should check the output for unexpected results to try to identify if bias exists.

One way to make algorithms less biased is to have a diverse team designing the algorithm and selecting the data to be used. Software development teams can also plan to use data from a variety of groups to ensure the output treats them similarly. Another way is to make the algorithm or data open for review from professional organizations or the public. However, many businesses would not want to share information that could give them a competitive advantage, so that is less likely to happen.

Day 156

Open access data does not have any restrictions on access, and it may have limited, if any, restrictions on use, such as copyright or other licensing. Using this data will save organizations money and time because they do not have to go collect it. They may also find access to data they would not have had otherwise.

Day 157

Citizen scientists can provide a lot of benefits. They can help provide data from locations across the globe that the scientists would not have the time or funding to visit. Citizen scientists can also provide data over a longer period when they live in an area being studied.

Citizen scientists may not always be reliable in providing the data the scientists requested. Some may also not provide the type of data the scientists were looking for. This can skew the results and require analysis, which takes time to track down that could have been better spent elsewhere.

Day 158

Crowdsourcing is a great way to connect people with a variety of needs, such as teachers needing classroom supplies or people seeking jobs, with those who are willing and able to contribute. One downside is that there are those who post false stories about needing funding. There are steps to try to ensure people are being honest, but it is difficult to identify them all.

Day 159

Anything created on a computer is just bits, so it's not always something you can hold, see, or use outside of a computing device (3D-printed designs are an exception). These belong to the person who created them or to an organization if it was created as part of a work assignment. Networks have given people new ways to share their intellectual property with a global audience. It's also easy to copy and paste or only slightly modify it and claim it as your own work without permission from or acknowledging the original creator and owner of the work.

Day 160

As the creator/owner of the design, you can assign a Creative Commons copyright license that allows others to use, either with or without attribution, but not modify or sell, your design.

Day 161

Today, people use peer-to-peer networks to share all types of digital software without paying for them. Often one person will have software, such as a game, and will share it with their friends so they can all play it. Others will purchase music and then share it through a peer-to-peer network for others to have for free. This is stealing, and the creators are losing income. People purchase one copy and do not have the legal right to share it with others. Think of the people who spent countless hours creating what you are enjoying and want others to enjoy too. It could also be you with your creations one day.

Day 162

This is a concern. Your data is often scraped from a site, such as a social media site, and sold to businesses and organizations who then analyze the data. They have data identifying you, and you now have no control over how that data is used or protected.

Day 163

Personally identifiable information is information about a person. Examples include gender, age, race, fingerprint scan, hobbies, and address.

Day 164

Tracking your web searches is a privacy concern. Your search history is stored, often sold, and used by other organizations. Suggested websites and products may provide you with additional stores to purchase from as a benefit. However, you may only be shown those sites and products that are similar to what you are searching for based on an algorithm's recommendations. Ads also pop up based on searches, so what you are searching for as a gift may show up in the ads or suggestions a family member sees. There goes the surprise!

Day 165

One benefit is that you can be found if you are in an accident or lost. Stories such as these are often in the news. Websites often offer incentives to shoppers to purchase items. Sometimes the incentive could be a lower price if you leave an item in your shopping basket for a while to entice you to buy it.

There are several potential downsides as well, mainly related to the loss of privacy. It is easy to be identified and for your information to be shared. You may receive unwanted ads or offers and other unwelcome attention.

Day 166

There is a lot of information about us available online. Some of it is public knowledge, such as our address. Some of it we post on our social media accounts, such as photos showing us in front of our favorite places to visit. Other information is private, such as our location, but can be identified as our cell phone pings off towers. Sometimes, information about us can be deduced from clues we inadvertently leave, such as a review we write about a restaurant we visited. It's easy to search for the restaurant, find the city, and get a general idea of where we may live since most of us visit restaurants near our homes or offices. Be cautious about what you post, especially if your accounts are open for anyone to view.

Day 167

There are frequent stories in the news about people receiving an e-mail that is unflattering about someone and then forwarding it on to others or sharing publicly. This also applies to tweets and other social media posts. Once it's there, it's next to impossible to completely remove. People can screenshot it and send it to others or to the news media. Colleges and future employers can and do view your social media accounts prior to accepting or hiring you.

Day 168

If thieves obtain your Personally Identifiable Information, they can use it in many ways to steal your identity and commit fraud in your name. Some of the things they can do are: open new credit card accounts or obtain bank loans and not pay them off, obtain a driver's license, or even use your information if they are arrested.

Always be cautious about sharing your personal information, and never make an online purchase without seeing "https" in the URL. The "s" stands for secure. You should also see a lock 🔒 by the URL to indicate it is secure.

Day 169

Password requirements needed to become more structured as many people used passwords that could easily be guessed, such as the current month and year, or their child's or pet's name. Information such as names can usually be easily found posted on social media. Additionally, many systems never required people to update their passwords. It is easy to write or find software that uses dictionaries to try to guess passwords.

As a result, passwords often have requirements such as:

- A length of at least 8 characters
- An upper and lower case letter
- A special character
- A number

Day 170

The three multifactor categories are:

- Knowledge. This is something people know, such as their password.
- Possession. This is something people have, such as when a code or token is sent to your cell phone for one-time use.
- Inherence. This is something people are, such as their fingerprint or retina, which can be used in a scan for comparison to grant access.

Day 171

Symmetric encryption uses the same key for both encrypting and decrypting a message. An issue is sharing the key so only the people who are sending and receiving the encrypted message have it. It is no longer used because it has become easier to intercept the key or to break the code even without the key. An example would be shifting letters over 5 spaces. Then the word "secret" would become "xjhwjy."

Day 172

Public key encryption uses one key for encrypting a message and a different key for decrypting it. Only the person decrypting has the key, so there is no longer an issue with sharing the key between the sender and receiver and having it intercepted. Also, the algorithm used for publickey encryption is published for everyone to have. They are considered one-way functions because they are easy to encrypt but difficult to decrypt. The keys are so long that, with our current computer processing power, they are unbreakable. This is how e-commerce is able to keep our credit card numbers safe.

Day 173

A Certificate Authority (CA) issues digital certificates to companies that purchase them. These certificates are installed and linked to the organization's website. They link the public encryption key of the organization to their name to confirm the site is who they say they are, versus a phishing site that looks like the real organization's site to trick people into entering account and password information or financial information.

The digital certificate allows people to be confident about sharing confidential information such as bank or credit card information on the site.

Day 174

The new releases or updates contain code to fix errors, add new features, and fix security vulnerabilities identified in earlier versions of the software. It's important to install these regularly to keep your software applications safe from hackers who may target people or organizations using older versions of the software.

Day 175

Malware, which is short for "malicious software," is often embedded in documents that are sent via e-mail or will download when you click on a link, such as a video, ad, or site offering something free. Malware can come in a variety of different forms, such as a computer virus. These can then start running on your device and can be destructive by deleting or damaging files or capturing data such as passwords and account information to send back to the malware source.

Day 176

Permission settings determine what data can be collected about you from your account. Websites now have to obtain permission to place cookies on your device that help track your visits to their site. This is because you can be identified through cookies, and organizations now have to have your permission to collect personal data through their website.

Permission settings for social media accounts can determine who can view your accounts. Your settings could change with updates made by the social media site, so check them regularly so only the people you want to view your posts are the ones actually able to see them.

Day 177

Phishing attacks work by creating an e-mail or website that looks exactly like the official website of an organization, such as a bank. Users may click on a link in the e-mail that takes them to the fake site, where they unknowingly think they are logging into their account, but they are actually entering their user ID and password into the fake site, where it is then captured and sold or used.

Day 178

Keylogging software collects all the keystrokes made on a device and stores them. Later, the file can be viewed or transmitted to another location for analysis. Usually, hackers are looking for account information and passwords to use later. Sometimes antivirus software can detect the keylogging software.

Using a virtual keyboard is one way to bypass some keylogging software. Multifactor authentication is another way to stop a keylogging attack. Hackers may have part of your credentials, but they cannot change anything without the additional credentials, such as a code sent to the account owner's phone.

Day 179

A rogue access point is one that is not being managed by the organization's network administrator. Unauthorized admittance to the network can be provided through the rogue access point. It can be used to intercept legitimate data and send copies of it back to the location of the person who placed the rogue access point on the network.

Day 180

Network administrators need to document the access points on their network. They then need to perform regular scans of the network to identify any new or unexpected connection points and investigate them to determine how they were placed on the network. Often employees may bring in an access point and connect it to their work network, trying to improve their work environment. However, hackers could also discover the rogue access point and use it to harm the organization.

Appendix

AP Computer Science Principles Exam Reference Sheet
Glossary

AP COMPUTER SCIENCE PRINCIPLES EXAM REFERENCE SHEET

As AP Computer Science Principles does not designate any particular programming language, this reference sheet provides instructions and explanations to help students understand the format and meaning of the questions they will see on the exam. The reference sheet includes two programming formats: text-based and block-based.

Programming instructions use four data types: numbers, Booleans, strings, and lists. Instructions from any of the following categories may appear on the exam:

- Assignment, Display, and Input
- Arithmetic Operators and Numeric Procedures
- Relational and Boolean Operators
- Selection
- Iteration
- List Operations
- Procedures
- Robot

Instruction	Explanation
Assignment, Display, and Input	
Text: a ← expression Block: `a ← expression`	Evaluates expression and then assigns a copy of the result to the variable a.
Text: DISPLAY(expression) Block: `DISPLAY expression`	Displays the value of expression, followed by a space.
Text: INPUT() Block: INPUT	Accepts a value from the user and returns the input value.
Arithmetic Operators and Numeric Procedures	
Text and Block: a + b a - b a * b a / b	The arithmetic operators +, -, *, and / are used to perform arithmetic on a and b. For example, 17 / 5 evaluates to 3.4. The order of operations used in mathematics applies when evaluating expressions.
Text and Block: a MOD b	Evaluates to the remainder when a is divided by b. Assume that a is an integer greater than or equal to 0 and b is an integer greater than 0. For example, 17 MOD 5 evaluates to 2. The MOD operator has the same precedence as the * and / operators.
Text: RANDOM(a, b) Block: `RANDOM a, b`	Generates and returns a random integer from a to b, including a and b. Each result is equally likely to occur. For example, RANDOM(1, 3) could return 1, 2, or 3.
Relational and Boolean Operators	
Text and Block: a = b a ≠ b a > b a < b a ≥ b a ≤ b	The relational operators =, ≠, >, <, ≥, and ≤ are used to test the relationship between two variables, expressions, or values. A comparison using relational operators evaluates to a Boolean value. For example, a = b evaluates to true if a and b are equal; otherwise it evaluates to false.

Instruction	Explanation
Relational and Boolean Operators (continued)	

Text:
 	
`NOT condition`
 	
Block:
 	
`NOT (condition)`
	Evaluates to `true` if `condition` is `false`; otherwise evaluates to `false`.

Text:
 	
`condition1 AND condition2`
 	
Block:
 	
`(condition1) AND (condition2)`
	Evaluates to `true` if both `condition1` and `condition2` are `true`; otherwise evaluates to `false`.

Text:
 	
`condition1 OR condition2`
 	
Block:
 	
`(condition1) OR (condition2)`
	Evaluates to `true` if `condition1` is `true` or if `condition2` is `true` or if both `condition1` and `condition2` are `true`; otherwise evaluates to `false`.

Selection	

Text:
 	
`IF(condition)`
`{`
`  <block of statements>`
`}`
 	
Block:
 	
`IF (condition)`
`   (block of statements)`
	The code in `block of statements` is executed if the Boolean expression `condition` evaluates to `true`; no action is taken if `condition` evaluates to `false`.

Text:
 	
`IF(condition)`
`{`
`  <first block of statements>`
`}`
`ELSE`
`{`
`  <second block of statements>`
`}`
 	
Block:
 	
`IF (condition)`
`   (first block of statements)`
`ELSE`
`   (second block of statements)`
	The code in `first block of statements` is executed if the Boolean expression `condition` evaluates to `true`; otherwise the code in `second block of statements` is executed.

Instruction	Explanation
Iteration	

Text:
 	
``
REPEAT n TIMES
{
 <block of statements>
}
``
 	
Block:
 	
REPEAT n TIMES
   block of statements
	The code in `block of statements` is executed `n` times.

Text:
 	
``
REPEAT UNTIL(condition)
{
 <block of statements>
}
``
 	
Block:
 	
REPEAT UNTIL condition
   block of statements
	The code in `block of statements` is repeated until the Boolean expression `condition` evaluates to `true`.

List Operations	
For all list operations, if a list index is less than 1 or greater than the length of the list, an error message is produced and the program terminates.	
Text: `aList ← [value1, value2, value3, ...]` Block: aList ◄─ value1, value2, value3	Creates a new list that contains the values `value1`, `value2`, `value3`, and `...` at indices `1`, `2`, `3`, and `...` respectively and assigns it to `aList`.
Text: `aList ← [ ]` Block: aList ◄─ []	Creates an empty list and assigns it to `aList`.
Text: `aList ← bList` Block: aList ◄─ bList	Assigns a copy of the list `bList` to the list `aList`. For example, if `bList` contains `[20, 40, 60]`, then `aList` will also contain `[20, 40, 60]` after the assignment.
Text: `aList[i]` Block: aList i	Accesses the element of `aList` at index `i`. The first element of `aList` is at index `1` and is accessed using the notation `aList[1]`.

Instruction	Explanation
List Operations (continued)	
Text: x ← aList[i] Block: (x ← aList [i])	Assigns the value of aList[i] to the variable x.
Text: aList[i] ← x Block: (aList [i] ← x)	Assigns the value of x to aList[i].
Text: aList[i] ← aList[j] Block: (aList [i] ← aList [j])	Assigns the value of aList[j] to aList[i].
Text: INSERT(aList, i, value) Block: (INSERT [aList, i, value])	Any values in aList at indices greater than or equal to i are shifted one position to the right. The length of the list is increased by 1, and value is placed at index i in aList.
Text: APPEND(aList, value) Block: (APPEND [aList, value])	The length of aList is increased by 1, and value is placed at the end of aList.
Text: REMOVE(aList, i) Block: (REMOVE [aList, i])	Removes the item at index i in aList and shifts to the left any values at indices greater than i. The length of aList is decreased by 1.
Text: LENGTH(aList) Block: (LENGTH [aList])	Evaluates to the number of elements in aList.

Text:
FOR EACH item IN aList
{
  <block of statements>
}
Block:
(FOR EACH item IN aList
  (block of statements))
	The variable item is assigned the value of each element of aList sequentially, in order, from the first element to the last element. The code in block of statements is executed once for each assignment of item.

Instruction	Explanation
Procedures and Procedure Calls	

Text:
 	
`PROCEDURE procName(parameter1,`
`                parameter2, ...)`
`{`
`  <block of statements>`
`}`
 	
Block:
 	
`PROCEDURE procName` `parameter1,`
`parameter2,...`
`block of statements`
	Defines `procName` as a procedure that takes zero or more arguments. The procedure contains `block of statements`. The procedure `procName` can be called using the following notation, where `arg1` is assigned to `parameter1`, `arg2` is assigned to `parameter2`, etc.:
	
	`procName(arg1, arg2, ...)`

Text:
 	
`PROCEDURE procName(parameter1,`
`                parameter2, ...)`
`{`
`  <block of statements>`
`  RETURN(expression)`
`}`
 	
Block:
 	
`PROCEDURE procName` `parameter1,`
`parameter2,...`
`block of statements`
`RETURN` `expression`
	Defines `procName` as a procedure that takes zero or more arguments. The procedure contains `block of statements` and returns the value of `expression`. The `RETURN` statement may appear at any point inside the procedure and causes an immediate return from the procedure back to the calling statement.
	
	The value returned by the procedure `procName` can be assigned to the variable `result` using the following notation:
	
	`result ← procName(arg1, arg2, ...)`

Text:
 	
`RETURN(expression)`
 	
Block:
 	
`RETURN` `expression`
	Returns the flow of control to the point where the procedure was called and returns the value of `expression`.

Instruction	Explanation
Robot	
If the robot attempts to move to a square that is not open or is beyond the edge of the grid, the robot will stay in its current location and the program will terminate.	
Text: MOVE_FORWARD() Block: (MOVE_FORWARD)	The robot moves one square forward in the direction it is facing.
Text: ROTATE_LEFT() Block: (ROTATE_LEFT)	The robot rotates in place 90 degrees counterclockwise (i.e., makes an in-place left turn).
Text: ROTATE_RIGHT() Block: (ROTATE_RIGHT)	The robot rotates in place 90 degrees clockwise (i.e., makes an in-place right turn).
Text: CAN_MOVE(direction) Block: CAN_MOVE [direction]	Evaluates to true if there is an open square one square in the direction relative to where the robot is facing; otherwise evaluates to false. The value of direction can be left, right, forward, or backward.

Abstraction Abstraction is the process of removing unnecessary details to focus on essential ones.

Algorithm An algorithm is a set of steps to do a task or solve a problem.

Analog data Analog data is a continuous series of data values that change smoothly over time.

API API stands for Application Programming Interface. APIs define how other programs can interface or interact with their programming module or application.

Argument An argument holds a value that is passed to a procedure when it is called. An argument can be a constant, a variable, or an expression to evaluate.

Arithmetic operators These are the symbols used in computer programs for mathematical operations.
+ addition
− subtraction
* multiplication
/ division
MOD modulus math results in the remainder after dividing

Assignment statement An assignment statement stores a value in a variable. The right side of the assignment statement is evaluated, and the result is stored in the variable on the left side of the assignment operator, which is the ← for this course.

Authentication Authentication involves verifying users requesting access to a system before providing admittance.

Bandwidth Bandwidth measures the amount of data that can be sent over a network in a fixed amount of time.

Bias Bias in computer science is the discrimination for or against certain groups or individuals. The bias can come from the data used or the way the code was written.

Binary number system The binary number system uses the values 0 and 1 and is used by computers at the lowest level to execute code.

Binary search A binary search is an algorithm that uses a "divide and conquer" process. The data must be sorted, and each iteration searches in the middle of the dataset. After determining if the value is higher or lower than the value at the current position, the half of the dataset that does not contain the value is no longer included in subsequent iterations of the search.

Bit A bit is a binary digit, which can only be 0 or 1.

Boolean values These are values that can only be true or false.

Byte A byte is made up of 8 bits.

Certificate Authority (CA) A Certificate Authority issues digital certificates that verify that the data encryption code belongs to the organization. This enables the transfer of confidential data such as passwords or credit card information on the associated website.

Citizen scientist Citizen scientists are volunteers who work with a scientific team to help collect or review data from their home, which can be in a separate location than the scientific team.

Clarity The clarity of a program means how easy it is to understand the code.

Classifying data Classifying data involves organizing and identifying categories that fit the data to make it easier to search for patterns and trends leading to insights.

Cleaning data Cleaning data is the process of identifying incomplete or duplicate data and ensuring the data is uniform (St. or street) without changing the meaning of the data.

Code segment A code segment can be a single line or a collection of lines of code that are part of a program.

Code statement Code statements are sections of a program with an action to be executed.

Collaboration Collaboration is people working together to produce a quality product.

Comments Comments are used to document a program. They should be used to include a brief description of the program, along with who wrote it and when, and to document complicated sections of code. Comments are for people and are ignored by the computer.

Computer virus A computer virus is spread by attaching itself to a valid file. It can then replicate and spread, either collecting or destroying data and programs.

Computing device A computing device is a piece of equipment that can run a computer program.

Computing network A computing network is a connection of computing devices that send and receive data.

Computing system A computing system is when multiple computing devices and programs work together for a specific purpose, such as managing the power grid.

Concatenation Concatenation is when strings are joined or "glued" together to form a new string.

Condition Conditions use the relational operators ($<, \leq, >, \geq, =$, and $\neq$) to compare two values, variables, or expressions and return true or false.

Creative Commons Licensing Creative Commons Licensing allows creators to assign different levels of copyright access to their intellectual property.

Crowdfunding Crowdfunding uses resources like the Internet to ask people across the globe to donate money to help fund their project or need.

Crowdsourcing Crowdsourcing provides opportunities for anyone with access to a site to participate in various ways, such as providing feedback, helping to solve problems, offering funding, or offering assistance finding employment.

Cybersecurity Cybersecurity protects our computing devices and networks from attacks and unauthorized access.

Data abstraction Data abstraction is assigning a data value to a list. The list can be used and updated without needing multiple copies of the data in the program or knowing the details of how it is stored.

Data mining Data mining analyzes large datasets to search for patterns that can lead to new insights for the organization.

Data stream Data streams are segments of data packaged in packets sent through a network such as the Internet.

Debugging Debugging is finding and correcting errors in a program.

Decidable problem A problem is decidable when an algorithm can be created that provides a yes or no answer for all instances of the problem.

Decision problem A decision problem only needs a yes or no answer.

Decryption Decryption is the process of deciphering an encrypted message so it can be read.

Digital data Digital data is made up of discrete data values. These look like stairsteps and can approximate analog data.

Digital divide The digital divide describes those who lack access to the Internet based on location, economic, or accessibility reasons.

Distributed computing system Distributed computing systems are when multiple computers are used to process a program or application. The computers each have their own processor and communicate over a network. The Internet is an example of a distributed computing system.

Efficiency The efficiency of an algorithm measures the amount of resources, such as memory and time, it takes to run.

Element Each data value in a list is an element. It is referenced through its index.

Encryption Encryption is the process of converting data into a coded format.

Event-driven programming Event-driven programming is when a program operates in a wait state and an action, such as pressing a button, provides input and triggers a section of code to run.

Expression An expression is a combination of variables or values and operations to be performed on them. Expressions are evaluated to determine a single value.

Fault-tolerant A system, such as the Internet, is fault-tolerant when redundancy is built in to ensure processing can occur even when sections of the system are not working.

Filtering data Filtering data involves selecting a subset of data, sometimes based on its classifications, to use for further analysis.

Heuristic A heuristic is a solution to a problem that is not optimal or the best but is close enough to work, especially when the optimal solution is unreasonable.

Hypertext Transfer Protocol (HTTP) The World Wide Web uses HTTP to send requested web pages across the Internet.

Hypertext Transfer Protocol Secure (HTTPS) HTTPS provides the secure processing of a web page. Always check for HTTPS before making a purchase online to ensure your credit card number is encrypted.

Incremental development process An incremental development process subdivides a program into small modules. Each section is coded, tested, and approved and then added to the larger application and tested with other completed parts of it.

Information Information is data that has been analyzed and has meaning applied to it. Information can guide decision-making for the data owners.

Intellectual property Anything a person creates using a computer is the intellectual property of that person.

Internet Protocol (IP) address An Internet Protocol address is a unique number assigned each time a device connects to the Internet. It is how the network knows where to find your device to get and send requested information.

Iterative Iterative means to repeat code a specified number of times or until a condition is true (for this course) using a loop structure.

Iterative development process The Iterative development process repeats the steps of coding, testing, and feedback to refine a section of code until it is complete.

Keylogging Keylogging software is malware that captures keystrokes and stores them in a file that is later transmitted to whoever planted the software.

Library A library is a collection of programs where the executable code is made available to other programmers. The entire library or a module from it can be imported into a program.

Linear search A linear search is a sequential search of a dataset. It starts at the beginning and checks each value to see if it matches the target value being sought.

Lists A list is a collection of data values stored in one variable. Each data value, or element, is referenced by its index position.

Logic error A logic error occurs when the code runs but produces incorrect results.

Logical operators The logical operators are AND, OR, and NOT and are used to create more complex conditions that evaluate to a Boolean value (true or false).

Lossless data compression Lossless data compression is a technique to make files smaller and allows the original file to be restored when the data is decompressed.

Lossy data compression Lossy data compression techniques can achieve more compression than lossless techniques, but some data is lost, and the original file cannot be restored.

Malware Malware stands for malicious software and includes anything placed on a device, unknown to the owner, for destructive purposes.

Metadata Metadata is data about data, such as the author of a document. It is used to help organize and find data.

Modularity Modularity is a style of programming that breaks the requirements into smaller pieces until each module does a specific task or set of tasks.

Modulus This operation provides only the remainder after dividing.

Multifactor authentication Multifactor authentication uses more than one method to ensure someone trying to access an account should be granted access.

Open access Data that is open access is freely available online with limited, if any, copyright restrictions.

Open source Open-source software is available for anyone to use or modify without restrictions.

Optimization problem An optimization problem attempts to find the best solution for the problem.

Overflow error An overflow error occurs when a number is too large for the number of bits the programming language allocates for it. The sign bit for the number is flipped as the number "overflows" out of its assigned range of bits.

Packets Packets are created by breaking data into same-size segments (except possibly the last one). A header is created with the sending and receiving IP addresses, the size of the packet, and its position in the reassembled data stream.

Parallel computing system Parallel computing systems use multiple computers to process a section of a program at the same time. The results are then combined for the complete solution. The devices in a parallel computing system share memory.

Parameter Parameters are used to accept data values into a procedure. The values are sent through arguments when the procedure is called.

Patterns in data Raw data is analyzed for patterns to help gain insights into its meaning.

PII (Personally Identifiable Information) PII is any information that identifies you.

Phishing A phishing attack uses messages and websites that look like another organization's official site to fool users into clicking on it and entering information such as passwords and account data.

Plagiarism Plagiarism is copying information or computational artifacts without direct permission from the owner/creator or without permission via the use of Creative Commons licensing.

Procedural Abstraction Once a procedure is defined, tested, and working, it can be encapsulated or protected so users of it only need to know the input to send it and the output to expect from it. The details of how the procedure accepts the input and produces the output do not need to be known and are abstracted away.

Procedure A procedure is a defined block of code that does a specific task or tasks. It does not run in a program until it is called in the program, and it can be called as many times as needed.

Program A program is a collection of code to perform a specific task.

Program behavior A program's behavior is how it performs when it is running and how users interact with the program.

Program documentation Program documentation describes a program's purpose and how it achieves it. Documentation is used by anyone who needs to review and understand the code. Documentation can also include the user's manual on how to use the program and help text to solve errors that occur.

Program input Program input is data sent to a program. It can be in a variety of formats, depending on what the program will accept.

Program output Program output is data produced by the program and sent by the program to a device such as a screen or printer or file.

Prototype A prototype is a draft or incomplete version used to obtain feedback from users and team members before allocating resources such as time and money to create the final version.

Protocols Protocols are rules. The Internet has protocols that are open for everyone to ensure that different manufacturers create equipment that can connect to and communicate with all other devices and equipment following the same protocols.

Pseudocode Pseudocode is a combination of natural language, such as English, and program code. It is used to design the structure or outline of a program prior to writing the code.

Public key encryption Public key encryption uses one key for encrypting data and another to decrypt it. The encryption key is public knowledge, and the decryption key is private to the person receiving the data.

Readability Making a program readable should be a goal of every programmer. The use of blank space and comments along with well-named variables and procedures help to make a program more readable.

Redundancy Redundancy, or duplication, is designed into the Internet to keep it operating even when sections of it are nonfunctional.

Relational operators The relational operators are the same as those used in mathematics: $<$, $\leq$, $>$, $\geq$, $=$, and $\neq$. They are used in comparisons to determine if the two operands match the operator or not and return the Boolean value of true or false.

Requirements Requirements are the specifications for the program to meet once it is complete.

RETURN statement The RETURN statement is used to immediately exit a procedure and return control back to the calling program. RETURN is also used to send values back to the calling program.

Rogue access point A rogue access point is one that is on an organization's secure network, but it is not managed by their network administrator.

Round-off or Rounding error A rounding error occurs because real numbers (those with decimals) are stored imprecisely in computer memory. 0.1 could be stored as 0.0999998.

Router A router manages the devices and routes packets to their destination along a network path. It can provide wireless access for smaller networks.

Runtime error A runtime error occurs when the program is executing. The error may not occur each time the program runs but only when certain conditions exist, such as trying to divide by zero.

Scalability Scalability in computer science means devices can be easily added or removed without interrupting service. The Internet is scalable because new devices and networks can be added without impacting the current operational structure.

Selection statement Selection statements are used to filter out sections of code that are only executed when a specified condition is true.

Sequential computing system A sequential computing system processes data by executing lines of code one after the other in order.

Sequential statement A sequential statement executes as soon as the program statement ahead of it finishes executing. These run one after the other in the order specified and should be in the correct order to avoid invalid results.

Simulation A simulation is a test environment of a model representing a real object or event.

String A string is a series of characters. These can be letters, symbols, or numbers. When numbers are part of a string, mathematical operations cannot be performed on them.

Substring A substring method returns a specified section of a string.

Symmetric key encryption Symmetric key encryption uses the same key to encrypt and decrypt data.

Syntax error Syntax errors break the rules of the programming language. A program cannot run until the syntax errors are corrected.

Targeted marketing Targeted marketing is when advertising is sent to a specific group of people, usually based on their prior searches and pages viewed.

Testing Testing involves executing a program to ensure it produces correct output that meets the program requirements.

Transmission Control Protocol/Internet Protocol (TCP/IP) Transmission Control Protocol/Internet Protocol are the rules that govern the breaking of information into packets, sending the data stream across the Internet to its destination, and reassembling the packets to display the information.

Traverse Traverse means to process all or part of a list's elements.

UDP User Datagram Protocol can be used in place of TCP to create and reassemble packets and work with IP to send the packets across the Internet. UDP does not send an acknowledgment that packets were received, whereas TCP does. UDP is faster than TCP.

Undecidable problem An undecidable problem is one where an algorithm cannot be written that returns a yes or no response for all inputs.

Unreasonable problem An unreasonable problem occurs when an algorithm to find the optimal solution takes too long or too much memory using current computing capabilities. Algorithms with exponential or factorial efficiency run in an unreasonable amount of time.

User interface The user interface includes all the ways a user would interact with a program, including providing input and reviewing output.

Variable A variable is a holding place for data.

World Wide Web (www) The World Wide Web is an application that uses the Internet to share web pages, files, documents, images, and other forms of data.

5 Steps to Teaching AP Computer Science Principles

TEACHER'S MANUAL

Julie Sway

AP Computer Science Principles teacher at the
Brookstone School in Columbus, Georgia

*Thanks to Greg Jacobs, an AP Physics teacher at Woodberry Forest School in Virginia,
for developing the 5-step approach used in this teaching Manual.*

Introduction to the Teacher's Manual

Hello, teachers! This guide is a combination of tips, suggestions, and observations from me and other AP Computer Science Principles teachers so you and your students can get the most out of your AP course.

Nowadays, teachers have no shortage of resources for the AP Computer Science Principles class. Classes are no longer limited to just the teacher and the textbook; today's teachers can utilize online simulations, apps, computer-based homework, video lectures, and so on. Even the College Board itself provides so much material related to the AP Computer Science Principles exam that the typical teacher—and student—can easily become overwhelmed by an excess of teaching materials and resources.

This book is a vital resource for your class because it explains in straightforward language exactly what a student needs to know for the AP Computer Science Principles exam. It provides a review program that students can use to prepare for the test, including questions to check for student understanding, explanations of the answers, and test-like practice exams. The book can be used to supplement your instruction in class or be used by students for assignments and review outside of class. It can be used along with any of the textbooks selected for use with the course.

This teacher's manual will take you through the five steps of teaching AP Computer Science Principles. These five steps are:

1. **Prepare a strategic plan for the course**

2. **Hold an interesting class every day**

3. **Evaluate your students' progress**

4. **Get students ready to take the AP exam**

5. **Become a better teacher every year**

I'll discuss each of these steps, providing suggestions and ideas of things that I use in my class. I present them here because over the years I have found that they work. You may have developed a different course strategy, teaching activities, and evaluation techniques. That's fine; different things work for different teachers. But I hope you find in this teacher's manual something that will be useful to you.

STEP 1

Prepare a Strategic Plan for the Course

In planning your course, you have to make time to teach the big ideas, prepare students for the Create Performance Task, and complete the Explore Curricular Requirement. First, it is important to understand the two components of the AP exam for this course:

1. **The Create Performance Task (CPT).** All Computer Science Principles AP classrooms have to provide a minimum of 12 class hours to work on the Create Performance Task project to make it equitable. This project is in lieu of free-response questions on the exam.

However, there are question prompts that students have to provide written responses to as part of the assessment. This is submitted by the student to the College Board via the digital portfolio site by the designated date set by the College Board each year. For the 2022 exam, the date was May 2, 2022, at 11:59 p.m. Eastern Standard Time. It counts for 30 percent of the final AP score.*

2. **Multiple-Choice Exam.** The multiple-choice exam is a two-hour exam with 70 questions. The exam is given without a scheduled break. It counts for 70 percent of the AP score, so each question is 1 percent of the total score.

The Create Performance Task (CPT)

You must provide your students a minimum of 12 class hours to work on this project. You can provide additional time in class if you choose; students can also work on their project outside of class. Students may work with a partner or partners to develop the program, as long as different parts are developed by each student independently. Teachers may *not* provide feedback to students on any part of the project content. Teachers are allowed to help with connectivity or other technical issues, saving files, or making the video, but not the content in it. Teachers can also clarify the prompts or submission requirements.

The CPT must be submitted in digital format to the online AP digital portfolio site by the deadline. As much as we encourage and cajole, there will always be students who wait until the last minute to finish and submit their projects. Students should realize the deadline is firm!

---

*Note that the College Board site specifies Eastern Standard Time, so if you are in another time zone, keep that in mind. I have read on social media that the time is 11:59 p.m. in each time zone, but I would not want to test that the hard way, although some of our students probably will!

The submission requirements include:

▶ **A video showing the program working**

▶ **A PDF of the program code**

▶ **Responses to written prompts**

Video Submission Tips

Because of the submission requirements, students need to practice making a video of code running more than once before they record the video of their CPT project. Remind students that they should not narrate their video. This was allowed prior to 2021, but no longer is; the College Board wants to remove any possibility of bias.

There is a size limitation for the video. It will *not* upload if it is too large! A message is displayed about the file size being exceeded on the College Board digital portfolio site, but I have had students completely overlook this message and simply state the site was not working. Show students how to check the file size. For practice, you can give students several files and have them document the file size to turn in or take a screenshot of the file size to submit to you.

Have students practice compressing video files. Students will also then need to view the compressed video. Some compression software versions provide tremendous compression capabilities, but the compressed video is then so blurry the AP readers would not be able to adequately view it. Sometimes the file becomes corrupt and is not viewable at all!

Program Code Screenshots and PDF

Students will also need practice during the course with taking screenshots of code to ensure it is readable. While the program code is not scored, it helps the AP readers if they need to check it to ensure a point can be awarded for a section of the rubric. Sometimes the program code snippets included in the written response are too small and become pixelated when the reader magnifies them.

The PDF of the program code is then checked. If neither is viewable, the readers send the file to the table leaders, but it's not likely they will have any better luck.

Remind students not to have their name or a partner's name in the code. They can say "my partner did this section of code" in their comment. This also includes user names on the screen when recording. The project will still be scored, but not having these reduces the potential for bias in the scoring process.

Rubric

The rubric for the CPT is posted online and available to all to view:

https://apcentral.collegeboard.org/pdf/ ap21-sg-computer-science-principles.pdf?course=ap-computer-science-principles. The College Board has sample projects posted online, along with an explanation of why the points were earned or not earned: https:// apstudents.collegeboard.org/courses/ ap-computer-science-principles/assessment/2021-create-performance-task-pilot-samples. Have students practice scoring the sample projects, projects you provide them, and their own work, especially if they do a mock CPT project. This helps them become familiar with the rubric and hopefully provide better written responses as a result. I'll never forget my student who created a wonderful program, but whose written responses rarely had more than one sentence. As a teacher, you can provide feedback on a mock project but not on the real one.

Written Response Section 3a

i. Many students confuse the **purpose** of their program with the **function** of it. Encourage students to use the word "purpose" in their description (and to give an accurate description). I recommend practicing this in writing prompts and discussions where you can provide feedback.

ii. Have students clearly label their input or output. Readers are not allowed to assume, and I have read many responses where students would write something general such as, "You can see the input and output for the program in the video." That would not earn the point.

Written Response Section 3b

iii. Many students include more than one list in their response. When this occurs, the AP readers are only allowed to consider the first one listed, even though it may not be the best one to use to earn the point.

iv. In a mock project or practice write-up, ensure students write about how the list helps their program specifically to manage complexity. Many students write about lists in general and do not include how using a list in **their project** expressly helps manage complexity.

Written Response Section 3c

v. A recurring issue in many projects is the use of an event handler as a student-created procedure. While students may use built-in procedures and event handlers in their programs, they will not count as a **student-created** procedure, which is one of the requirements. Students select the procedure to write about and include screenshots of the function. It's dismaying as a reader to see student-written procedures in their code that they did not select to write about! Drive this point home early and often!

vi. The algorithm described can be spread out among other procedures called. Therefore, the selection statement, IF (condition) can be in one procedure, and the iteration (loop) example can be in a different one that is called by the procedure being described.

Written Response Section 3d

vii. Students need to show the results of two calls to their procedure using parameters. The values passed to the procedure must cause different code to execute. An easy way to show this is using an IF/ELSE statement; one call should cause the condition to be true, and the other should cause it to be false so the code in the ELSE block would execute.

```
IF (condition)
    < code to execute >
ELSE
    < code to execute >
```

Many teachers are able to incorporate a mock CPT where they are able to provide feedback to students to help them better prepare for the actual CPT. One way to help students better understand the scoring would be to have small groups teach or present an evaluation of a mock CPT or one from a prior year. There are sample projects on the College Board site if you are a new teacher and do not have access to projects from prior years. I do not use projects from students who are still at school and always keep the name anonymous.

I also have students score their own practice project using the rubric, and I score it as well. My hope is that this will motivate them to improve their work on the actual CPT. Many students are very optimistic and think they have covered everything to earn a point, but alas, they have not. I meet individually with each student to compare our scoring and discuss differences. It takes time, and I have to start early to provide feedback to everyone before they start the actual CPT.

Another technique is to give students three to four sample CPT submissions and have the students rank them based on the score they think the projects would earn. Some are a little harder to grade than others, so it is also good practice.

These activities all help students study the scoring rubric, see correct and incomplete responses, and experience what it really takes to earn a point! Several points on the scoring rubric have multiple steps, and all of the steps must be completed to earn the point.

Teachers are required to view student submissions after they are marked as final in the College Board digital portfolio and report projects submitted that students received feedback on, such as a mock project, or those they suspect of plagiarism.

Explore Curricular Requirement

There are three Explore curricular activities to be covered during the AP Computer Science Principles course. You can do these all at the same time or spread them out over the course duration. It's easy to forget about them if you get pressed for time, so include them in your pacing schedule.

The Explore curricular requirement gives students a scenario in the format of a paragraph and accompanying information, such as a chart, flowchart, or other diagram, to analyze.

There are five questions related to the reading and diagram analysis. Areas in which to prepare students for questions include:

Input/Processing/Output

Input is data external to the program that feeds into it. The program processes the data in some way and produces output. Students need to carefully distinguish between data and the device that collects it. For example, a camera is not data. It is the device, and the picture it takes is the data. Sensors are devices, and the data is what they record, such as light, sound, and distance, to name a few.

Analyzing Data

Many students confuse the difference between privacy and security. Privacy deals with our personal information and protecting it from being collected and used or sold without our knowledge or consent. Security deals with access to data of any type and can include our personal data. We only want a few people who need access to be able to update or delete data. Others may only need view-access to the data, while some do not need access at all.

One way to address these gaps would be for students to present an innovation to the class in five minutes or less and discuss why it is a computing innovation, what the data is, where it comes from, and any storage, privacy, or security issues. The ensuing discussions should help all students reach a solid grasp of these frequent areas of misunderstanding.

This book has two practice scenarios in Chapter 6: one in the description and the other in the review section. There is also a scenario and set of questions in the diagnostic exam and both practice exams.

Order of Units

The College Board uses the Big Ideas to organize the course; this book generally follows this order. For a more in-depth description of these Big Ideas, go to the Course and Exam Description used by the College Board: https://apcentral.collegeboard.org/pdf/ap-computer-science-principles-course-and-exam-description.pdf.

Here are the five Big Ideas of the course in the order that the College Board presents them:

> Big Idea 1: Creative Development
>
> Big Idea 2: Data
>
> Big Idea 3: Algorithms and Programming
>
> Big Idea 4: Computer Systems and Networks
>
> Big Idea 5: Impact of Computing

However, I teach the course information in a different order, and you may decide to do that too. I always start with Big Idea 3: Algorithms and Programming, because most students need the time to process the concepts in this unit, especially if it is brand new to them. They need this material to be able to do the CPT, which includes writing a program in the programming language of their choice (although it's likely they'll use the one you teach in class). Also, this Big Idea accounts for the largest number of questions on the AP exam. Early and longer exposure to and review of the concepts should translate to a better score.

Following Big Idea 3, I cover sections from Big Idea 1: Creative Development interwoven with other Big Ideas. Next I cover Big Idea 2: Data, followed by Big Idea 4: Computer Systems and Networks, and finally I finish up with Big Idea 5: Impact of Computing. Although this section also has a high percentage of multiple-choice questions, many elements of the unit are more intuitive for my students. If necessary, it can be covered more quickly, just in case we do not have the time to cover the material as thoroughly as I'd like.

The chart below shows an overview of my class both in terms of the order of topics and the amount of time spent on each topic. My class is a one-semester class, but there is also a breakdown of time if your class is a year long course. The chart also shows the pages in this book that relate to each of the topics.

TOPICS	YEAR DURATION	SEMESTER DURATION	PAGES IN THIS BOOK	BIG IDEA
Binary number conversions	3 days	2 days	pp. 80–85	Big Idea 2
3 types of algorithms	4 days	2 days	pp. 99, 106–113	Big Idea 3
SDLC: Iterative development cycle Incremental development cycle Function versus purpose	2 days and review throughout	1 day and review throughout	pp. 68–74	Big Idea 1
Flowcharts/Pseudocode	2 days	1 day	pp. 99–100	Big Idea 3
Use code snippets to introduce: Variables Lists Data Types Operations	6 days	3 days	pp. 100–105	Big Idea 3
Introduce programming language and write first program together	4 days	2 days	pp. 100–124	Big Idea 3
Practice written response 3a			pp. 73, 85–86	Big Ideas 1 and 2
IF/ELSE IF/ELSE	4 days	2 days	pp. 106–110	Big Idea 3
Logical Operators: AND, OR, NOT	2 days	1 day	pp. 104–105	Big Idea 3
Loops: REPEAT UNTIL ( )	4 days	2 days	p. 111	Big Idea 3
Loops: REPEAT n TIMES Practice compressing a video	4 days	2 days	p. 110	Big Idea 3
Procedures: RETURN Parameters/arguments Practice written responses 3c and 3d	8 days	4 days	pp. 121–123	Big Idea 3
Robots/Algorithms	4 days	2 days	pp. 113–114	Big Idea 3
Lists: Index Elements Built-in methods FOR EACH loop Linear and binary search Practice written response 3b	10 days	5 days	pp. 115–121	Big Idea 3
Practice Create Performance Task (CPT)	4 days	2 days		
Real CPT	12 class hours*	12 class hours		

(continued)

TOPICS	YEAR DURATION	SEMESTER DURATION	PAGES IN THIS BOOK	BIG IDEA
Submit to College Board digital portfolio portal	1 day	1 day		Big Idea 2
Analog data Lossless/lossy data compression	2 days	1 day	pp. 86–87	Big Idea 3

Analyzing algorithms
    Heuristics
    Undecidable problems
	2 days	1 day	pp. 125–127	Big Idea 2

Processing data: Cleaning, filtering, classifying, patterns Bias Correlations Metadata	4 days	2 days	pp. 87–90	Big Idea 3
Simulations	2 days	1 day	p. 125	Big Idea 4
Internet	8 days	4 days	pp. 138–141	Big Idea 4
Sequential versus distributed computing systems	2 days	1 day	pp. 141–142	Big Idea 5
Digital divide Crowdsourcing Creative Commons Open-source Open access Analytics Data mining	2 days	1 day	pp. 150–154	Big Idea 5

Personally identifiable information (PII)
    Privacy
    Security
Public key encryption
Certificate of authority
	2 days	1 day	pp. 154–158	

Explore curricular requirements #1, #2, #3	3 days	3 days	pp. 57–63	
Review	4 days	2 days		
Diagnostic Exam	2 days	2 day	pp. 15–34	
Review based on Diagnostic Exam results	2 days	1 day		
Practice Test 1	2 days	1 day + after school	pp. 165–189	
Review based on Practice Test results	2 days	1 day		
Practice Test 2	2 days	1 day + after school	pp. 191–211	

*16 days with 45-minute classes

Using This Book in Your Classroom

Whether you are new to the course or an experienced AP teacher, you will find that this book covers each of the topics and complements the material from the College Board. You can use this book to supplement your textbook.

Review Questions

Each section of this book has review questions. The first section of questions reviews student understanding of the concepts. The second section of questions tests their application of the concepts. Have students review these sections as you go through the Big Idea. It helps them get used to the style of the questions on the exam. It also provides the opportunity to help students think through the answer options, so they don't panic if they see an unfamiliar term or one they have seen but can't remember.

Vocabulary

Vocabulary words are included at the beginning of each Big Idea section. Many of you have likely used a variety of ways to help students learn the vocabulary words. My best success over several years has been to have students write the definitions on paper, so there is no copying and pasting from an online source. Then I let them use their handwritten definitions on vocabulary quizzes. The online version of this book has vocabulary flashcard practice quizzes for students (see the back cover of this book for instructions for accessing the Cross-Platform Edition).

Diagnostic Exam

Some teachers give the diagnostic exam at the beginning of the course to see where students are. Since this course does not require prior programming knowledge or experience, I mainly have students who are brand new to all of the material. Some of these students are demoralized taking the diagnostic exam early in the term.

I want all of the students to know that they can be successful learning the material. Therefore, you may want to give the diagnostic exam after the content is finished but before reviewing for the exam.

I give the diagnostic exam over three class days. I then share the correct answers and have students fill out the diagnostic performance summary sheet. I recommend collecting these summary answer sheets from students after they view them to make a copy. I find it helpful to see what topics need be reviewed in depth for most of my students. It helps my students so much to understand why the wrong answers are wrong. The answer section also includes which Big Idea each question belongs to.

Practice Exams

The practice exams present a different story. Some teachers give these right after school, on a school evening, or on a weekend day when students can have the full two hours. My school uses a rotating class schedule, so I time this for a day my class is last, and then we keep going right after school. I usually give Practice Exam 1 right after we finish the course content and have reviewed a little. We then focus on the subjects for which most students need more review. I give Practice Exam 2 a few days before the actual exam.

Exam Reference Sheet

Students receive a copy of the Exam Reference Sheet when taking the AP exam. I do not give my students the Exam Reference Sheet to use for the diagnostic exam. I don't even tell them it exists until after we've completed the programming unit, so no one is tempted to use it as a crutch. Inevitably, when they learn about it, someone will say something like, "Now I don't have to study!" I cringe every time I hear that.

STEP 2

Hold an Interesting Class Every Day

Students are usually interested in taking AP Computer Science Principles, *and* they are a little apprehensive because computer science is the "big unknown" for many of them. I tell them the content is not that difficult; they just haven't had much, if any, exposure to it.

I give homework most nights, but I try to keep it to a minimum most of the time and ensure it is relevant to the topic at hand. I assign a little reading and one to two questions related to it. They will have a couple of vocabulary questions to answer each night as well.

I use "Bell Ringers" with questions that cover concepts from the previous or recent days to help them focus on our class and see what they remember and understand about the topic. What they don't always realize until test time is that they are building a review guide as we go, so it is to their benefit in multiple ways to correct their responses and to be thorough.

As we progress in the course, I often include one or more practice questions from prior released exams for review during class. I start with easier ones to help build their confidence. I have students hold up fingers for the answers, 1 for A, 2 for B, and so on, or use small white boards and markers to record their answer and show them all at the same time to get a feel for how many got it right. I then go over the answer and explain why the other responses are incorrect. This only takes a few minutes, but the payback has been big in helping students become familiar with the test question format.

Big Idea 1: Creative Development

The concepts covered here include the software development process, collaborating with others, documentation for applications, and testing.

Students can collaborate on their Create Performance Task (CPT) to an extent. This topic is a good time to start talking about that and to ensure they understand the limits of the collaboration allowed. Students can work together on the design of the program. However, each student has to develop part of the code independently. Students can also test each other's code to help identify errors.

Students tend to be very optimistic with their programs. If it runs without syntax errors, some students think their program produced correct output. Developing good testing habits from the start will help them with their debugging on their CPT.

Students also need to get in the habit of documenting their programs. As I teach the basics, I require them to include a header at the top of the program with their initials, the date, and a brief description of their program. I also have students comment sections of code, such as defining functions, variables, and important sections of code.

Big Idea 2: Data

This Big Idea is all about various aspects of data. It includes number conversions from decimal to binary and vice versa. I have taught these for several years, and the method I outline in this book has worked best for my students. It really seems to help conceptually to having them think of different ways they already use to denote "how many" of something they have. After that, they just have to follow the algorithm. There are other ways to teach the converting process, and some of my students immediately make the leap to dividing by two to do the conversion. If that's easier for them, I let them keep with it.

Data compression with lossless and lossy techniques is a good time to have students practice using compression software to see how it works. I always use a video since their CPT video may need to be compressed. They need to know how to see the size of the file before and after compression. Also, have students view the compressed version to ensure it is not blurry.

When covering correlations, I use Tyler Vigen's "Spurious Correlations" website, https://www.tylervigen.com/spurious-correlations. He includes silly correlations that the data show. Some are quite hilarious, and students can easily see that there is no correlation.

Big Idea 3: Algorithms and Programming

This is a key chapter covering algorithms and programming. A specific programming language is not required for this course. Some teachers cover more than one programming language, usually one block based and another text based. If the programming language you teach starts index positions at 0 for strings and lists, you need to let students know that the exam questions will all start at index position 1. Once they have submitted their CPT to the College Board digital portfolio portal, all of our practice and review questions only use the AP exam format of indices starting at 1.

One activity I like to do for algorithms is to describe the steps to sketch an object. At first, when given vague instructions, I do a terrible job. After students complain and tell me why, I get better, and then I have students draw a slip of paper with an object's name on it. They then write the algorithm for someone else to sketch the object. This is an effective way to help students realize how detailed an algorithm needs to be!

A similar activity is to put students in groups and have them create a flowchart for a board game. They then have to switch flowcharts with another team and play the game following the flowchart only and provide feedback to the original team. Thrift shops are a great place to find inexpensive board games to keep in your classroom.

Selection statements (IF statements) and the REPEAT UNTIL (condition) loop reinforce each other. I teach the IF statement first and then follow with the REPEAT UNTIL, since both statement types use conditions. I then introduce lists and follow them with the FOR EACH loop. Lists use several built-in procedures that students must know, and practicing these with the FOR EACH loop helps reinforce both structures. I also like to teach the common algorithms students need to know, such as finding the average of a group of numbers, with both FOR EACH and REPEAT UNTIL loops. Students learn the common algorithms better if they work with them twice, and more practice with both loop types never hurts!

The linear and binary search algorithms are fun to do in class. I usually start with the binary search by telling students I can guess any number between 1 and 100 in seven guesses or less and then prove it. They see that I'm guessing in the middle each time quickly. They then try out the algorithm with classmates.

My students had trouble with the idea of parameters and their scope. Even though I don't explain the details until a little later, I started using procedures in sample code for other concepts, so students get used to seeing them used earlier. They also struggle a bit with sending a value back to the calling procedure with RETURN. Many of them regularly forget to store the value in a variable. I've started introducing that in sample code before explaining it in detail so they get used to seeing it. A brief explanation is given as we use it, and that has helped when we go over it in detail later in the programming unit.

Google Maps is a good way to explain APIs since so many websites and apps have it as a feature.

It is really helpful for students to see other students' code. I regularly hold gallery walks for students to view and provide feedback in the form: "I really like how . . ." and "I wonder if you . . ." I also do gallery walks using code with errors. Groups of students rotate through them to find and discuss the errors.

If you have time, simulations can be fun to do as a programming activity if you have access to micro:bits or other microprocessors. Sometimes we'll just use Popsicle sticks or straws and build structures for an earthquake simulation. It's a fun way to get the important points across. There are some traveling-salesman simulations on the web that can be used when you cover reasonable and unreasonable algorithms.

Big Idea 4: Computing Systems and Networks

I have two favorite activities in this unit. One is to take the class on a tour of the school's network infrastructure. Students often think their data is floating around in "the cloud," waiting to be summoned for some purpose. Seeing the main server room, the IDF closets in every building, and where the cable comes in from our ISP helps them see how hardware-driven the school network and the Internet are. Many are often quite stunned at the realization.

There is an excellent activity posted multiple places online where students act out sending a message across the Internet in packets. I use puzzle pieces in an envelope with a header written on them. Sometimes there is a virus in a packet. I can always tell if we need to further review the different aspects of the Internet based on how they do or how much guiding I have to provide. It gets them up and moving, regardless!

Big Idea 5: Impact of Computing

This unit generates several good discussions in class. These include the digital divide, how bias makes its way into data and algorithms plus its impact, and illegally copying and sharing digital versions of games, music, and movies. Anything we can do to make students more aware of and protective of their personally identifiable information (PII) is a good outcome from this course!

We use some of the online sites that show how quickly passwords can be broken, although I do tell students to only use old passwords or something similar while doing this. It makes me nervous otherwise!

One activity I like with symmetric ciphers is to have students make one by cutting out a template with the letters and different shifts to see what they would become. Another helpful activity for public key encryption is to use a box with a slot to put in something and a padlock on it. Seeing that the recipient is the only person with the right key and the designated eavesdropper can't get to the message helps them understand it. You can add the concept of Certificate Authorities to this activity.

There are videos that use paint to show how public key encryption works. Rather than paint, I've used craft dough to demonstrate how this works. You might need to have the "do not throw craft dough" talk before you start!

There are lots of opportunities from the real world to share with students that incorporate the concepts this section covers. This helps make it more relevant to many students when they are impacted, either positively or negatively.

Finally, you can create an escape-room activity that brings all the Big Ideas together. The clues to the locks include a binary number conversion, a robot grid pathway, network sections, and a cybersecurity puzzle to solve. It is a lot of fun and a good way to review.

5 Steps to a 5 AP Computer Science Principles: Elite Edition

The Elite Edition of this book provides additional questions that can be used in your class. It contains 180 activities and questions that require five minutes a day. While they are primarily intended to be used by students studying for the test, you can use these as daily warm-ups in your course.

UNIT	QUESTIONS/ACTIVITIES IN THE ELITE EDITION
Big Idea 1: Creative Development	1–28
Big Idea 2: Data	29–51, 107
Big Idea 3: Algorithms and Programming	52–106, 108–123
Big Idea 4: Computer Systems and Networks	124–150
Big Idea 5: Impact of Computing	151–180

STEP 3

Evaluate Your Students' Progress

In class, I start having students read code early and often. I give a lot of formative assessments, since the material is brand new to most of my students. We go over practice questions, including those in this book. I don't use questions from AP Classroom for this; those are saved for quizzes and tests.

Occasionally we do a vocabulary review game. There are many posted online if you are looking for new ideas. I have the words on cardstock folded over with the definition on the other side; you can fold them with either side visible. We make outer and inner circles. Students each have a card and either give the word or the definition for their partner to give the corresponding word or definition. One circle rotates clockwise one person over, and the process repeats.

I give quizzes fairly frequently to help keep students on track, as well as to see how they are doing with their understanding of the concepts. I always include a couple of questions from a prior quiz, usually the ones students had problems with so they will keep reviewing. I sometimes include a binary number conversion or have students set up a REPEAT or FOR EACH loop, among other topics, to keep it fresh in their minds. The quizzes do not take the entire class period and are only 10 to 15 questions each.

I mainly use secure questions from AP Classroom for tests. Students have told me that using questions in the AP format helped them on the exam, as they became used to seeing them. I also include questions from prior sections on tests to keep students reviewing. I allow test corrections, because I want students to learn the material. They have to provide an adequate explanation for why the correct answer is correct and why their response was incorrect to earn points.

STEP 4

Get Students Ready to Take the AP Exam

To review for the exam, I start about two weeks before the test is given. I teach the course in a semester, and there is not as much time as I would like for review, so I incorporate it all semester with the bell ringers, practice questions, and repeat questions on quizzes.

I usually give Practice Exam 1 right after we finish the course content. We then focus on the areas most students need more review on in class. I have create and collected additional practice questions over the years for all areas, so students can take those and review them independently as well. These questions are in the AP format but are not from AP Classroom.

I give Practice Exam 2 a few days before the actual exam. We continue to review the areas needed most, but I focus most on the algorithm and programming questions, since most of the exam questions are from this area. We also do a refresh on what is in the Exam Reference Sheet, which is provided to students during the exam. Then students can remember to reference it for exam questions as needed.

We also practice robot questions, and students are encouraged to take a penny to the exam and use Lincoln's head to ensure they are facing the right direction or to put a face on their pencil eraser or finger and use it the same way. This is not considered cheating and came from an AP Summer Institute course instructor!

We go over test strategies for eliminating some responses and continuing to mark their best guess on the answer sheet. This way, they are less likely to put answers on the wrong line on the answer sheet, and it gives them a chance to go back and check those they were not sure about. **Remind students often that there is no penalty for wrong answers!**

STEP 5

Become a Better Teacher Every Year

Becoming a better AP Computer Science Principles teacher involves a growth mindset. A growth mindset will allow you to seek out better instructional strategies and ideas to improve your AP classroom each and every year. The best AP teachers are not ones who believe they have "figured it out," but ones who look to improve through self-reflection and growth.

Always make notes about what you would change the next time you teach the course. Sometimes I read about a great lesson another teacher taught and use that idea as well! There are many creative teachers who share their ideas on social media. I've listed some groups on social media below.

Two reports from the College Board also are very helpful in planning for the next year:

▶ The Chief Reader for each AP exam prepares a report with information about areas students were weaker in, common errors, and some resources to address these areas.

▶ The Instructional Planning Report is specific to your students compared to all students taking that exam. It can help you find areas to keep doing what you are doing and those you may want to shore up.

The AP Summer Institutes sponsored by the College Board are also excellent places to share resources, review textbooks, and meet your peers. The College Board also holds shorter workshops during the year that are usually one to two days in length. There is also an online series that takes you through the Course and Exam Description (CED), AP Classroom, the scoring rubric, and strategies to better understand course expectations and College Board resources.

Another way to grow as a teacher is to apply to be an AP reader. This course has seen incredible growth, and readers are usually needed each year. It's a great way to see student work from classrooms everywhere and meet, virtually, other teachers to share ideas. It is not as easy to meet and share ideas as it once was because the AP Computer Science Principles reading is now mainly done online.

Additional Resources for Teachers

The websites listed here can be easily accessed through a web page that I created: https://bit.ly/apcspresources.

College Board Resources

AP Teacher Community

This community is free to join through the College Board site. Teachers can post questions and receive ideas and suggestions from teachers and college professors worldwide.

AP Classroom

The College Board has greatly enhanced the resources available to teachers through AP Classroom. There are practice questions and secure questions you can use. There are also daily videos. These are a new addition, are five to ten minutes long, and generally cover one topic. It can be helpful to hear the same content from someone else in a different way.

Conceptual Framework

I have students mark the Essential Knowledge columns as we go. They check those they are confident about and feel they have mastered, mark with an asterisk those they did not know, and then add + or − to indicate their current level of understanding of the concept, as we continue to review them. Similar to using the Conceptual Framework, you can create benchmarks or checklist items for students to use as a timeline for reviewing the material.

Other Websites

Code.org and Khan Academy

These sites provide freely available resources and curriculum. I often use videos from both sites to explain concepts for students. It's refreshing for them to hear the same concept in a different way and in a different voice. They can view the videos multiple times, and the videos are much more "hip" than I am.

Facebook Groups

AP Computer Science Principles Teachers

AP CS Principles Teachers

AP CS Principles Educators

Teaching Aids

Egg cartons work for list and string indices along with Scrabble letters as the list element.

Dice are an easy example of random number generators. There are also many digital versions of dice, or you can use the Google random number generator.

Shower curtains marked off with blue painter's tape can be used to make a grid to use with robots. This is a fun activity that helps students who can't remember their left from their right and helps others to remember that turns do not also move forward.

Good luck to you and your students. You've got this!